Strategies for Human Resource Management

Strategies for Human Resource Management

A Total Business Approach

EDITED BY
MICHAEL ARMSTRONG

Coopers
&Lybrand

KOGAN
PAGE

2 0 1100044 01

First published in 1992
Reprinted 1992, 1993 (twice), 1995, 1996

Apart from any fair dealing for the purposes of research or private study, or criticism or review, as permitted under the Copyright, Designs and Patents Act, 1988, this publication may only be reproduced, stored or transmitted, in any form or by any means, with the prior permission in writing of the publishers, or in the case of reprographic reproduction in accordance with the terms of licences issued by the Copyright Licensing Agency. Enquiries concerning reproduction outside those terms should be sent to the publishers at the undermentioned address:

Kogan Page Limited
120 Pentonville Road
London N1 9JN

© Michael Armstrong, 1992

British Library Cataloguing in Publication Data

A CIP record for this book is available from the British Library.

ISBN 0 7494 0537 6

Typeset by Books Unlimited (Nottm), Sutton-in-Ashfield, Notts
Printed and bound in Great Britain by
Biddles Ltd, Guildford and King's Lynn

CONTENTS

CONTENTS

LIST OF FIGURES

LIST OF TABLES

ACKNOWLEDGEMENTS

The editor and authors would like to thank Lynda Patterson, a Human Resources consultant with Coopers & Lybrand, for co-ordinating the preparation of this book and progressing it through to publication.

THE CONTRIBUTORS

Philip Albon holds an MA in Management Learning and specialises in organisation and management development. His previous experience includes being an internal consultant and training manager with British Telecom. He has worked on a wide variety of consultancy assignments in the UK, Europe and North America. Philip has particular expertise in designing creative interventions to develop organisations and the people who work in them.

Michael Armstrong has written many best-selling books on human resources and general management topics. His *Handbook of Personnel Management Practice* is a standard text for students preparing for Membership of the Institute of Personnel Management. After a career in management and consultancy, Michael was a General Manager at Book Club Associates (BCA) with responsibility for a number of business functions as well as personnel. Following his retirement from BCA, Michael Armstrong now works as a consultant, especially for voluntary sector organisations. He also continues to write, and his latest book, *Human Resource Management: Strategy and Action* is being published in 1992 by Kogan Page.

Alan Cave began his career with a major pay and benefits consultancy and currently works on all aspects of reward management. He also has extensive experience of industrial relations having been Head of Research and Policy at the GMB Union and an Assistant Secretary of the TUC. Alan has a PPE degree from Oxford University and an M Phil in Industrial Relations from the London School of Economics.

Ron Collard is London personnel partner for Coopers & Lybrand, responsible for the personnel management of several thousand staff. Having been awarded a prize to study approaches to Total Quality in Japan, he wrote the best-selling book *Total Quality Management* and is widely recognised as an authority in the field. As a consultant he has advised many leading companies — including Sony — on quality management.

Roger Cooke has over twenty years' experience with Coopers & Lybrand as a consultant to major companies and organisations, both in the UK and overseas. He leads the UK Organisation and Human Resources practice of Coopers & Lybrand, where he specialises in strategic issues in these fields. Roger began his career with the Ford Motor Company, and took an MBA at the Warton School of Finance in the US before becoming a management consultant.

Denis Crowe specialises in remuneration management. He has worked on many assignments in both the public and private sectors, including top management pay, pay and benefits surveys, job evaluation and performance-related pay. Denis was previously editor of a leading journal dealing with all aspects of managers' pay and benefits and is a steering committee member of the IPM's Compensation Forum.

Kelvin Hard specialises in the design of organisations and in managing the process of change and development for organisations to meet their business needs. He previously worked on personnel and organisation matters in central government, including two efficiency scrutinies for the Prime Minister. Kelvin was educated at Cambridge and Oxford universities and at the London Business School. He is a member of the Institute of Personnel Management and of the Institute of Management Consultants.

Jan Morgan now works as a consultant with Coopers & Lybrand in Australia. While working with Coopers & Lybrand in the UK, she specialised in helping organisations to develop personnel information and management systems to meet their business needs. Jan, who previously worked for Granada TV Rental, holds an MA and a degree in Economics and Statistics, and is a Fellow of the Institute of Personnel Management.

Lawrie Philpott began his career in local government, where he held a variety of posts, including Head of Management Services at the GLC. He now specialises in the communications, energy, water and transport sectors, where he has extensive experience of leading a wide range of human resource assignments. As well as reward management, Lawrie has taken a particular interest in the assessment and development of top managers and those with the potential to rise to that level.

Martina Platts gained wide experience of human resource management with the Courage Group, United Glass and Nabisco. She has worked on many assignments, with a particular focus on relating personnel policies and programmes to strategic business needs. Martina holds an MBA (with distinction) from Warwick Business School in addition to her first degree, a Diploma in Personnel Management and Membership of the Institute of Personnel Management.

Louise Sheppard gained experience in all aspects of human resource management with Unilever Plc, where she worked for Lever Brothers Limited and Brooke Bond Group. She has extensive experience of performance management, training design and delivery and change management. Louise has an Economics and Politics degree from Bristol University, a postgraduate diploma in Personnel Management and is a Member of the Institute of Personnel Management.

Anne-Marie Southall began her career in the automotive industry, where she worked for both the Rover Group and Unipart. She has extensive experience of employee relations and communications, both as a consultant and as a front-line personnel manager. Anne-Marie holds a degree in Business Studies and is a Member of the Institute of Personnel Management.

Ruth Spellman is Director of Personnel at the NSPCC, having previously worked as a management consultant with Coopers & Lybrand. An economist by background, Ruth has focused on developing imaginative responses to resourcing issues and labour market problems. After Cambridge University (where she was secretary of the Union) Ruth worked for British Coal and for NEDO, where she helped to produce *Competence and Competition*, the seminal study of how the relative failure of the UK labour market puts us at an economic disadvantage compared with competitor countries.

Michael Stanton studied at INSEAD in preparation for the development of a single market in Europe, and has played a leading role in developing an integrated Organisation and Human Resources practice for Coopers & Lybrand across Europe. He has over ten years' experience as a management consultant, having previously worked in a variety of personnel roles for aero engine makers Rolls Royce. Michael is a Fellow of the Institute of Personnel Management and has been active in Institute affairs at both branch and national levels.

Peninah Thomson specialises in human resource management issues in the public sector, where she has focused particularly on organisation culture, change management and improving the quality of service delivery. Peninah previously worked for Marks & Spencer in France, for NATO and for Oxford University. She is a Fellow of the Royal Society of Arts, a govenor of a London polytechnic and holds a first-class degree from Oxford University.

Garnet Twigg launched and ran his own consultancy business prior to joining Coopers & Lybrand. He specialises in management development and change management through a wide range of process interventions, including team building, top management workshops and changing leadership styles and organisational culture. Garnet holds degrees in both Psychology and Law, and has worked extensively both in the UK and overseas.

INTRODUCTION

Michael Armstrong

The aim of this book is to explore the directions in which human resource management will be going, taking into account changes arising in the business and economic environment, nationally and internationally, and the implications of organisational and technological developments within companies.

The book has been written by a team of experienced Coopers & Lybrand management consultants and is intended to be a practical guide for chief executives, line managers and personnel professionals on trends in human resource management and what they should do about them. The book starts with an overview of human resource strategy, which provides a framework for an analysis in the next seven chapters of how strategies can be developed in each of the key areas of human resource management: organisation, resourcing, performance management, human resource development, reward management, employee relations and communications.

The book continues with four chapters which examine broader but significant areas of human resource management in the 1990s — the implications of the single European market, the particular factors affecting human resource management in the public sector, total quality management, and how information systems can be developed to provide a basis for strategic human resource management. Finally, the book assesses how human resource strategies and policies can be implemented, taking into account the respective roles of top and line management and the members of the personnel function.

The aims of this introduction are to:

- analyse the context within which these aspects of human resource management take place — the changing external and internal environment;
- define what we mean by the concept of human resource management;
- identify the themes which underlie each chapter.

THE CONTEXT OF HUMAN RESOURCE MANAGEMENT

Human resource management as a strategic and organisation-wide approach to managing people has achieved prominence over the last decade. Its rise and future development can be related to environmental changes arising outside and within organisations.

The external environment

The most important environmental factor is increased competition, within the UK and from European and global businesses. The search for competitive advantage and added value (two phrases which entered the human resource manager's vocabulary during the 1980s) has led to the belief that people must be treated more as assets than as costs and that all managers in the organisation are equally concerned in gaining the greatest return possible from investment in those assets.

Strategies for investing in human resources may focus first on the harder areas where measurable returns can be made. These comprise:

- resourcing — getting the right people, training them in the particular skills needed by the business and ensuring that those worth retaining stay with the organisation;
- human resource development — supplying the people and skills required in the future;
- performance and reward management — developing performance management and pay systems which provide both incentives and rewards: incentives to join and stay with the organisation and to improve performance, and rewards for delivering the required results.

Human resource investment strategies, however, will also address the softer areas of human resource management when the aim will be to create an environment which is conducive to commitment, team working and quality enhancement. These 'softer' areas will include organisation and job design, culture management, communications management, broader education and training activities covering such matters as leadership, team working, interactive skills and total quality management, and the development of a cooperative climate of employee relations. Some of the 'harder' approaches such as performance management may support these softer areas by providing for performance to be measured not only by reference to the achievement of quantified objectives but also with regard to, first, the degree to which the behaviour of managers upholds such values as team work, quality and customer service and, secondly, how they manage their teams in terms of leadership, involvement, communications and the development of individual abilities and potential.

The other key factor is change, which can produce conditions of turbulence, even chaos. There is no sign of the rate of change diminishing in the 1990s and strategies for managing change are playing an increasingly important part in human resource management.

The internal environment

Competitive pressures have accentuated the need for managements to concentrate on innovation, quality enhancement, customer service and cost reduction. This has influenced the way in which organisations have been structured and managed. The need to be more responsive to external events has resulted in a greater emphasis on operational flexibility, and the need to make managers more accountable for results has resulted in more decentralisation and devolution of authority.

The impact of new technology, especially information technology, has enabled organisations to eliminate layers of management and supervision in the interests of a quicker and more flexible response to new demands, increased accountability and, of course, cost reduction. Cellular manufacturing systems, for example, have encouraged the creation of autonomous work groups, which reduces the need for supervisory and quality control staff as well as enhancing team accountability and, importantly, cohesiveness.

The new 'flexible firm' is one in which teamwork is more important but it also means the setting up of core groups of employees consisting of managers, technicians, knowledge workers and multi-skilled craft workers. These groups are supported as and when required by contract staff and part-timers. The creation, development and control of teams of core workers operating in a state of constant change places even greater demands on all managers and it is these demands which have accentuated the need to adopt a human resource management approach as described below.

HUMAN RESOURCE MANAGEMENT

Human resource management (HRM) is an approach to the management of people which is based on four fundamental principles:

1. People are the most important assets an organisation has and their effective management is the key to its success.
2. Organisational success is most likely to be achieved if the personnel policies and procedures of the enterprise are closely linked with, and make a major contribution to, the achievement of corporate objectives and strategic plans.
3. The corporate culture and the values, organisational climate and managerial behaviour emanating from that culture will exert a major influence on the achievement of excellence. This culture must be managed, which means that strong pressure, starting from the top, needs to be exerted to get the values accepted and acted upon.
4. Continuous effort is required to encourage all the members of the

organisation to work together with a sense of common purpose. It is particularly necessary to secure commitment to change.

Human resource management in the 1990s will be both business and people orientated. It emphasises that human resource strategies must be built into the fabric of the business and support the achievement of business objectives. But it also recognises that people cannot be treated like other resources. They have their own needs and expectations, which may not be consistent with those of the organisation, and they are certainly becoming more demanding, both as individuals and collectively, on what they see as acceptable treatment by their employers. Managers concerned with human resource management, and this means all managers, must have a deep understanding of the values which guide and motivate employees, and must develop their approaches to managing people accordingly. It is necessary to take a pluralistic point of view, recognising that people have different interests than those of the organisation. An autocratic management style may still work in some circumstances — for example in a group where strict operational or financial disciplines must be exercised from the top, but increasingly, the human resource management approach aims to create a 'climate of consent'.

UNDERLYING THEMES

The main themes that have emerged from our analysis of developments in human resource strategies in the 1990s are:

- The need to achieve 'strategic integration', ie ensuring that there is good fit between business and human resource strategies.
- The need for a coherent approach which links the various aspects of human resource management together to provide more powerful support for the achievement of organisational objectives.
- The importance of recognising that human resource management processes can provide a number of levers for change.
- The need to adopt a flexible approach to managing people which will vary according to the situation — there are no sure-fire solutions and no quick fixes.
- The importance attached to managing corporate culture.
- An emphasis on the importance of commitment and mutuality which involves a shift towards concentrating on individuals and working groups rather than on representative bodies.

Strategic integration

Strategic integration is the process of linking human resource management policies and activities to explicit business strategies. This integrating process will aim to match available human resources to the ever changing requirements of the organisation. It will also establish the competencies required at all levels in the organisation to ensure that business strategies are implemented and will then take the human resource development initiatives required to provide those competencies. Finally, it will provide the levers required to manage strategic change.

A coherent approach

The history of personnel management, in fact management generally, over the last two decades is littered with techniques and nostrums such as management by objectives, job enrichment, OD (organisation development), systematic training, career planning, job evaluation, merit rating, assessment centres, psychometric tests, performance related pay, performance management, quality circles and competency analysis. These have usually been introduced piecemeal and have too often failed to make any real impact on performance. Each of these techniques can play a part in improving organisational effectiveness but not if used in isolation and without the full backing of top management as something *they* recognise as being important in helping them to get things done.

A coherent approach means linking and, as necessary, coordinating the various techniques available to ensure that added value is obtained from their combined impact. For example, a performance management system will generate data on development needs, indicate where competency-related training is required, provide the basis for performance related pay, help managers to lead their teams more effectively, clarify the results expected of individuals and teams and assist with career and management succession planning.

A coherent approach to human resource management is, however, only possible where the whole top team works together in developing and managing the process. In this situation, the human resource professional acts as an enabler and facilitator, providing ideas, drawing the threads together, and helping his or her colleagues to put the ideas into practice.

Change management

Human resource strategies should help the organisation to move forward in the direction set by business strategies. They do this first, by providing various levers for change through the introduction of integrated resourcing, human resource development, performance and reward management systems and secondly by seeing that change is managed properly.

Change management programmes should be driven from the top but their implementation requires the support and involvement of people at every level in the organisation. They are sometimes related to abstractions such as participation or culture and are based on the belief that the place to begin is with the knowledge and attitude of individuals. In fact, as Beer, Eisenstat and Spector[1] point out: 'Individual behaviour is powerfully shaped by the organizational roles that people play. The most effective way to change behaviour, therefore, is to put people into a new organizational context which imposes new roles, responsibilities and relationships on them.' They suggest a six step approach to effective change:

1. Develop commitment to change through joint analysis of business problems.
2. Develop a shared vision of how to organise and manage for competitiveness.
3. Foster consensus for the new vision, competence to enact it, and cohesion to move it along.
4. Spread revitalisation to all departments without pushing it from the top, ie don't force the issue, allow departments to find their own way to the new organisation.
5. Institutionalise revitalisation through formal policies, systems and structures.
6. Monitor and adjust strategies in response to problems in the revitalisation process.

Flexibility

In each area of human resource management it is necessary to develop flexible structures, climates, systems and organisations which enable the organisation to respond readily to change. Organisations need to embrace the motto 'constancy towards ends but flexibility about means'. Greater operational flexibility must, of course, be achieved within a strategic framework which maintains a strong sense of direction, but there is usually plenty of scope within that framework to develop organisation structures which are adaptive and receptive to innovation. The thrust is towards functional flexibility which can be achieved by one or more of the following approaches:

- work-based — job related flexibilities concerned with multiskilling and the removal of demarcation boundaries;
- contract-based — employee contracts which specify flexibility as a key aspect of terms and conditions and job descriptions which specify outputs but do not attempt to hamper employees by over-rigid descriptions of how they are expected to achieve results;
- team-based — the use of project teams, task forces and autonomous work groups;
- organisation-based — the use of contract workers and part-timers;
- time-based — the use of flexible hours: daily, weekly and annual.

Values

Peters and Waterman[2] wrote that if they were asked for one all-purpose bit of advice for management, one truth they could distil from all their research on what makes company excellency, it would be: 'Figure out your value system. Decide what the company *stands* for.' And Selznick[3] emphasised the key role of values in an organisation when he wrote: 'The formation of an institute is marked by the making of value commitments, that is, choices which fix the assumptions of policy makers as to the nature of the enterprise, its distinctive aims, methods and roles.'

Successful companies are value driven, whether those values direct the beliefs and actions of the chief executive officer or whether, preferably, they permeate the whole organisation. Each aspect of human resource management discussed in this book can be enhanced if it is underpinned by a set of values which may refer to such areas as care and consideration for people, care for customers, competitiveness, enterprise, excellence, flexibility, growth, innovation, market/customer orientation, performance orientation, productivity, quality, social responsibility and teamwork.

Commitment

The effectiveness of any aspect of human resource management depends largely upon the extent to which it will increase commitment, motivation and, ultimately, performance. A strategy for commitment is therefore necessary to support each aspect of the overall human resource strategy. The aims of a commitment strategy will be:

- **Identification** — Increasing the identification of every member of the organisation with the mission, goals and core values of that organisation.
- **Mutuality** — Developing unity of purpose and a shared belief that what is good for the individual is good for the organisation and vice versa. Mutuality therefore involves integrating the needs of those who work in the organisation with the needs of the organisation.
- **Individual creativity and energy** — Unleashing the latent creativity and energy of individuals throughout the organisation. Note the emphasis on individuals. While good teamwork is vital, and a commitment strategy will aim to enhance it, what must *not* be inferred from the development and application of such a strategy is that the organisation wants to create a colony of clones who will slavishly conform to norms and standards imposed on them by the company. As John Harvey-Jones[4] says, it is 'the individual's unique and personal contribution that matters.'
- **Ownership of change** — Managing change by getting people to 'own' it. This means trying to ensure that those affected by change feel the project is theirs and not one imposed upon them by outsiders which will conflict with their values or be detrimental in any way.

REFERENCES

1. Beer, M, Eisenstat, R and Spector, B (1990) 'Why change programmes don't produce change', *Harvard Business Review*, November-December.
2. Peters, T and Waterman, R (1982). *In Search of Excellence*, Harper & Row, New York.
3. Selznick, P (1957) *Leadership and Administration*, Row, Evanston, Illinois.
4. Harvey-Jones, J (1988) *Making it Happen*, Collins, London.

1

HUMAN RESOURCES STRATEGIES FOR BUSINESS SUCCESS

Roger Cooke

THE BASIS OF HUMAN RESOURCE STRATEGY

Why is it that so few organisations have articulated human resources strategies? Why are companies that have shown the way in developing strategies at corporate, business unit and functional level so much slower to develop strategies for the management of their people?

The answer is not that human resources are seen as too unstrategic to merit a strategy: on the contrary, all the evidence suggests that more and more chief executive officers (CEOs) regard people-related issues as amongst the most critical facing their organisations. The transformation of 'personnel' into 'human resources' reflects this. The key to the paradox is that a central tenet of human resource management is that local managers should be responsible for selecting, motivating and developing staff, rather than the personnel department whose role increasingly is to provide specialist advice and services rather than actually to take decisions. It is an unexpected, even perverse, result that this generally positive development may have made it less, and not more, easy for organisations to develop strategies for the management of their people, because the focus for human resource management has become diffused.

Let me introduce the subject of this chapter with two statements about HR strategy:

- *Human resource strategy is concerned with those decisions which have a major and long-term effect on the employment and development of people in the organisation and on the relationships which exist between its management and staff.* An HR strategy will express the intentions of the enterprise about how it should manage its human resources. These intentions provide the basis for plans, developments and programmes for managing change.

- *HR strategy exists to support the achievement of the business strategy.* This support should be both proactive and reactive:

  — *Proactive* in the sense that it suggests how the organisation can maximise the added value provided by its human resources. Michael Porter[1] has suggested that the skills and motivation of a company's people and the way they are deployed can be a major source of competitive advantage. A proactive approach will identify the human resource strengths of the organisation so that business strategies can be created which take into account how these strengths can be utilised and developed.

  — *Reactive* in that when the HR implications of established business strategy are assessed, decisions can be reached on what directions should be taken to help achieve it. Those decisions can take the form of resourcing, development, reward, employee relations, motivation or commitment strategies.

Ideally, an iterative approach is adopted in which those responsible for HR strategy are both proactive and reactive — helping to shape business strategy and also ensuring that 'strategic fit' is obtained between the business strategy and that relating to human resources.

Much has been written and spoken about human resource strategy, but there is little evidence of what has actually been done about it. The overall purpose of this book is to illustrate, on the basis of the authors' practical experience as consultants and managers, how particular aspects of HR strategy can be developed. My particular aim in this chapter is to take a wider view of HR strategy as an integrating force and to discuss how this can be achieved. To do this I shall first, examine briefly what business strategy is, how it is developed and the forms it takes, as a basis for understanding where HR strategy fits. Secondly, I shall assess how HR strategy can be integrated with the business strategy, and finally, I shall consider the components of HR strategy and approaches to its development.

BUSINESS STRATEGY[1]

What it is, and what it is not

Experts in business strategy tell us that business strategy determines the direction in which the enterprise is going within its environment in order to achieve sustainable competitive advantage — strategy is a declaration of intent which is concerned with the long-term allocation of significant company resources. It is the means of addressing critical issues or success factors at the level of the company as a whole or an aspect of it — for example, a business unit or major function such as manufacturing or information technology (IT). Thus, strategic decisions aim to make a major and long-term impact on the behaviour of the organisation.

Strategists distinguish strategy from business objectives, plans, financial projections, targets for shareholder value or key result areas. These latter are simply outcomes or expressions of strategy. The ingredients and outcomes of a business strategy are summarised in Figure 1.1.

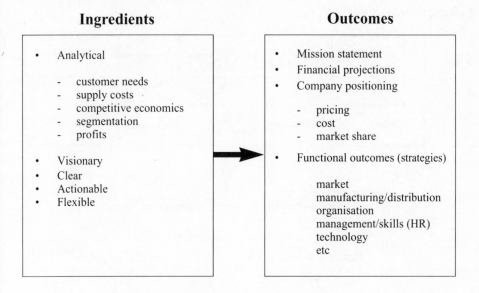

Figure 1.1 Ingedients and outcomes of business strategy

Clearly, there are no universal rules on how business strategy should be developed or expressed. Within the same organisation there will be different levels of strategy, and the approach to strategy formulation and the style used to manage it in diversified companies will vary.

Levels of business strategy

There are two levels of business strategy. At the *corporate* level, strategy is likely to be concerned in general with the composition and performance of the portfolio of businesses which make up a company. In particular, corporate strategy is concerned with:

- the company's mission;
- the cohesiveness of that portfolio;
- mergers, acquisitions and divestments;
- the ethos of how to manage and control the business.

At *business unit* level, strategy is concerned mainly with answering the question 'where and how are we going to compete in order to earn sustained high returns?' This means making decisions on how, in the longer term, the business can develop superior effectiveness, a superior cost position and superior quality, coupled with the ability to meet customers' real needs. The key elements of this process are illustrated in Figure 1.2.

Key elements

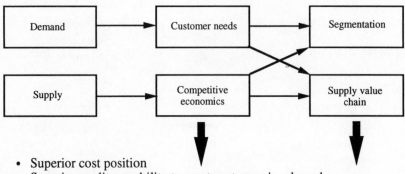

- Superior cost position
- Superior quality or ability to meet customers' real needs
- Superior effectiveness

Figure 1.2 Business unit strategy — key elements

Business unit strategy puts corporate strategy into effect at the competitive level and refers to definition of the business, growth and profitability objectives, product/market scope, marketing approach and competitive position.

These business unit considerations are also the ones most likely to concern medium sized or smaller independent companies which, however, are less likely to have an articulated business strategy.

Approaches to strategy in diversified companies

On the basis of their research into how the corporate offices of 16 British-owned diversified companies managed their relationships with their business units, Goold and Campbell[2] discussed how the corporate centre tackles its roles of setting and reviewing strategies, allocating resources, reviewing plans and controlling and auditing performance. They refer to Lorsch's[3] view that superior performance in diversified companies depends upon the ability of each business unit to attain its objectives, strategies and culture within its competitive environment. The problem is achieving a balance between the strategies of business units, which are tailored to local circumstances, and the role of the centre in providing policies and a structure which integrates the divisions into a corporate whole.

Goold and Campbell identified three styles of managing strategy. Each addresses how this balance is achieved by means of a different corporate approach to influencing business unit strategies. The three styles are those adopted by:

1. **Strategic planning companies** which believe that their corporate centres should participate in and influence the development of business unit strategies by establishing demanding planning processes and making contributions of substance to strategic thinking. The centre is at its best in helping businesses to embark on strategies to build long-term competitive advantage. The centre encourages a wide search for the best strategies, is willing to coordinate between businesses if needed, and provides a buffer against capital market pressures. It believes that the best approach to defining strategy and motivating management is cooperative and collabora-tive between the business and the centre with an emphasis on shared purposes. Companies with this style are BOC, BP, Cadbury Schweppes, Lex, STC and UB.

2. **Strategic control companies** which are concerned with business unit planning but believe in organising around independent profit-responsible business units, and leaving as much as possible of the initiative to business unit management. The centre therefore focuses more on establishing demanding planning processes, and on reviewing and challenging business unit proposals, than on advocating particular strategies. Tight control is exercised against results achieved, taking into account both financial and strategic objectives. Companies with this style are Courtaulds, ICI, Plessey and Vickers.

3. **Financial control companies** where the centre sees its main tasks as sanctioning expenditure, agreeing targets, monitoring performance against the targets, and taking action to reorganise management teams which are performing poorly. They have no formal planning systems and are concerned mainly with financial results which they control against annual targets. This contrasts with strategic control companies which try to measure strategic achievements and take a longer term view of performance against targets. Companies with this style are BTR, Hanson Trust, GEC and Tarmac.

Goold and Campbell conclude by developing the model summarised in Figure 1.3 which shows that the strategic management style adopted by the centre with regard to its business units should be shaped by the nature of each unit's business and the resources available to the corporation as a whole.

Development of business strategy

Analysis of the concept of business strategy as a basis for HR strategy has to take account not only of the different levels and styles of strategy but also of the diversity of ways in which strategy is formed. It is generally assumed that strategy formulation is an analytical, systematic and rigorous process. But this is not

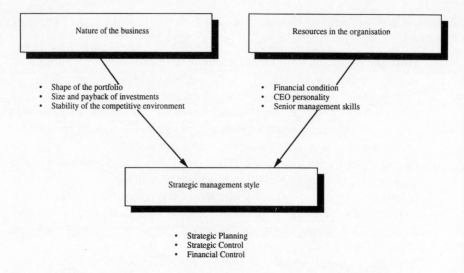

Figure 1.3 Model for development of a strategic management style

Reproduced with permission from Strategies and Styles, Michael Goold and Andrew Campbell, Blackwell 1987

necessarily so. As Johnson[4] comments: 'Strategic decisions are characterised by the political hurly-burly of organizational life with a high incidence of bargaining and a trading off of costs and benefits of one interest group against another; all with a notable lack of clarity in terms of **environmental** influences and objectives'.

Goold and Campbell also emphasise the variety and ambiguity of influences which shape strategy:

> Informal understandings work alongside more formal processes and analyses. The headquarters agenda becomes entwined with the business unit agenda, and both are interpreted in the light of personal interests. The sequence of events from decision to action can often be reversed, so that 'decisions' get made retrospectively to justify actions that have already taken place.

Strategy formulation is not necessarily a rational and continuous process, as was pointed out by Mintzberg.[5] He believes that, rather than being consciously and systematically developed, strategy reorientations happen in brief quantum leaps. Strategies, according to Mintzberg, are not always deliberate. In theory, he says, strategy is a systematic process. 'First we think, then we act. We formulate then we implement.' In practice, 'a realised strategy can emerge in response to an evolving situation' and the strategist is often 'a pattern organizer, a learner if you like, who manages a process in which strategies, and visions, can emerge as well as be deliberately conceived.'

Articulating business strategies

Business strategies are not necessarily expressed in writing, although there are advantages in doing so from the point of view of having a defined point of reference for planning and control purposes. Strategic management and strategic control companies are more likely to prepare formal, long-term strategic plans, but financial control companies will rely on one year budgets with interim reforecasts as required.

A business unit or independent company may have a formal strategy but it is more likely, especially in the case of a financial control company, to have an unwritten strategic orientation which is based on an assessment of future market opportunities. In Mintzberg's phrase, these organisations 'craft' their strategies, being responsive to changing situations as they emerge while still taking a view on the general direction in which they are going.

INTEGRATING BUSINESS AND HUMAN RESOURCE STRATEGY

Strategic integration is necessary in order to provide congruence between business and human resource strategy so that the latter supports the accomplishment of the former and, indeed, helps to define it. The aim is to provide strategic fit and consistency between the policy goals of human resource management and the business.

Problems of integration

However, integrating the two is easier said than done for the following reasons:

1. **Diversity of strategic processes, levels and styles** — as described above, the different levels at which strategy is formulated and the different styles adopted by organisations may make it difficult to develop a coherent view of what sort of HR strategies will fit the overall business strategies and what type of HR contributions are required during the process of business strategy formulation. In other words, it may be difficult to focus HR strategies.
2. **The evolutionary nature of business strategy,** which may make it difficult to pin down the relevant HR strategies.
3. **The absence of written business strategies,** which adds to the problems of clarifying the strategic business issues which human resource strategies should address.
4. **The qualitative nature of HR issues** — business strategies tend, or at least aim, to be expressed in the common currency of figures and hard data on portfolio structure, growth, competitive positioning, market share, profit-ability etc. HR strategies may deal with quantifiable issues such as resourcing

and skills acquisition but are equally likely to refer to qualitative factors such as commitment, motivation, good employee relations and high employment standards. And, as John Purcell[6] has written:

If it were possible to demonstrate that 'enlightened' or progressive approaches to the management of people were invariably associated with higher productivity, lower unit costs and improved profit, life would be easier for the human resource planner. As it is, little can be proved because of the complexity of the variables and the impossibility of monitoring and measuring all the relevant dynamics and relationships.

Approaches to dealing with these problems

These are serious problems and it may be difficult for the HR strategist to overcome them completely. But the attempt should be made and the following approaches are available.

1. **Understand how business strategy is formed**
    The HR strategist should take pains to understand the levels at which business strategy is formed and the style adopted by the company in creating strategy and monitoring its implementation. It will then be easier to focus on those corporate or business unit issues which are likely to have HR implications.
2. **Understand the key business issues**
    The key business issues which may impact on HR strategies include:

    — intentions concerning growth or retrenchment, acquisitions, mergers, investments, divestments, diversification, product/market development;
    — proposals on increasing competitive advantage through productivity, improved quality/customer service, cost reduction;
    — the perceived need to develop a more positive, performance-orientated culture;
    — other culture management imperatives associated with changes in the philosophies of the organisation in such areas as moving from 'control' to 'commitment', mutuality, communications, involvement, empowerment, devolution and teamworking.

Business strategies in these areas should not be over-influenced by HR factors. HR strategies are, after all, primarily about making business strategies work. But the business strategy must take into account key HR opportunities and constraints.

Business strategy, therefore, sets the agenda for HR strategy in the following areas:

*   resourcing;
*   skills acquisition and development;
*   culture, values and attitudes;

- commitment;
- productivity;
- performance management;
- rewards;
- employee relations.

While these may all arise at *business unit* level, there are a number of strategic issues which exist at the *corporate* level and are likely to have a decisive influence on HR strategy. These are:

- corporate mission;
- corporate values, culture and style;
- organisational philosophy and approach to the management of people;
- top management as a corporate resource.

Some organisations such as IBM, Hewlett-Packard and Marks & Spencer will have clearly articulated strategies in these areas. Others will not, until events force a re-evaluation of the mission, values, philosophies and structure of the organisation, as has happened in such companies as British Airways, BP, Thorn EMI and ICL. These changes have often taken place following the appointment of a CEO with a new vision of where the organisation should be going and how it is going to get there.

3. **Establish methods of linking business and HR strategy**

   Business and HR issues influence each other, and in turn influence corporate and business unit strategy. It must be remembered, however, that in establishing those links account must be taken of the fact that strategies for change have also to be integrated with the changes in the external and internal environments. This is illustrated in a model developed by Professor Andrew Pettigrew and his team at the Centre for Corporate Strategy and Change, Warwick University (Figure 1.4).

This model shows in general the relationships between HR and business strategy and the environment, but how can specific links be achieved?

To achieve a link in rigorous terms would require a means of quantifying the resources allocated to human resource development, both overall and at the level of each element of HR strategy, and then measuring and comparing the marginal return (in terms of higher profit) on investing in each element. But, to echo Purcell's point, such an approach is unlikely to be practicable. The link must therefore be judgemental, but it can still be rigorous. Conceptually, the approach would be to develop a matrix as illustrated in Figure 1.5 which, for each of the key elements of business strategy, identifies the associated key elements of HR strategy.

While it may seldom, if ever, be possible to devise a complete expression of these relationships in matrix form, at least this approach will ensure that the implications and interrelationships of business and HR strategy are analysed systematically. The following is a disguised example of a real life statement of business strategy which has been distilled into an HR strategy statement, which in turn has been expanded into an expression of its key elements.

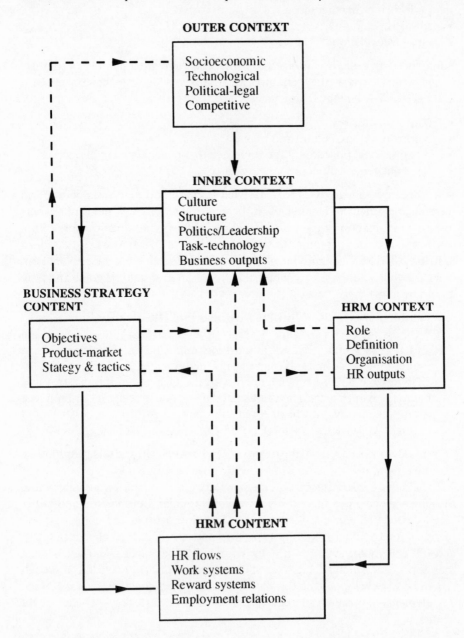

Figure 1.4 Model of strategic change and human resource management

Key elements of business strategy

Key elements of HR strategy		1	2	3	4	5
	A					
	B					
	C					
	D					
	E					

Figure 1.5 A conceptual approach to linking key elements of business and HR strategies

Statement of business strategy

A strategic mission has been developed for Division A to provide a clear direction for its business into the 1990s. The chosen strategy recognises that A is uncompetitive in three of its product groups and that a major restructuring of its manufacturing base and product support is necessary.

The strategic mission for Division A is to acquire and integrate businesses B and C into Division A to become the leading worldwide competitor in specialist automatic gearbox systems for heavy duty off-road vehicles:

- wheeled military applications;
- construction applications;
- agricultural applications.

A major investment programme in alloy and other non-ferrous castings and a minor reinvestment in oil seal technology is to be adopted. It is not intended to be involved in new basic designs.

The X factory facilities for components will be relocated at Y factory, and those for future assembly and test at Z factory, the X factory being closed before expiry of the lease.

The product support business is to be reorganised to form a separate profit centre located in Z factory.

The cellular manufacturing strategy will be continued which, together with the overall reduction in business complexity and improved control, will remain the basis for the necessary improvements in operating performance.

In order to fund this reinvestment programme, P and Q businesses will be divested by Division A. It is proposed, however, to expand the profitable business, R, as a hedge against declining turnover.

Finally, to establish Division A as a leading supplier in the specialist automatic gearbox systems markets, this strategy envisages integrating the relevant activities of B and C to form a formidable competitor on a worldwide scale.

HR strategy statement — Division A

The chosen business strategy involves:

- acquisition of two businesses and integrating them with Division A's businesses;
- a major capital investment programme in new product technology;
- continuing development of the Division's cellular manufacturing strategy to simplify the business;
- closure of one site and relocation to a second site;
- reorganisation of one business unit.

In the light of the selected business strategy the Division's strategic HR objectives will be to:

- integrate the organisation structure and management teams of businesses B and C into Division A;
- maximise our investment in new technologies through targeted programmes for developing skills, maximising staff productivity and effectiveness, and minimising waste;
- manage the downsizing and restructuring of staff cadres humanely and responsibly;
- establish a clear ethos and culture for the division based on values relevant to the business strategy.

The key elements of our HR strategy will be:

- organisational restructuring and management training to support:
  — integration of two acquired businesses
  — repositioning of product support;
- high performance work design at Y and Z sites incorporating multi-skilling and autonomous working groups;
- new performance management and performance-related pay systems at all sites;
- new early retirement policy for management;
- 'hard-to-refuse' relocation packages for selected staff at X;
- sensitive redundancy programme for other staff at X which improves on current best industry practice;
- reaffirmation and roll out of TQM and customer care programmes across the Division to provide a firm philosophic basis for integrating new businesses and establishing a clear ethos and culture.

DEVELOPING HR STRATEGY

To summarise my argument thus far, HR strategy can be used as an integrating force, linking various strands together into an overall strategic thrust which complements and is consistent with the overall business strategy. In some circumstances this may be highly desirable; for example, when Book Club Associates, a leading mail order book club, embarked on a programme of sustained growth and diversification, it developed an integrated HR strategy aimed at achieving significant cultural change in four main areas — communications, involvement, performance management and reward management. The links between each aspect of this strategy were emphasised and new communications channels were developed and used to ensure that everyone knew and could discuss the implications of the business strategy.

The key requirements of HR strategy are that it should be:

- justified from the business strategy;
- imaginative and innovative;
- clear and actionable;
- selective, focusing on priorities;
- flexible.

There is, however, no standard format for a statement of HR strategy; it will depend entirely on the circumstances. Strategic HR thinking may indeed concentrate on one area such as resourcing or performance management, although it would be important to ensure that the implications of change in one direction are considered for other aspects of human resource management. For example, the development of a performance management system raises questions about career development, training and performance related pay.

Key issues

Of all of the requirements of HR strategy referred to above, perhaps the most critical is that HR strategy should be justified by business strategy. Without this, HR strategies will be seen by top management and line managers as of little relevance to the real priorities of the business, and the credibility of the HR function will be in doubt.

It is, therefore, instructive to consider the views of senior business executives on how they rank HR issues among the key business issues that their organisations face. The survey summarised in Table 1.1 provides some insight.

Organising and managing HR strategy development

Effective integration of HR strategy is best achieved if the personnel director is closely involved at top management level with the formulation of business strategy. One would expect the head of the personnel function to be a member

Table 1.1 View of CEOs on key business and HR issues

In 1989 Coopers & Lybrand assisted the Management Consultancies' Association to survey the views of 100 chief executive officers on HR and business issues. The survey established that 84 per cent of the respondents ranked HR as one of their top three concerns, while 93 per cent marked HR as one of their top five concerns. The three most important issues of all types mentioned were:

- recruitment (67 per cent of replies);
- skills (42 per cent);
- productivity (35 per cent).

The issues mentioned most frequently were:

- people availability (42 per cent);
- 1992 (31 per cent);
- customer care (25 per cent);
- competitiveness (25 per cent).

Despite the emphasis given to HR issues, it is interesting to note that one of the issues which was mentioned least frequently was industrial relations (7 per cent).

CEOs' views on the actions needed to address these issues were distributed as follows:

- training/retraining (mentioned by 56 per cent of CEOs);
- rewards/incentives (41 per cent);
- employment of older people (27 per cent);
- use of new technology (25 per cent);
- flexible conditions (21 per cent);
- communications (20 per cent).

The emphasis, therefore, was on specifics such as resourcing, training and motivation through rewards.

of an executive or management committee, or at least to have access to the CEO, in order to obtain information about the direction business strategy is taking and make contributions at an early stage on any HR implications.

HR strategies should be based on information concerning:

- the business strategy and plan;
- the external environment, with particular reference to the supply of people (demographics) and the availability of skills;
- the internal environment, including the implications of product develop-

ment and new technology, the requirement for increased flexibility and the need for new skills and multi-skilling;

- HR issues related to productivity, motivation, communications, commitment, involvement, employee relations etc.

HR strategy should be backed up by a computerised personnel information system as described in Chapter 10. This will provide basic data on human resource stocks and flows, and decision support data on other aspects of human resource management including the availability of skills, productivity and basic indicators of motivation and commitment such as employee turnover and absence.

HR STRATEGY AREAS

Let me now turn to specific aspects of HR strategy which, collectively, will form the building blocks of overall HR strategy development. No two organisations will face quite the same issues, and each will address in its own way those issues that it does face. Nonetheless, it may be helpful to look at some of the issues that will be relevant to many organisations, each of which is elaborated in subsequent chapters of this book.

Fundamental questions

First however, I should emphasise that a human resource management strategy should provide answers to three fundamental questions which relate to all the specific aspects discussed below:

1. How are we going to acquire and retain the number and quality of people required to meet the forecast needs of the organisation?
2. How are we going to ensure that we have a well motivated and fully committed workforce?
3. What actions will be needed to train, develop and fit people for greater responsibility and responsiveness to change and the resulting demands for different skills and abilities?

Acquisition and retention strategies

A starting point in the development of a human resource strategy is often the identification of the long-term human resource requirements of the organisation. These have to be assessed in general terms to provide the basis for more detailed human resource planning processes. The aim of HR acquisition and retention strategies should be to ensure, on the one hand, that the achievement of corporate objectives will not be inhibited by human resource shortages or inefficiencies and, on the other, that impending surpluses can be dealt with in good time with the minimum individual hardship and disruption to employee relations.

At this stage broad questions need to be answered concerning:

- Human resource requirements:

    — how many employees are needed? — over what period?
    — what kind of abilities and skills will be required?

- Availability:

    — what is available now inside the company?
    — what would be made available from inside and outside the company?

- Retention:

    — what is the company's experience in retaining staff?
    — what are the problems and how can they be overcome?

- Human resources utilisation:

    — how well are human resources used in the company?
    — what is the scope for increasing productivity?

Motivation strategy

Motivation strategy should aim to increase the effective contribution of members of the organisation in achieving its objectives. Motivation strategy will refer to the performance management and reward systems, and in particular to the type and scale of financial incentives which are to be provided. But it will also be concerned with other processes which should yield favourable attitudes, including job design, participation, joint objective setting, career development, and any other processes relating to the individual's need to achieve and maintain a sense of personal worth and importance. Motivation is also affected by the quality of leadership in an organisation; therefore the selection, training and development of effective leaders should be part of the strategy.

Human resource development and training strategies

A human resource development strategy is concerned with the longer term programmes needed by an organisation to improve operational performance at all levels, in accordance with the additional demands which the business strategy will place on people in the future. The strategy will provide continuous development processes linked closely with the programmes designed for the organisation as a whole to implement its product, technology and market development strategies.

The associated training strategy will be concerned particularly with the development of new or existing competences, and with multi-skilling. For example, it will take account of the introduction of new technology and of increased demands for 'knowledge workers', and for 'systems technicians' on production lines. The training strategy may be linked to the reward strategy by the development of skills or competency-based payment systems.

Organisation development strategy

The aim of an organisation development strategy should be to ensure that an effective organisation is maintained which will respond appropriately to changes in its internal and external environment and make the best use of the individual and collective capacities of its members. The main strategic areas in which organisation development takes place are:

- the implications of change and the actions required to ensure that the organisation will continue to function effectively when subjected to pressures resulting from change.
- changes in organisation structure as well as values and culture development programmes, and changes in organisation climate and management style.
- the proper integration of increasingly diversified activities which are likely to result from change.
- team development.
- the management of conflict.
- work on planning and objective-setting processes for individuals and teams.

Reward strategy

A reward strategy will be concerned with:

- developing a positive, performance-orientated culture;
- underpinning the organisation's values, especially those relating to excellence, innovation, performance, teamwork and quality;
- conveying a message to prospective high-calibre employees that the organisation will satisfy their reward expectations;
- ensuring that the right mix and levels of reward are provided in line with the culture of the organisation, the needs of the business, the needs of employees and the economic, competitive and market environment in which the business operates;
- linking reward policies, systems and procedures to the key business and human resource strategies for innovation, growth, development and the pursuit of excellence;
- developing a strong orientation toward the achievement of sustained high levels of performance throughout the organisation by recognising successful performance and increases in levels of competence, thus contributing to the processes of empowering, enabling and energising all employees;
- indicating to existing employees what types of behaviour will be rewarded

and how this will take place, thus increasing motivation and commitment and improving performance.

Employee relations strategy

The aim of an employee relations strategy is to develop policies, systems and procedures which maximise the degree to which management and employees will co-operate to their mutual benefit, and minimise the causes and effects of unnecessary conflict or restrictive practices.

The employee relations strategy will be concerned with enhancing 'mutuality', improving relationships and establishing and maintaining the rules and procedures which govern the management and discussion of issues affecting the company and its employees. It will encompass strategies for union recognition or de-recognition, and for any collective bargaining arrangements. It will also cover the strategies for negotiations and for involving employees in the affairs of the company as well as for communicating to them information about the company's performance and future plans.

IMPLEMENTING AND EVALUATING HR STRATEGY

So much for the content, developed in later chapters of this book, of specific aspects of HR strategy. The development of a strategy is, of course, only part of the story. Without effective implementation and marketing even the best prepared HR strategy will fail.

In this context there are, in my experience, three inherent problems relating to HR strategies. First, they become ends in themselves — all the effort goes into their creation rather than their implementation. Secondly, HR strategies are expressed as bland statements with which everyone can agree but no one need do anything about. Thirdly, no systematic attempt is made to evaluate them.

Avoidance of these problems depends on two key requirements. First, determined efforts must be made to inject realism into the HR strategy by, in a sense, building it into the fabric of the business strategy, so that the contribution the HR strategy is designed to make is evident from the business strategy and progress made in its implementation can be evaluated against defined objectives. Much of this book is concerned with how this should be done.

Strategies for securing commitment to change

Secondly, and this is a critical overlay that is only now becoming properly recognised, an organisation that is serious about achieving strategic change through people will require a *commitment* strategy — a strategy for winning the hearts and minds of its people, for harnessing their skills and abilities in the search for competitive advantage and superior performance, and for enabling and empowering them to develop themselves in the interests of both themselves and the organisation.

A commitment strategy is inherently long term. Extensive work is now taking place on both sides of the Atlantic, and in Japan, to develop frameworks, approaches and techniques for securing commitment — for example by ODR, an Atlanta-based research and training consultancy that has developed a behaviourally-based process for securing commitment to and internalising change. My aim in the concluding paragraphs of this chapter is to outline how organisations should approach developing their commitment strategies.

A strategy for gaining commitment to change should cover the following phases:

- **Preparation** — In this phase, the person or persons likely to be affected by the proposed change are identified and made aware of the fact that a change is being contemplated.
- **Acceptance** — In the second phase, more specific information is provided on the purpose of the change, how it is proposed to implement the change and what effect this will have on those concerned. The aim is to achieve understanding of what the change means and to obtain a positive reaction. This is more likely if:

    — the change is perceived to be consistent with the mission and values of the organisation;
    — the change is not thought to be threatening;
    — the change seems likely to meet the needs of those concerned;
    — there is a compelling and fully understood reason for change;
    — those concerned are involved in planning and implementing the change programme;
    — it is understood that steps will be taken to mitigate any detrimental effects of the change.

    It may be difficult, even impossible, to meet these requirements. That is why the problems of gaining commitment to change should not be underestimated.

    During this phase, the extent to which reactions are positive or negative can be noted and action taken accordingly. It is at this stage that original plans may have to be modified to cater for legitimate reservations or second thoughts. As Pettigrew and Whipp[7] concluded from their recent research into change in a number of British firms in the automobile, publishing, financial services and insurance industries, implementing change 'may include clusters of iterative action in order to break through ignorance or resistance'. Change, as they put it, is an 'iterative, cumulative and re-formulation-in-use process'.

- **Commitment** — During the third phase, the change is implemented and becomes operational. The change process and people's reaction to it need to be monitored. There will inevitably be delays, setbacks, unforseen problems and negative reactions from those faced with the reality of change. A response to these reactions is essential so that valid criticisms can be acted upon or explanations given of why it is believed that the change should proceed as planned.

Following implementation, the aim is to get the change adopted as, with use, its worth becomes evident. The decision is made at this stage on whether to continue with the change or whether it needs to be modified or even aborted. Again, account should be taken of the views of those involved.

Finally, and after further modifications as required, the change is institutionalised and becomes an inherent part of the organisation's culture and operations.

NOTES

1. *I am indebted to my colleagues in Outram Cullinan & Co (OC&C), the strategy consulting arm of Coopers & Lybrand, for some of the material in this section.*

REFERENCES

1. Porter, M E (1987) 'From competitive advantage to corporate strategy', *Harvard Business Review*, May-June.
2. Goold, M and Campbell, A (1987) *Strategies and Styles*, Blackwell, Oxford.
3. Lorsch, J W and Stephen, A (1973) *Managing Diversity and Interdependence*, Division of Research, Harvard Business School.
4. Johnson, G (1987) *Strategic Change and the Management Process*, Blackwell, Oxford.
5. Mintzberg, H (1987) 'Crafting strategy,' *Harvard Business Review*, July-August.
6. Purcell, J (1989) 'The impact of corporate strategy on human resource management,' *New Perspectives on Human Resource Management*, ed Storey, D Routledge, London.
7. Pettigrew, A and Whipp, R (1991) *Managing Change for Competitive Success*, Blackwell, Oxford.

2

DEVELOPING THE RIGHT ORGANISATION

Kelvin Hard

INTRODUCTION

It is widely recognised that how well a company or institution is organised is a major determinant of whether or not it will be successful. Yet very few organisations have a section or even an individual whose job it is to be expert in organisational matters and to advise top management on such issues. Organisational change tends to be the responsibility of managing directors or general managers, whose knowledge is usually based mainly on their own experience, perhaps mixed in with some selective reading or else some prejudices or nostrums about organisation gained during the course of their managerial careers.

As a consultant specialising in organisational issues, I am frequently confronted by very senior managers with an extremely one-dimensional view of organisational issues. Some see organisation as exclusively about structure, and seem to believe that organisation is a mechanical concept susceptible to immutable laws, such as 'six direct reports is the maximum span of control' or 'matrix structures never work'. Others are the victims of various fads or fashions in management science, and so (for example) believe that the only thing that matters about an organisation is its culture. The managerial 'culture vultures' have often been inspired by books such as *In Search of Excellence* to analyse the culture of their own organisations, and then come up against the fact that it is much easier to describe an organisational culture than it is to change it, and are disappointed that there is no two-month action programme which can be recommended to achieve this.

In this chapter, we consider the range of organisational issues which companies and other bodies face and the role which the personnel or human resources function should play in helping to manage such issues. The Coopers & Lybrand management consultancy has an Organisation and Human Resources practice, recognising the close links which exist between their two sets of issues. In the US, the personnel function of major corporations quite often has specific responsibility for organisation matters. But as yet, very few personnel functions in the UK (whether in the private or public sector) have an overt role, acknowledged by others, as active advisors on organisation issues. This is a fundamental weakness because:

- it deprives the company of a source of systematic advice on this subject and a continuous review of how effectively it is organised;
- it reduces the effectiveness of the personnel function, because it means that vital areas of human resource management tend to be seen as technical personnel issues (eg, reward being about job evaluation and salary surveys) rather than in their wider organisational context.

In the UK, many management services (or similar) functions undertake 'efficiency' studies which bear on organisational issues. In other companies, this role is fulfilled by the internal audit function. However, neither of these functions is likely to be well placed to integrate organisation issues into the wider human resources context.

HISTORY OF ORGANISATIONAL ISSUES

In order to understand how the present situation arose, and to point the way to how the gap between organisational and personnel issues came about, it is helpful to consider briefly the history of thinking about organisations.

For many hundreds of years there were only two types of large-scale organisations in existence, the church and the armed forces. The fundamental missions of both organisations were very slow to change, as were the basic principles by which they were organised. Most of the early thinking about management derived directly from the military, for example the distinction between line and staff functions. The term 'personnel' itself derives from the military vocabulary, being one of the two components of an army, namely its people (the other component — materiel — was the army's physical resources). But as the 'personnel management' function began to emerge in the early part of the twentieth century, it tended to focus on three areas:

1. personnel administration, such as payment of wages and personnel records
2. the provision to individuals of what might broadly be termed a welfare service
3. acting as a focal point for dealing with the workforce collectively, especially through their trades unions (ie, labour relations).

Thus the personnel function did not attempt to deal systematically with all the different issues which we now understand to be involved in 'organisation', because it is only much more recently that any such holistic concept of the term 'organisation' has emerged. The first recorded use of the term 'organisation' in anything like its modern sense is by Herbert Spencer in 1873. In the 120 or so years since then, a variety of approaches or models for looking at organisations has emerged. Each has dominated for a while, only to be replaced by the next dominant model, but each has left a continuing mark on how we think about organisations. Some of the main approaches are characterised — in approximately chronological order — in Table 2.1.

Table 2.1   Some approaches to thinking about organisations

Approach	Characteristics
Structural	Concerned with hierarchical relations, divisions of tasks and roles to achieve organisational ends
Bureaucracy	Concerned with authority as a means to completing tasks efficiently. Uses sociological insights
Human Relations	Concerned with the achievement of managerial goals through meeting the social needs of the workgroup
Organisational Psychology	Concerned with matching organisational needs to individuals' needs for personal satisfaction and fulfilment
Systems (or Contingency) Theory	Concerned with how organisations adapt to meet the differing demands of the market, technology and individuals
Action Theory	Concerned with how individuals influence organisations by making sense of, and giving meaning to, their own actions
Organisational Culture	Concerned with the unwritten norms which influence how people behave in organisations. Uses anthropological insights

Best practice today in managing organisational issues is not to chose one model or way of thinking about organisations but to take account of all the models and dimensions of 'organisation' which are relevant to a particular situation.

WHAT IS AN ORGANISATION?

In most companies if you ask its managers to describe the organisation, this will be done principally in terms of structure. Almost certainly, organisation charts will be produced which depict organisation structure by setting out the division of roles and reporting lines. In terms of the approaches outlined in Table 2.1, this represents a mixture of the structural and bureaucratic models, and is normally underpinned — consciously or unconsciously — by a set of beliefs about organisations:

- Each person should receive orders from a single superior.
- There should be a single chain of command running from top to bottom of the organisation for the purposes of communication and coordination.
- The number of people reporting to one supervisor must be limited, so as to enable effective control and coordination.
- There should be a clear distinction between 'line' functions (eg, production or operations) and 'staff' or advisory functions (eg, personel).
- Tasks should be differentiated according to different specialisms so as to focus expert knowledge and ensure tasks are done efficiently.
- Individuals should be given *responsibility* for certain tasks and the requisite *authority* to carry these responsibilities out.

While some or all of these beliefs may still be found to apply in even the most leading edge organisations, the fact is that organisations are much more complex than these principles imply. It is essential, therefore, that the human resources manager works with a model of what an organisation is which can engage systematically with that complexity. One such model is shown in Figure 2.1. It does not purport to be the only or definitive model of what an organisation is; but it is a model which encompasses all of the main elements which are currently thought to make up an organisation. Let us now look at the main issues which arise with each element.

Mission and strategy

An organisation's *mission statement* defines why the organisation exists, and what purposes it seeks to fulfil. Examples of mission statements are:

> 'To supply high technology products within committed cost, time and market quality and delivery requirements.'
>
> *ICL Manufacturing Operations*

> 'Lamb Technicon is a world-wide leader in the design and manufacture of automotive manufacturing systems. Our mission is to continually improve our products and services to meet our customers' needs, allowing us to prosper as a business.'
>
> *Lamb Technicon*

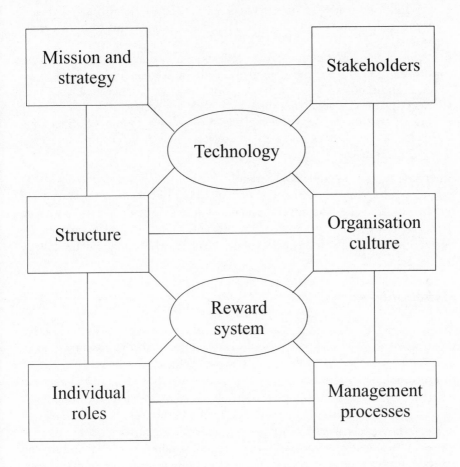

Figure 2.1 Elements of an organisation

The mission statement is an important element of an organisation because the other elements should be arranged and managed so as to fulfil that mission statement. In this way, the mission statement should provide a key reference point as to whether a particular organisational change or development is desirable. Organisations that do not have a clear mission statement risk confusion or ambiguity: disagreements about organisation and strategy can often be traced back to different opinions about what an organisation's mission should be in the absence of a clear statement of what it *is*.

Some guidelines for the development of a mission statement are:

- Ensure that the mission statement encapsulates the fundamental *purpose* of the organisation (normally to be in certain markets and to fulfil certain values).
- Have a mission statement that reflects the *particular* nature of your organisation, not a bland statement (eg, 'to be the leading company in the such-and-such market') which could apply equally to other organisations.
- Keep the mission statement short, clear and memorable.
- Ensure that the mission statement is supported by a strategy (including critical success factors) and a set of core values which are clearly understood and communicated.

An organisation's strategy is a declaration of intent which is concerned with the long-term allocation of company resources to fulfil its mission. An increasing number of strategies do cover human resources issues such as employee numbers, costs and skills. However, very few strategies yet encompass the organisational changes and developments which may be required if the strategy is to be achieved.

Stakeholders

Though they are very useful, mission statements do carry with them the risk that they focus too much on the purposes or interests of too narrow a group of stakeholders, ie, the employees and/or owners of the organisation. The concept of a stakeholder is a useful one. It means anyone who has a legitimate interest in what an organisation does. From the stakeholders' perspective, the boundaries of an organisation are actually much wider than a standard organisation chart implies. The stakeholders of a commercial company might, for example, include owners, employees, employees' spouses and families, customers, company pensioners, distributors, suppliers of goods and services, business and domestic neighbours of the company's sites, anyone affected by the environmental impact of the Company's operations, and government (local, central and EC). It is increasingly important for organisations to identify and manage actively the whole range of stakeholder relationships with which they are involved. For example:

- A key component of Marks & Spencer's success is its relationships with its suppliers. Manufacturers are helped and encouraged to become efficient and successful; in return, Marks & Spencer expect keen prices and a higher degree of responsiveness to its wishes than is normally available.
- When the London Business School established its part-time MBA pro-gramme, extensive international research showed that bosses and spouses were the key influence on whether students completed a demanding and lengthy part-time course. The school therefore invested considerable resources in gaining ownership and commitment from these two groups by inviting them in for regular briefings and social events.

- The London Docklands airport could not become profitable unless the runway were extended to enable longer-range aeroplanes to use it. A long — and ultimately successful — campaign was mounted to persuade the planning and regulatory authorities and to try to allay the fears of local residents.

Technology

In the organisational context, 'technology' means any plant or equipment that an organisation uses to help it transform inputs into outputs. The extent to which technology determines organisation varies according to the nature of the core technologies which the organisation uses. For example:

- In a continuous process plant such as a steelworks, the part of the organisation directly supporting that plant cannot be readily varied without investing in new plant.
- In a major assembly plant, like a car factory, organisation is similarly plant-determined, but one sub-assembly area can be altered without necessarily affecting the others.
- Service operations such as banks have some jobs which are technology-influenced (eg, computer staff) but considerable freedom elsewhere in terms of how to organise.
- A professional services organisation, (eg, an advertising agency or a management consultancy) can be organised with relatively little regard to the technology employed.

The number of people actually engaged on highly technology-determined work such as manufacturing is steadily falling in advanced countries. Even major manufacturing companies tend to employ only a minority of their workforce on actual *manufacturing*. The focus of the human resources (HR) manager thinking about the effects of technology on organisation has tended to turn away from manufacturing and towards information technology, and away from technology as an influencer of structure towards technology as a determinant of strategy and culture.

There are several ways in which technology now influences organisations: Sophisticated information technology networks such as widespread electronic mail and voice messaging systems tend to 'democratise' organisations by cutting across line management channels of communication. This can facilitate flatter hierarchies and better project working across a 'networked organisation', but can also cause shifts of power and influence which need to be carefully managed.

Shifts in technology can pose radical questions about how companies are organised and staffed. For example, First Direct's tele-banking operation may, if it is very successful, call into question much of the need for the branch network run by its parent, Midland Bank (and similarly for other retail banks).

Flexible manufacturing techniques are reducing the minimum efficient plant size for various processes and products, so reducing some of the technical constraints on organisation for those companies which make best use of these advanced techniques.

Structure

For many managers, the terms 'organisation' and 'structure' are almost synonymous. It therefore follows that when a manager wants to improve the performance of an organisation, some alteration to the formal structure will usually feature high up the list of favoured interventions. We argue strongly that all the elements of an organisation set out in Figure 2.1 above need to be considered in a *holistic* manner. Nevertheless, changes to organisation structure are one of the most powerful — and tangible — interventions that can be made to improve organisation performance.

Some of the basic structures most frequently found in organisations are set out

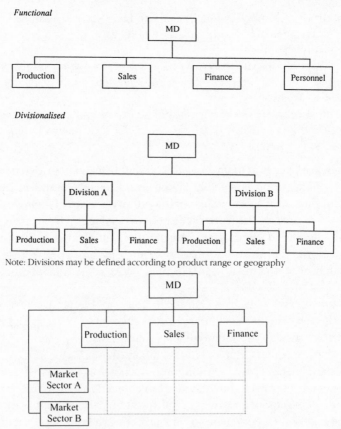

Figure 2.2 Basic organisation structure

in a simplified form in Figure 2.2. Most organisations begin with a simple, functional structure: increasing size and/or complexity are what usually drives organisations to change their basic structure.

There is no simple set of decision rules which determine when any particular form of organisation will lead to optimum performance. It is often said that structure should be in line with strategy; but many changes in business strategy imply no particular structure more than another. In practice, any organisational structure represents a compromise between conflicting pressures, a necessary over-simplification of the complexities which any organisation has to deal with. An organisation structure is one of the ways in which that organisation tries to shape and make sense of its world. Changing the structure normally reflects the fact that the organisation considers its world has changed, that certain things have become more important than they were before, and that it is time to focus on them. This is illustrated by the following case study, which exemplifies a re-structuring designed to respond to changing business forces.

Case Study — British Shoe Corporation

The British Shoe Corporation (BSC) owns many of the best-known High Street shoe shops, including Dolcis, Saxone, Freeman Hardy Willis and many more. BSC was built up by Sir Charles Clore, who stripped out the separate managements and established a single, functional structure, with buying, finance, distribution etc being undertaken by the same set of people for all of some 2,500 outlets. This enabled BSC to maximise economies of scale and purchasing power and so to be very price competitive. But all this changed with the retail revolution of the 1980s; success now lay not in shaving 50p off the price of a pair of shoes but in having a well-designed retail format which would persuade customers to pay £5 more. The mass market, driven by price, had fragmented into various niches, based on the lifestyles and needs of different customer groups.

BSC responded by reorganising into four market sector divisions: volume (ie, low price), family, fashion and quality. Each was headed by an MD with control over all key functions including buying and retail formats and operations. Only distribution remained centralised, because the economies of scale were great and implied few constraints on divisions' ability to focus on their target sectors. Interestingly, the new structure was no more expensive to operate than the old one (though it did demand more managerial talent, eg, five MDs instead of one) and led to increased profits before the early 1990s recession hit BSC and most other retailers.

It is important to remember that there are substantial frictional costs in restructuring any organisation, eg, distraction of management time, investment in new systems and procedures and time taken by people to get to grips with new roles. The key task for the human resources strategist is to spot when restructuring really is needed in order to capitalise on new opportunities or, just as likely, to remain competitive at all.

Organisation culture

An organisation's culture comprises the shared beliefs, attitudes, assumptions and expectations which guide behaviour when there is no explicit rule or procedure to be followed — and in most organisations that means the majority of managerial situations. Culture is determined largely by what an organisation has learned from its successes and failures. Culture can be a powerful source of identity, common purpose and flexible guidance. But it can also become a barrier to change, especially when organisations cling too long to what has made then successful in the past, like generals who always plan to fight the last war.

An organisation's culture manifests itself in a variety of ways:

norms:	the unwritten (often unspoken) rules of behaviour
values:	beliefs about what is important and good for the organisation
management style:	the ways is which managerial authority is (and is not) exercised
artefacts:	layout of buildings, corporate image etc.

Managers are increasingly recognising that important though culture is, it is much easier to characterise an organisation's culture than it is to change it. A traumatic external event (eg, privatisation, take-over or collapse of performance) can open up the possibility of rapid and major change, but otherwise, it is best to accept that an organisation's culture is likely to change only slowly, and is unlikely to change via a full frontal assault. Most adults are very reluctant to change their beliefs when directly challenged, as any televised debate or saloon bar discussion tends to show.

A much more promising approach is to intervene in some of the other elements of organisation (eg, structure or management processes) in order to change behaviour in line with the desired culture. These types of intervention can also affect the organisational climate (including employee motivation and morale) which is more susceptible to change than the underlying culture.

For example, a financial services company wanting to make its branch managers more entrepreneurial encouraged them to spend up to £1,000 each on local initiatives to increase business volumes. Some schemes succeeded, others failed; but the only managers who were criticised were those who failed to take up the challenge at all. Through this experience, managers learned that it was fun and sometimes very successful to be entrepreneurial; that taking risks inevitably includes the risk of failure (which can also be a learning experience) and that in current markets, having more successes than failures is a surer way to profits than being so cautious that you have no failures — but no successes either.

Reward system

The reward system is an integral part of any organisation. Reward systems fulfil a variety of purposes, including:

- encouraging people to become and remain members of the organisation;
- securing commitment to the organisation and effort on its behalf;
- encouraging behaviour likely to lead to organisational success;
- supporting flexibility, creativity and innovation.

By reward system we mean:

- the formal reward system, ie, how individuals' pay and benefits are determined;
- the intrinsic rewards of a job, eg, the opportunities for self-expression and fulfilment; and
- the recognition system, ie, the type of behaviour that is approved of, as shown by peer group praise or by being promoted.

Chapters 5 and 6 of this book deal respectively with performance management and individual reward. These are largely the province of the formal reward systems, such as pay and benefits and appraisal and promotion systems. We shall focus, therefore, on the need to manage some of the more important of the *informal* reward systems which exist in all organisations. The human resources manager needs to recognise that informal rewards can sometimes provide more powerful and less expensive levers to improve organisational performance than the formal reward system.

Recognition can be a very powerful reward and for many high achievers is a much greater motivator than a marginal increase in income. Managers should therefore make much better use of what is still an under-exploited tool of organisational management. The type of recognition used will vary according to the situation and culture of the organisation, but examples include:

- positive feedback, eg, via appraisals;
- internal and external publicity;
- symbolic tokens or gifts (whether a bunch of flowers or a weekend in Paris);
- a personal message from the MD or someone very senior;
- 'Employee of the month' and similar schemes.

The following examples demonstrate the successful use of recognition within a reward system.

A multi-disciplinary professional services firm offering a wide range of advertising, PR and media services wished to increase its cross-selling and team working, so as to exploit the synergy between its services. However, senior staff achieved recognition by their personal volume of sales, even though this did not directly determine their salaries. Little progress was made until the MD began celebrating each multi-disciplinary sale and made clear that only those with a demonstrated commitment to multi-disciplinary working could expect to be promoted.

Brewers Joshua Tetley were convinced that a key determinant of pub profitability was having a large group of 'regulars' who felt known and welcomed by bar staff (who typically have high turnover rates). Recognition badges were awarded to those bar staff who could name and know something about 100, 200, 500 and even 1,000 customers. Recognising this critically important behaviour not only increased customer loyalty and spend per head but also improved bar staff's commitment to the company.

In many organisations, *access to training opportunities* has become a part of the reward system. Clearly, training activity and resources should be primarily devoted to building competencies relevant to business success. But because individuals increasingly recognise the importance of continual upgrading of their skills to job security and career development, they now regard access to training as a key element in the overall reward package. Managers need therefore to recognise that how training resources are seen to be allocated, who is selected to go on high prestige courses and programmes, and the skills and knowledge which the organisation is seen to encourage its members to acquire will be read as powerful leading indicators of how top management see the future of the organisation and, consequently, may be used to transmit strong messages in this field.

There are various other informal rewards which managers have at their disposal, including:

- allocation to a high-profile project;
- secondment as assistant to a much more senior person;
- giving someone a 'mentor' relationship with a more experienced colleague;
- managing perceptions of which organisational units are seen as well-regarded and the most career-advancing to work in.

It should also be remembered, of course, that virtually all informal rewards form a zero-sum game and that one person's recognition also implies an element of non-recognition for all those who are not so recognised, and that the consequences of having winners and losers, while almost inevitable, need to carefully managed.

Individual roles

All organisations are made up of individual people whose roles interact. The design of individual roles is an important — but often neglected — area of concern for the human resources manager seeking to ensure an effective organisation.

One feature which has tended to distort the design and communication of individual roles is the prevalence of job evaluation systems in large organisations. Some of the more cumbersome proprietary job evaluation systems demand that jobs be analysed into as many as eight different factors.

In the first place, this means that role definitions (job descriptions) are written so that they can be readily assessed against the supposedly universal job evaluation factors, irrespective of their relevance to that particular role or organisation. Worse still, because what somebody earns may be largely determined by the points clocked up on the job evaluation system, roles are often defined with more attention being given to getting the right result out of the job evaluation system than to ensuring that the role plays an effective part in the organisation. At worst, role definitions become a statement of what the individual will *not* do: 'that's not in my job description'. This subversion of the proper function of role definitions is best avoided by having reward systems which do not rely on elaborate job evaluation systems or, alternatively, by ensuring that job descriptions written for job evaluation purposes are used only for that purpose and that other role definitions exist to specify what each post should contribute to the organisation.

Classic job descriptions tend to deal in activities, eg, 'To supervise the five clerks in the despatch section'. It is actually much more useful to think of individual roles in terms of outputs or objectives, eg, 'To ensure that all orders are despatch within 48 hours'.

For relatively simple and junior jobs, defining the key objectives of the role may be relatively straightforward. But given the way that all the elements of an organisation interact, the formal definition of someone's role is by no means the only determinant of how the person will actually behave within that organisational role; other factors, especially the reward system and the organisational culture, will also have a major impact.

For example, a production line worker in a car factory may have as his key objective the fitting of a particular component. But it may make a big difference to efficiency and productivity if that worker regards minor maintenance of his equipment and routine problem solving as a part of the role. Moreover, if the factory has an embedded culture of continuous improvement, then the worker will regard it as part of his role to seek out ways of improving quality and efficiency in his job which, by definition, he knows better than anyone else can.

The same is even more true of more complex and senior roles. At managerial levels, organisations need to be flexible, fast-moving and responsive, which means that rigid definitions of individual roles are inappropriate. Much more effective is a fairly short list of clear, and mainly measurable, objectives combined with a culture and a reward system which encourage the type of behaviour likely to make the organisation successful. The ideal way of defining managerial roles is as part of the business planning process. This should help ensure that all parts of all roles contribute to one or more organisational objectives; and responsibility is clearly allocated to specific people for achieving everything that will be required for the organisation to achieve its objectives; and lastly that activities which do not directly contribute to organisational objectives are discontinued and the resources devoted to them reallocated or saved.

Management processes

Most of the important things in organisations take place *across* the functional hierarchies depicted on diagrams of organisational structures. It is increasingly recognised that stewardship and optimisation of these key processes is a vital component of organisational management.

The typical types of key processes which exist in many organisations include:

- planning and budgeting;
- sales order processing;
- new product development;
- new systems development;
- managing relationships with key customers/clients;
- total quality management;
- succession planning and management development.

Because these (and other) key processes are usually multi-functional and multi-disciplinary, they are often organisational 'orphans' with no single person clearly responsible for their health and well being. It is therefore vital that the business-oriented human resources manager should ensure that procedures

---

Case Study — General Foods

General Foods (GF) — now Kraft General Foods — in the UK is part of the world's largest consumer goods company. Its products include Maxwell House, Café Haag and Kenco Coffee and the Bird's range of desserts. As part of a wider exercise of performance improvement, GF recognised the need to improve its new product development process so as to get new products to market more quickly and profitably.

Analysis of the new product development process showed various opportunities for improvement, of which the two most important were:

- Having a much clearer 'fast track' for product innovations such as sugar-free versions of existing desserts which involve responding quickly to changing customer needs rather than exploiting fundamental technical innovation.
- Changing from a system where members of new product teams were solely responsible to their functional interests (eg, the manufacturing member would be concerned with ease of manufacture) to one where the primary responsibility of all team members was for the successful and timely launch of the new product, with bonuses determined partly by new product team leaders as well as by functional heads.

---

exist to define what the organisation's key processes are and to analyse those key processes against key criteria such as:

- time taken;
- resources consumed;
- quality;
- flexibility to meet future needs.

In addition, procedures should exist to continually improve the organisation's performance in its key processes to at least match (and ideally exceed) the benchmarks set by its competitors and peers.

It is not, of course, for the human resources manager to be personally responsible for all the key processes *as such*, but rather to ensure that some appropriate person *is* responsible for each of them.

The preceding case study shows how one organisation tackled a key process with the help of external consultants.

CONCLUSION: THE MANAGEMENT OF CHANGE

The human resources strategist for the 1990s and beyond must look holistically at all of the elements which make up an organisation. But what is equally important is to look at these elements in a dynamic rather than a static fashion. In other words, it is the *change* from one organisational state to another which requires most attention and effort.

Virtually all organisations are increasingly subject to challenges from a variety of influencing factors — markets, technology, regulatory environment, social environment, demographics, competitors — each of which requires change if the organisation is to respond effectively.

Change management has tended to fill the vacuum left by the relative demise of Organisational Development, which was behavioural-science based and focused on group dynamics, conflict resolution and notions of job enrichment. Change management attempts to integrate these behavioural factors with all the non-behavioural elements of organisation (systems, strategy, structure, etc) to provide a comprehensive model of how organisations adapt.

The management of change is a complex topic which cannot be fully dealt with in the scope of this chapter. But in seeking to manage organisational change some of the key points to be kept in mind are:

- Establishing *what* change is required is normally much easier than determining *how* to achieve it.
- People do not generally resist change — often they are crying out for it — but they do resist *inept* management of change.
- The fear that 'I may not be able to cope' is the biggest barrier to change, but will often be expressed in the form of more 'rational' objections.
- Change always involves a shift of power and the politics of this must be managed carefully.

- Hard evidence and data on the need for change are the most powerful tools for change (the Titanic's passengers did not see the need to take to the boats until they realised the ship was listing).
- Change will always involve failure as well as success: the failures must be expected and learned from.
- It is much easier to change *behaviour* by changing, for example, structures, processes and reward systems rather than to change organisational culture directly .
- The success of an organisation will increasingly depend on its total ability to manage continuous change successfully.
- Change can be painful, but often the only thing more painful than change is to maintain the status quo.

'The management of change' has become a management buzzword of the 1990s. It is often used as though the successful management of change was principally a matter of good communications, or else required little more than a programme of workshops to explain and gain commitment to change. Important though these are, successful change must involve the active management of all the different elements of organisation referred to in this chapter, as well as all the other dimensions of human resource management dealt with elsewhere in this book. Only in this way will managers be alert to all the possible barriers to successful change — as well as to all the potential levers for achieving it.

3

GAINING A COMPETITIVE ADVANTAGE IN THE LABOUR MARKET

Ruth Spellman

Resourcing strategies provide guidance on what the organisation must do to obtain, retain and develop the human resources it needs to achieve its goals. Their aim is to enable the enterprise to build upon its capacities and strengths through the people it employs.

Increasing competition in UK, European and world-wide markets puts greater pressure on companies to achieve competitive advantage through their business strategies for innovation, quality enhancement and cost reduction. The implementation of these strategies depends ultimately on having the right mix of skills at all levels in the organisation. And these skills are scarce.

The importance of having a resourcing strategy which will help in the achievement of competitive advantage is fully recognised. A survey conducted by Coopers & Lybrand and the Management Consultancies' Association (MCA) in 1989 of 100 large private sector companies, public enterprises and local authorities revealed that chief executives believed the key business or organisational issue for the 1990s would be people availability. And on human resource issues, their main concern was staff recruitment.

These issues cannot be handled by the use of short-term crisis measures. A strategic approach is required which defines the longer term intentions of the organisation on how it will meet its human resource requirements; intentions that can be converted into realistic plans. This strategy should be based on the analysis and understanding of the internal and external factors affecting the demand for and supply of people.

This chapter deals initially with approaches to analysing the internal factors which affect resourcing strategies, the external environment as it affects the demand for and supply of people, and the international, UK, regional and local labour markets. Methods of creating a human resource database and using it to prepare manpower forecasts are then examined. Finally, the factors to be considered in developing strategies for recruitment, retention, human resource development and downsizing are considered.

ANALYSIS OF INTERNAL FACTORS

The first step is to achieve the integration of business and resourcing strategies. The subsequent analysis of the human resource implications of business plans leads to further analyses of stocks and flows. These can be supplemented by surveys of why people join, stay with or leave the organisation.

Integrating business and resourcing strategies

Business strategy indicates the direction in which the organisation is going. It should reveal human resource needs in terms of:

- numbers required in relation to projected activity levels;
- skills required on the basis of technological and product/market developments and strategies to enhance quality or reduce costs;
- the impact of organisational restructuring as a result of rationalisation, decentralisation, delayering, mergers, product or market development, or the introduction of new technology, for example, cellular manufacturing;
- plans for changing the culture of the organisation in such areas as ability to deliver, performance standards, quality, customer service, teamworking and flexibility which indicate the need for people with different attitudes, beliefs and personal characteristics.

Resourcing strategies exist to identify the people and skills required to support the business strategy, and they should also contribute to the formulation of that strategy. Personnel directors can play a vital role in contributing to the business strategy and have an obligation to point out to their colleagues the human resource opportunities and constraints that will affect the achievement of strategic plans. In mergers or acquisitions, for example, the ability of management within the company to handle the new situation and the quality of management in the new business will be important considerations which will influence the business outcome.

Stocks and flows analysis

This analysis describes how people move into and out of the organisation and how they progress between the various levels or grades. It records stocks — the number of people employed in each occupation or grade in lengths of service or career bands, and flows — leavers, recruits and promotions, again by occupation and grade and according to length of service.

This information describes the human resource system, and modelling techniques can be used to evaluate the outcomes of alternative assumptions about the future behaviour of the system.

The stocks and flows analysis and data on future requirements and the potential of existing employees can be used to produce management succession schedules and for planning career moves and development programmes.

Internal Surveys

Attitude surveys can be used to provide 'barometer' checks on current employees — why they joined, stay or might want to leave. Special surveys of ex-employees can be carried out to establish reasons for leaving, thus supplementing the (often unreliable) information obtained from leaving interviews. In addition, surveys can be conducted of groups who are regarded as at risk, such as those who have recently started work or those possessing key skills, especially at managerial levels where skill and experience may be at a premium in the external labour market and difficult to replace. Organisations can also benefit from a regularly coordinated skills analysis, enabling them to identify the pool of resources available internally, before resorting to external recruitment.

ENVIRONMENTAL ANALYSIS

In spite of the recession, employers are finding it hard to match internal vacancies to external labour availability. This problem applies particularly amongst the highly skilled, mobile members of the labour market, and is acute in the South East. Demographic trends are partially responsible but there are also severe mismatches caused by:

- under-investment in training (as measured by investment in craft training, number of days per year spent in training, figures available on private sector spend). The impact of the recession has aggravated the problem;
- a fall in the population of graduates (which will start to climb again in the mid-1990s);
- labour demand moving away from unskilled or semi-skilled manual workers towards knowledge workers (see Figure 3.1);
- a major change in the age composition of the labour force. There will be a million fewer 16–19 year olds in 1993 than in 1983. Figure 3.2 illustrates this point. The hardest hit employers are likely to be in the south. At the same time there will be a rise in number of women in the labour force, and a substantial increase in the availability of labour in the age group 45–54;
- a labour force which is increasingly diverse and segmented.

The causes are many and various as have been the responses by employers. A recent survey conducted jointly by Coopers & Lybrand and the British Institute of Management showed the impact of shortages of key skills on employers in the East Region. Many of them considered that skill shortages and the unavailability of skilled labour generally could be a key threat to the growth prospects of the region. Most employers had not adjusted their recruitment and training strategies to meet their needs or to accommodate changes in the labour market. The overwhelming response to staff shortages still appears to be upward pressure on salaries (see Figure 3.2). However there is little evidence to suggest that increasing the wage/salary bill has a long-term positive impact upon recruitment. Also, employers are still targeting their recruitment efforts at those already in work and to labour sources in short supply rather than reaching towards the labour reserve (see Figure 3.3).

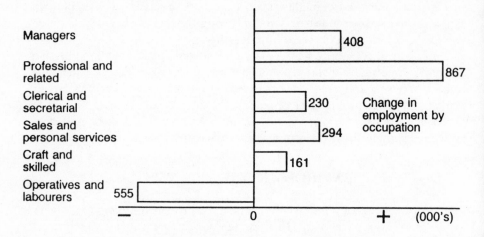

Figure 3.1 Changing demand — occupational structure (1986-95)

Source: Employment trends

This evidence put forward by the BIM is strongly supported by CBI Industrial Trends survey reports and by work undertaken by the Regional Town Planning Institute, which regularly surveys key issues affecting economic growth.

The thesis that labour shortage, particularly amongst key skill groups, can act as a brake on economic development is not restricted to the late 1980s and early 1990s. Overheating in the economy has usually been identified as a causal factor. However it is difficult to sustain the overheating argument at present and human resource professionals are being pressed increasingly to develop resourcing strategies which combat skill shortages.

The international experience and the wider investment issues

Human resourcing strategies, if they are to be effective, must increasingly take note of international competition for scarce resources, including labour resources. In addition, the quality of the labour and managerial resources will be

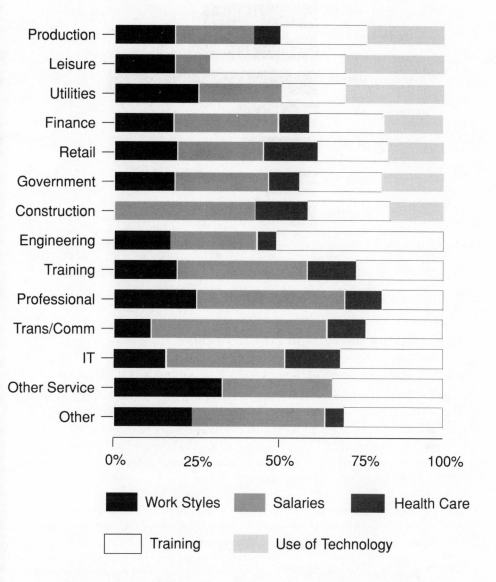

Figure 3.2 Company activity vs methods to combat staff shortages

Source: BIM (C&L) survey, March 1990

a key competitive differentiator in markets for goods and services. There has been, and will continue to be, an increasing emphasis on high quality, high technology products requiring fewer people but a more highly qualified labour force.

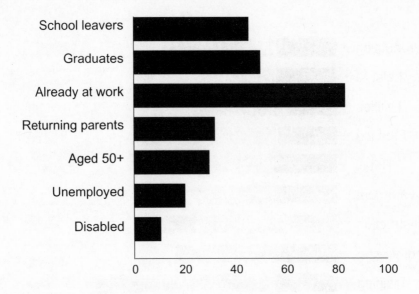

Figure 3.3 From which group do you expect to draw staff in the next five years?

Source: BIM (C&L) survey March 1990

Developing the human resource base

Critical issues for the continuing growth and development of the human resource base will be:

- private and public funding of training and development. This includes public commitment to high levels of vocational and educational achievement, commitment from employers to developing the talents of their employees, and the opening of retraining and learning opportunities for skilled and unskilled employees;
- the development of an education and training infrastructure to support development activity. At the moment resources are thinly spread and the ground is unevenly covered. Other countries are more successful in generating the right quality of labour supply, and more successful in catering for key skills required, eg, the number of foremen and supervisors who are properly trained in management roles is only a quarter of the number trained in Germany. In the UK only 24 per cent of senior managers have degrees compared with 88 per cent in Japan[1].

The success of companies in tackling the training agenda will depend upon supply side issues, ie the quality of young people leaving schools, educational attainment and learning aptitude, and the availability of high quality further education to supplement the skills base of economically active adults.

In some areas it will be necessary to expand the available labour pool by means of policies which are targeted on the economically inactive, eg older workers, women returners, disadvantaged groups and the long-term unemployed.

The power of example

The recently launched initiative 'Investors in People' (IIP) creates a kitemark to which companies are invited to respond. The aim of IIP is to get organisations to take training and development seriously, and to evaluate the cost effectiveness of their investment in human resources. IIP is supported by training and enterprise councils (TECs) and follows a number of government/TEC initiatives aimed at improving the quality and quantity of training provided in the UK.

However the market penetration of these initiatives is so far small, and the efforts of individual companies to grow their own skills for the future will be critical. A recent CBI Industrial Trends survey showed that company spend on training programmes has not been the first casualty of the recession. Nevertheless there are widespread skill shortages. There is a deficit to address and it will require continued commitment and consistency from the public and private sectors to address quality of resourcing issues and the real skills agenda.

The way in which human resources are deployed and managed should reflect new patterns of behaviour from the boardroom to the shop floor. The fundamental characteristics of HR strategy which are likely to feature in the 1990s include:

- devolution of management control (to reduce tiers of management);
- increased line involvement;
- high status and profile for HR;
- fewer people employed overall;
- more emphasis on training and development;
- increased professionalism in recruitment and retention;
- greater flexibility in the use of labour resources;
- horizontal as well as vertical career patterns, ie job enlargement to take on additional responsibilities.

All these features must be accommodated within the resourcing strategy of the employing organisation.

LABOUR MARKET ANALYSIS

The environmental analysis should identify overall economic, business and demographic trends. Against this background, more specific analyses of the labour markets in which the firm is operating can take place. Most large companies in the UK operate in a number of labour markets — international, national, regional and local. Behaviours within these markets will influence the company's resourcing strategies and plans.

The international market

The international labour market is divided into two parts: UK nationals who are willing to work abroad and nationals of other countries who would be available to work locally or elsewhere.

There are no published data in the UK on the availability of people to work overseas. Companies operating internationally should, of course, have ample information on stocks and flows. Other firms have to make specific enquiries with the help of recruitment consultants or by advertising. International published statistics can give only a broad indication of the supply of suitable people abroad. To obtain more precise information it will again be necessary to conduct special enquiries — locally based consultancies should be able to help.

UK labour market

The following questions should be answered by companies to understand how the UK labour market is likely to affect the demand for and availability of staff:

- What are the main influences upon supply and demand for key skills for the next five years?
- What are industrial employment prospects like?
- What changes are taking place in work patterns and the use of new technology nationally and what are the implications on the demand for skills?
- What implications are there for this organisation in national trends in occupational structuring?
- What impact does the single European market have for the recruitment strategies of this organisation?
- What role should this organisation be playing in national initiatives in training and development?
- With which national institutions (academic and commercial) should this organisation forge links?

Regional labour market

Answers should be obtained to the following questions concerning the supply of and demand for people:

- **Supply:**
    - What are the key population trends for the region?
    - What is the potential supply of re-entrants to the regional labour market?
    - What is the current and future supply of school leavers likely to be?
    - How many unemployed people are there and with what skills?

- **Demand:**

  — What is the employment structure of the region?
  — Are there retraining facilities and grants available?
  — What are the existing job vacancies?
  — What are comparative terms and conditions of employment like in other regionally based companies?

- **Labour market issues:**

  — How are other employers responding to recruitment and retention difficulties?
  — What trends are there in the growth of small businesses?
  — What is the effect of the London labour market on the region?
  — What major infrastructural projects are underway and/or planned which will affect this company either directly or through competition for skills?

- **Occupational trends:**

  — What demographic and skill changes are affecting relevant skills groups?
  — What implications do these trends have for this department/organisation?

Local labour market

When analysing the local labour market it is first necessary to define its boundaries by reference to the catchment area from which employees can travel to work and the transport facilities available. A survey of the travelling arrangements of existing staff should help to define the area. It is also necessary to establish what transport facilities are available.

When studying local supply and demand factors the questions set out above for the regional market should be answered. In addition, it is helpful to assess the factors which have influenced recruitment in the local labour market and to analyse the background of current staff (especially recent joiners) and recent leavers in terms of their previous employment, skills and qualifications, mobility and travel patterns.

CREATING A HUMAN RESOURCE DATABASE

The purpose of a human resource database is to store the information collected from the internal and external analyses so that demand and supply forecasts can be made and the opportunities and constraints that may affect resourcing strategies can be assessed.

Contents of the database

The internal database consists largely of employment and personnel records, job histories (including performance appraisals), data on training received and data on labour wastage (turnover and stability indices), sickness and absenteeism. It will also include information obtained from surveys such as those described earlier in this chapter. The external database should contain information on overall manpower trends and labour markets.

Responsibility for the database

Responsibility should be assigned for the resourcing database and for maintaining links between it and other business and human resource databases. The following steps are necessary:

1. Define user requirements.
2. Install a software package capable of analysing and manipulating human resource data.
3. Update and refine current manpower statistics.
4. Allocate responsibility to someone in the personnel department to manage the database, provide and analyse data and generate stocks and flows analyses and manpower forecasts.

Development of overall resourcing strategies

The human resources database should provide the information needed to prepare demand and supply forecasts and to decide how the manpower requirements generated by the business strategy will be satisfied. The overall resourcing strategy can then establish the extent to which human resource targets can be met by recruitment, retention or development programmes respectively. If necessary, it will also cover how potential surpluses of manpower will be dealt with by, for example, considering methods of avoiding compulsory redundancy or, if that is unavoidable, mitigating its effects. In some recent studies of companies undergoing rapid change, the development of manpower plans for each functional area facilitated transfers of relevant skills from one area to another. In many respects managerial competencies are generic and can be transferred from one department to another. This gives benefits in terms of reducing net redundancy costs, career development, increasing cross-discipline working, and networking.

RECRUITMENT STRATEGY

The aim of a recruitment strategy is to decide how quality people can be attracted to the organisation so that the recruitment targets contained in the overall resourcing strategy can be met.

The strategy should take account of:

- the factors that are likely to attract or deter people from joining the organisation;
- the basis upon which the organisation competes with other employers for high quality staff (competitive resourcing);
- alternative methods of meeting human resourcing requirements;
- what selection techniques are most likely to deliver the best recruits.

The factors affecting decisions to join the organisation

There can be no doubt that rates of pay and the total benefit package — existing or anticipated — have a considerable effect on decisions to apply for jobs and accept offers of employment. Pay is obviously a key factor in extracting good people from other organisations.

But there are many other factors besides pay which affect recruitment and, indeed, retention, and these include:

- career opportunities — these are particularly relevant to the recruitment of young people;
- the existence of a career and training plan to which the company is committed;
- the opportunity to use existing skills;
- the opportunity to acquire new skills;
- access to high level education and training, both on and off the job;
- a responsible and rewarding job in which performance is recognised;
- an attractive working environment;
- being treated as a person not a machine;
- an open management style;
- a high level of involvement;
- being a respected and useful member of a cohesive team;
- a belief that what the organisation is doing is worthwhile, that it knows where it is going and is led effectively;
- the overall reputation of the organisation for innovation, quality products, level of service to clients and customers, social responsibility and its philosophy on how people should be treated;
- a big and respected company name to appear on a CV.

Recruitment and, as we shall see later, retention strategies must address all these factors.

Competitive resourcing

There is acute competition for high quality staff. To ensure that a flow of talented people enters and progresses through the organisation it is necessary to understand the basis upon which it competes with other employers and how it can exploit any competitive advantage it enjoys in its labour markets.

The starting point will be pay. It is essential to track market rates in order to develop and maintain a competitive pay structure. It is also necessary to formulate remuneration policies which establish the company's 'pay posture', that is, where its pay levels should be placed in relation to market rates.

Pay policies will also have to be developed to provide guidance on the approach to be adopted if it is only possible to attract a good quality individual by paying him or her significantly more than existing employees in similar jobs. Ideally, this should not be necessary — the organisation should do its best to develop its own staff's skills and promote from within. In practice, the latter often does not happen, especially when the company is developing new products, markets or technologies. In these circumstances, the policy may be that the inevitable has to be accepted, although it is to be hoped that in an expanding organisation, existing staff will be given the opportunity to acquire new skills and thus catch up with those brought in over their heads. Hence the importance of skills development training programmes (including multi-skilling) and skills based pay systems.

Competitive resourcing also means the creation of strategies for providing better career and training opportunities than other employers and for ensuring that potential employees know that these opportunities exist.

Alternative methods of meeting human resource requirements

Recruitment strategies must consider alternative sources of recruits. Some companies have targeted certain sections of the labour force which may be crucial to their business. For example, Tesco and others in the food retail business have targeted older workers both in their recruitment advertising, and in terms of the training, employment packages (principally pay and benefits) which they are prepared to offer.

It is interesting to note that employers' arrangements for working mothers are failing to keep pace with increasing demand. Less than 5 per cent of working mothers receive any special treatment — despite the fact that twice as many mothers are going back to work within a few months of giving birth as they were a decade ago. At the same time there has been little improvement in childcare facilities, a decrease in the number of nursery school places, and little increase in flexible working or career break schemes in companies. These findings have been published in a recent report by the Policy Studies Institute. The fact that any growth in labour supply over the next 10 years is likely to come from female re-entrants pinpoints the need to think through a strategy for employing mothers as part of the future work force in many organisations and industries.

It will also be necessary to face up to the increasing demand for graduates and to target and to influence both male and female graduates. Most students are looking for a well defined career path, good training and interesting work. A survey from the Universities Central Services Unit shows that meaningful work counts far more than starting salary in attracting graduates, who will become an increasingly scarce resource in the mid-1990s. ICL has recently revamped its recruitment image to stress investment in people and career and training opportunities.

When reviewing recruitment strategies it may be necessary to consider wider issues of resourcing strategy. Alternative methods of meeting future human resource requirements such as the six approaches listed below should be considered.

1. **Organisational** — moving in the direction of a 'shamrock' organisation as described by Charles Handy. This would contain a core of key workers and relies on a 'contractual fringe' of contract workers and a flexible labour force consisting of temporary staff. Use may also be made of teleworkers.

2. **Flexibility** — developing a strategy which incorporates four kinds of flexibility:

   — functional flexibility, which gives employees appropriate training or retraining so that they can be redeployed quickly to different activities;

   — numerical flexibility, which uses subcontracting, temporary employees and part-timers to enable the organisation to increase or decrease employee numbers quickly in response to short-term changes in the demand for labour;

   — flexible working hours which may vary the daily pattern according to typical workloads, or may provide for longer weekly hours to be worked at certain peak periods during the year. A longer term approach is to introduce an annual hours system which reduces the need to keep on underemployed staff or to recruit part-timers at peak periods. This is achieved by scheduling employee hours on the basis of the number of hours to be worked over the year, with provision for the increase or decrease of hours in any given period according to seasonal activity levels;

   — financial flexibility, which involves the establishment of payment systems that reinforce the organisation's greater requirement for flexibility, for example, skills-based or flexibility pay.

3. **Training** — more emphasis on internal training programmes to provide the skills required.

4. **Career management** — installing management development and career planning programmes to provide for management succession from within the company.

5. **Productivity planning** — planning for improved productivity and therefore reduced employment costs. This can be done by improving or streamlining methods, procedures and systems, investing in new technol-

ogy, introducing better financial incentives and developing more effective managers and team leaders. In addition, greater commitment from employees to performance improvements can be gained by involvement programmes (eg quality circles) and special working arrangements such as autonomous work groups or high performance work design.

6. **Downsizing** — stripping out unnecessary layers of management, ensuring that the introduction of new technology (especially information technology) really does save jobs and recognising that the extension of teamworking may reduce the need for the number of supervisors currently employed. It would, of course, be essential to ensure that a downsizing strategy as described later in this chapter incorporates plans to mitigate the effect on individuals, and that unavoidable redundancies are dealt with humanely.

Selection techniques

The recruitment strategy should cover the introduction or extension of selection techniques such as psychometric tests, biodata and assessment centres to improve the quality of recruits.

RETENTION STRATEGY

In the debate about labour shortage, competition for scarce skills and constraints on labour market mobility there may have been a tendency to concentrate on labour supply to the exclusion of labour demand.

Yet in many companies experiencing the greatest degree of difficulty, one of the most cost effective tactics in the battle for scarce resources is to retain the most able and skilled employees within the organisation. Retention, perhaps more than recruitment, depends upon concerted action by line managers as well as personnel professionals. Effective solutions also depend upon an understanding of the causes of labour turnover and a willingness to change attitudes and behaviours. In some specific studies undertaken by Coopers & Lybrand, we have identified the need for personnel professionals to pinpoint retention as a business issue, to spell out the cost implications for particular departments, and to concentrate on prevention mechanisms rather than recruitment activity.

There is, in many companies, a close correlation between peak recruitment and peak wastage. If the additional costs incurred because of the increased likelihood of new recruits leaving were added to recruitment costs, then management would become much more interested in retention. This interest would be accentuated if they appreciated that time delays in filling vacancies and the costs of induction and training increase the true cost of labour turnover and significantly add to employment costs. A cost centre approach to recruitment, where recruitment costs are attributed to the relevant employing department, would help to increase awareness of these costs and to pinpoint the need for corrective action.

Understanding the retention problem

It is of course important to note that some level of labour turnover is healthy and desirable. However for each company and for each skill category, the desirable base line figure may be different and typically lower than the levels which are actually achieved. Surveys of labour turnover conducted by the National Economic Development Office in the early 1980s showed variable patterns within industries, sometimes comparing companies competing for employees from the same pool of labour. Variations bore no overall relationship with local patterns of economic activity, but reflected a list of factors which were internal to the companies concerned.

In the 1980s it was not uncommon for large employers to live with labour turnover amongst craft and professional grades in excess of 20 per cent per annum. There is little evidence, however, that the employing organisation regards this level of turnover as 'healthy', although line managers may have formed the view that it is inevitable. We have discovered that a number of in-house myths are created to justify excess labour turnover, or to rationalise a lack of company initiative to tackle the problem.

The surveys which have been done on the causes of labour turnover show that the potential range of reasons include poor career prospects, boredom, not being interested in the work, being treated like a cog in a machine, not being valued as an employee, not having enough to do, not being properly rewarded, lack of status, poor working environment, and, of course, inequitable or uncompetitive pay structures. In fact, pay systems can be a major cause of dissatisfaction and therefore labour turnover if they do not provide appropriate reward for contribution and responsibility, and do not satisfy reasonable expectations on the appropriate return for the employee's investment of skill, effort and time.

Such survey results tend not to vary with fluctuations in the level of economic activity. By conducting surveys at different levels of line management, facilitating group discussions with stayers (to understand their motivations for staying) and by surveying those who have actually left, it is possible to build up a convincing and informative picture of why people stay, why people leave, and what action may be appropriate to improve retention. It is also possible over a period of time to establish the characteristics of those who stay with an organisation, and to identify those categories of employee who are more at risk from poaching, or from other temptations to leave the company. By understanding internal labour markets it is also possible to shed light on how external labour markets behave and to take the action which is most likely to attract future recruits. The development of an integrated and intelligent database on stayers and leavers can be an important tool not only for HR professionals, but also for line managers within organisations. This can help to inform selection decisions, and it can help managers to become better custodians of human resources.

The overall care of employees may also become a significant issue in European labour markets post-1992. There are already worries in the business community about the impact of 1992 on labour mobility within a single European market: this was revealed in the Management Consultancies' Association survey mentioned earlier. Lack of linguistic training cannot be regarded as a long-term barrier to enhanced mobility of UK nationals in Europe.

Strategies for the improvement of retention rates

Strategies for improving retention should address the following ten areas:

1. **Pay** — problems arise because of uncompetitive or unfair pay systems. Possible actions include:

    — review pay levels on the basis of market surveys;
    — ensure that individuals are paid according to their market worth;
    — introduce job evaluation or improve an existing scheme to provide for equitable grading decisions;
    — review performance-related pay schemes to ensure that they operate fairly.

2. **Rewards** — 'one man's meat is another man's poison'. A reward strategy can help companies to identify rewards which may be applicable to certain target groups, eg men or women with parental responsibilities may regard time off in lieu as a better way of compensating for out of hours work than traditional overtime. Other rewards may include cash or non-cash benefits such as length of service bonuses, business related to individual or team outputs, assistance with transport costs, or the provision of on-site facilities, eg company creches.

3. **Jobs** — dissatisfaction results if jobs are unrewarding in themselves. Jobs should be designed to maximise skill variety, task significance, autonomy and feedback, and they should provide opportunities for learning and growth.

4. **Performance** — employees can be demotivated if they are unclear about their responsibilities or performance standards, do not receive feedback on how they are doing, or feel that their performance appraisals are unfair. To counteract this reaction, a performance management system along the lines described in Chapter 5 should be introduced.

5. **Training** — steps need to be taken to reduce the number of resignations because people feel that they have not been trained properly, or consider that demands are being made upon them which they cannot reasonably be expected to fill without proper training.

6. **Career development** — dissatisfaction with career prospects is a major cause of turnover. The steps that can be taken include providing advice and guidance on career paths, introducing more systematic procedures for identifying potential such as assessment centres, and developing more equitable promotion procedures.

7. **Commitment** — defined as identification with the organisation and a

desire to remain with it, commitment can be enhanced by explaining the organisation's mission, values and strategies and by encouraging employees to discuss and comment on them. In addition, the organisation should seek and take into account the views of people at work and develop a comprehensive communications strategy as described in Chapter 8

8. **Lack of group cohesion** — teambuilding programmes can be introduced which aim to reduce the tendency for employees to feel isolated and unhappy if they are not part of a cohesive team.

9. **Dissatisfaction with management and supervision** is a common reason for resignations. It can be dealt with by the improved selection and training of managers and supervisors and by introducing better procedures for handling grievances and disciplinary problems.

10. **Recruitment, selection and promotion** — rapid turnover can result simply from poor selection or promotion decisions. It is necessary to ensure that selection and promotion match the capacities of individuals to the demands of the work they have to do.

11. **Overmarketing** — creating false expectations about varied and interesting work and career and training opportunities can lead directly to dissatisfaction and early resignation. Care should be taken not to oversell the firm and/or position.

HUMAN RESOURCE DEVELOPMENT STRATEGIES

Human resource development strategies, as described in Chapter 1, should be designed specifically to support the need for new or enhanced skills, multi-skilling and increases in competence required to achieve business strategies.

Training strategies

Training strategies are concerned with:

- the training philosophy of the organisation;
- the key strategic (longer term) issues that training is required to address;
- the shorter term training needs which are to be met;
- the priorities to be attached to meeting long- and short-term needs;
- the resources that will be made available for training;
- the allocation of responsibility for developing and implementing training plans.

Management development strategy

The management development strategy should set out how the organisation intends to:

- undertake regular and disciplined assessments of high-potential talent on a national and international basis;
- adopt a common language for management development, building upon models of leadership excellence and competence dimensions;
- introduce selective and planned job rotation;
- use the performance management system as a major lever for developing competencies.

DOWNSIZING STRATEGY

Downsizing strategy will be based on an analysis of the strategic plans for reducing employment levels as a result of organisational restructuring, new technology, the need to achieve cost reduction targets, office or plant closures, product or market withdrawals and the impact of mergers or acquisitions.

The strategy will be concerned mainly with methods of achieving staff reductions with the minimum of hardship and disruption. It will incorporate provisions for:

- informing and consulting with employees in good time;
- financial or other inducements to encourage voluntary redundancy;
- financial inducements for key staff to remain with the company;
- arrangements for retraining employees or transferring them to other jobs;
- the steps to be taken to help redundant staff to find new jobs or spend their redundancy pay wisely by the provision of counselling or the services of outplacement consultants.

CONCLUSION

This chapter has emphasised the importance of developing resourcing strategies that are consistent with the strategic direction of the firm. Once this has been established, an analytical, integrative and innovative approach is required.

The initial analysis of environmental trends, labour markets and internal stocks and flows provides the inputs to the database needed to prepare human resource forecasts. The different approaches to meeting the targets derived from these forecasts — recruitment, training and management development — need to be balanced so that an integrated strategy is evolved. This strategy should incorporate innovations on methods of satisfying requirements and sources of recruits.

In this way, resourcing strategies can make a major contribution to improving bottom-line performance.

REFERENCES

1. Coopers & Lybrand (1985) *A Challenge to Complacency: Changing Attitudes*

to Training, Report to the Manpower Services Commission and the National Economic Development Office, Imprint, Sheffield.

4

HUMAN RESOURCE DEVELOPMENT AND BUSINESS STRATEGY

Garnet Twigg and Philip Albon

INTRODUCTION

The facts are clear: in Britain we do not invest enough money or time in developing people; most of our competitor countries (for example Japan and Germany) do. Curiously, this is at a time when a large proportion of the management gurus, and many leading industrialists, recommend a 'human resources' or 'people development' route to improving organisations. However, the attitudes of British managers may well be changing.

In 1985 Coopers & Lybrand published a report, *A Challenge to Complacency*,[1] which described the poor state of vocational training in the UK. The report suggested that many firms viewed training more as an overhead than as a response to the fundamental need to compete. Later (in 1989) a Deloitte Haskins & Sells report for the Training Agency, *Training in Britain*,[2] found that the need to improve competitiveness was identified most frequently (56 per cent of companies) as an influence that encouraged training. Could this finding suggest a significant shift in attitudes towards training?

We believe that Human Resource Development (HRD) is at last becoming accepted as an important priority in Britain. But it seems that the usual corporate approach to training belies this attitude change. *Training in Britain* found that few companies planned, budgeted or monitored training activity effectively. Fewer than 20 per cent of those surveyed had a formal written training plan.

A central problem is that many companies waste much of the money they do commit to HRD through failing to recognise the need for their HRD strategy to be driven by business strategy. As a result they establish inappropriate or, in the worst cases, no real objectives for their training. Moreover, the training functions of those companies that *do* value HRD find it difficult to respond to demands placed on them by changes in the marketplace. As the pace of industrial change quickens, training functions can all too often become a bottleneck on major initiatives. Consider the following examples:

- A major British plc takes over six years to complete the initial training of its large workforce for its customer care training programme.
- A major international company's Total Quality programme is severely hampered by a slow and expensive programme of classroom-based training courses.
- HRD plays no part in the integration of a new company formed by the merger of two long-standing competitor firms. Instead the two predecessor training functions vie for position.

Both of the authors of this chapter work in the Coopers & Lybrand management consultancy practice and are specialists in HRD, in particular in the field of using HRD to support organisational change. We often work with clients whose business managers, ie those who have profit and investment responsibility, feel that their training managers are insufficiently business-orientated and are unable to support them in changing the organisation. We are also familiar with training managers who feel marginalised by business managers who, they consider, ignore the true potential of people in their pursuit of productivity or short-term profit. We are so struck by this polarisation that we refer in this chapter to *two worlds* — one of business managers and another of HRD managers.

Later in the chapter we describe fresh approaches that will bring together these two worlds to foster joint working that will deliver high returns on training and development investment and thus help to secure long-term investment in HRD. If you see people development as essential to business success — read on. If you do not, please read on also — we may convince you.

INTEGRATING HRD WITH BUSINESS STRATEGY

What is integration?

Simply handing down business strategy to a training department and charging them with supporting the implementation of the strategy is not integration. Neither is it when training and development act in isolation from resourcing and performance management. HRD managers need to be involved in the thought processes and decisions that underpin strategy. We believe that HRD managers should contribute to the development of strategy, as well as implementing strategy, because in most cases an important factor to consider when making strategic decisions is the competence of staff and managers. Effective integration of HRD into business strategy is therefore characterised by three features:

1. HRD managers are involved in a two way dialogue with business managers before business strategy is finalised.

2. Strategy is supported by HRD on a number of fronts; HRD is not simply a 'quick fix' training programme.

3. HR processes have a common architecture — thus, the appraisal scheme seeks to measure the same things that the development programme sets out to develop; the same things that the pay system seeks to reward.

Many organisations realise that by integrating all key HR processes with business strategy, dramatic changes in culture and performance can be achieved. For example, British Airways in its *Putting People First* programme was able to foster customer orientation in its staff not only through training but also via other HR processes, for instance by changing recruitment criteria in the interests of recruiting people more likely to care for customers, and by introducing innovative reward schemes to recognise excellent customer service.

What's involved?

One barrier to such integration, perhaps, is how people define human resource development. HRD is a loose term often used to mean any training activity. Correctly defined however, HRD is a set of processes for developing people at work which should be linked to business strategy and integrated with other major business processes such as supplier management or purchasing.

The processes involved in HRD are:

- **Training and development** — all activities aimed at promoting learning from formal courses to informal counselling or advice.
- **Performance management** — goal setting and appraisal processes, linked to reward through performance-related pay and promotion.
- **Resourcing** — all processes aimed at managing the 'stocks and flows' of an organisation's human resources including manpower planning, recruitment and career management.

It is one thing to assert that HRD should integrate with business strategy but it may be quite another to achieve this in practice. Consider the following example which shows how integration can be the key to successful business strategy implementation.

Case Study

This case study concerns one of the country's building societies which over a decade ago was planning to diversify and take advantage of deregulation promised by the incoming Conservative government. An early step was to seek to increase the sales by branches to the society's customers of a range of financial services products. The branch managers were to have the key role in this sales drive.

Traditionally branch managers had been involved in or had sight of all major transactions such as mortgage loans and were well placed to spot and,

---

so the theory went, exploit opportunities to sell extra services. The feasibility of a new strategy based on this was discussed and the main barrier was thought to be the limited skills and experience of branch managers in selling. The training function was not involved in this debate but was subsequently charged with assisting in implementing the new strategy.

Pleased to be involved in such an important strategic drive, the training function immediately set about commissioning a high profile sales training programme for branch managers. This training programme was run by a leader in the field of sales training and the courses were well received by branch managers.

Senior management were pleased with this response and waited eagerly for branch sales to improve, but as the months went by it was hard to discern the effects of the programme; there was a slight increase in sales performance which eventually tailed off, and the programme seemed to have failed to have made any significant impact.

What had gone wrong? The strategy seemed well founded, the training function was involved and a large investment in training had been made — a model of integrating HRD and strategy?

Investigation by the company revealed that although the branch managers may have acquired new selling skills, two particular factors thwarted the sales drive. Traditionally promotion through the ranks had depended on having good audit reports prepared on the branch. This had led to branch managers taking on a role of overseeing and checking on all activities rather than one of business development. At the time the sales drive was introduced, the criteria for promotion were not changed: sales success would not improve a branch manager's chances of promotion. Secondly, the appraisal process remained unaltered and sales performance was not taken into account either in the appraisal forms or in the appraisal interviews.

Two key processes, therefore, were driving branch managers in an almost opposite direction to that which the training programme was promoting. Eventually those key processes were also adjusted and the strategy was achieved.

It can be seen that the notion of integrating HRD processes with strategy has a certain simple elegance when represented in diagrammatic form (Figure 4.1) and it also makes sense as demonstrated by practical examples. Why is it, therefore, that so many companies struggle to achieve the kind of integration between HRD and strategy that is needed?

BUSINESS MANAGEMENT AND HRD — TWO WORLDS?

One factor militating against the integration of HRD and business strategy appears to relate to the scale and complexity of the organisation. For example,

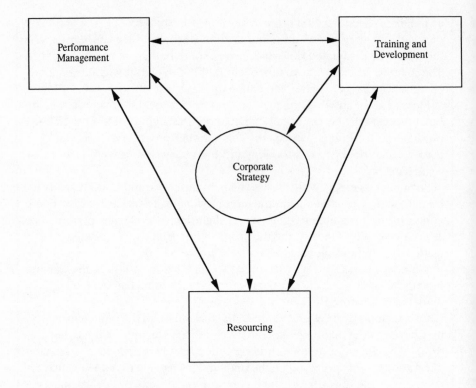

Figure 4.1 Integrating human resource development procedures

in many of the small growing companies we deal with, an entrepreneur/owner is able, through hands-on control, to ensure that HRD supports business strategy. However, a simple 'small is beautiful' prescription is of no use to large organisations which are seeking to compete in an increasingly globalised market.

We submit that the problem is not just one of scale but that, in many large organisations, the managers who drive strategy and those who drive HRD are polarised. The larger the organisation, the greater the risk that this will occur.

Are the two groups different?

Is it just popular prejudice that business managers and human resource developers occupy two worlds? Whilst it seems obvious to observers and management writers that training and development should be linked to strategy, it is a formidable task to those responsible for effecting the link, not least because of the different interests held by the two groups.

Consider the differing areas of interest of the two groups:

Business managers 'own'	*HRD managers 'own'*
Strategy	Training plans
Profit and investment	Training budgets
Business processes and systems	Courses
Career decisions	Education
Appraisal and reward decisions	Seminars } Process intervention
	Workshops
	Career planning procedures
	Appraisal records

Clearly HRD, when run as an isolated function, can be peripheral to general business management. Add to this a fundamental difference in background, training and values between the managers on each side of this divide, and you have a situation in which the training department can be actively marginalised by the rest of the business. Consider the following stereotypes:

A business manager stereotype	*A HRD manager stereotype*
Profit centre or earnings per share responsibility.	Budget holding responsibility.
Strongly cost conscious.	More focused on people than costs.
Strong short-term focus with a variable strength of longer term focusing.	Concern with development leading to a longer term focus.
Interpretation of human motivation/behaviour founded on rules of thumb based on practical experience.	Interpretation of human motivation/behaviour founded upon behaviourial science.
High pay linked to business performance which can be influenced directly.	Lower pay with any bonus linked to HRD objectives rather than business objectives.
High power and direct authority can make things happen.	Influences events indirectly and through others.
Focus on technology and business systems, hence views programmes such as TQM as 'methods and technologies'.	Focus on people and social systems, hence views programmes such as TQM as 'culture change and personal empowerment'.

Whither the 'HRD CEO'?

It is perhaps unsurprising that few HRD specialists reach CEO level while other specialisms such as sales, marketing, engineering, manufacturing and finance are well represented among the UK's population of CEOs. We have all met the 'marketing CEO' who is strong on product mix and marketing strategy, the 'financial CEO' strong on financial disciplines and processes, or the 'manufacturing CEO' strong on technology and systems. But do we know a 'HRD CEO' who is strong on gaining competitive advantage by developing his or her people? The idea raises a wry smile when we put it to CEOs — but is it so preposterous?

In the United States commentators have detected a trend towards HR-orientated CEOs in recent years. In 1987 Mr Randy Thurman was appointed CEO of Rorer Pharmaceuticals (now Rhone Poulenc Rorer). This appointment caused a certain amount of surprise. He had no background in finance or marketing and he was not a line manager. Thurman was an HR professional who had joined Rorer in 1984 from Exxon. He had some significant achievements under his belt such as guiding Rorer company through a successful merger with Revlon Healthcare. Skills such as managing culture change and achieving company-wide changes in behaviour are making HRD professionals more and more valuable in organisations. But HR managers must step up to meet challenges like this one from Philip Crosby, an American guru on Total Quality in 1991: 'Most HR executives are still tied up with being a regulatory agency. Many times they act like robots. HR executives have to get a dollar sign in there somewhere'.

We submit that in order to bring the two worlds together a new agenda needs to be created, one that breaks down the stereotypes, changes mindsets and encourages managers to stop thinking in a binary manner about HRD and business, and start focusing on how to combine their talents for the good of the whole organisation.

CREATING A NEW DEVELOPMENT AGENDA

The vision

Organisations will have to form a common agenda to which both sides can subscribe. To a large extent that agenda has already been set by external factors in the business environment which demand a step change in how organisations should be managed. These external factors are so well known that we will not dwell on them here, other than to say that all organisations now have to manage change, and that fundamental to managing change successfully is building on organisation that learns from its experiences. We say this because innovation and risk are essential elements in a culture that is effective in managing change. For innovation and risk-taking to be nurtured, a learning climate needs to be developed in which experiences, whether successful or not, are rapidly assimilated by others and form the basis of learning how to cope with change. Organisational learning is the common agenda which draws the two worlds together.

World class organisations continually learn from their past experiences and from creative individuals or teams. Good ideas take hold quickly. Past ones that worked are refined and reapplied. In such organisations learning seems to take place informally or habitually rather than in a structured formalised manner. Usually they have worked hard at developing informal learning processes, and in doing so they have come to recognise that adults usually don't learn much in classroom settings. They resist being 'students' or 'trainees'. They complain about the unrealistic or theoretical nature of courses. They observe that what they have learnt often cannot be implemented because systems infrastructure or management support is missing.

Such companies have bid farewell to 'sheep dip' training initiatives where hundreds of employees are put through a single training course, without preparation and without debriefing. In the 'sheep dip' syndrome, managers do not explain why that course is important because nobody has told *them*: worse, they even complain of losing their staff member for the duration of the course. When trainees come back to work, their managers make no attempt to discuss how their new skills can be applied. In this situation, the 'half life' of any learning achieved is short, and even that learning may not be put into practice.

World class companies recognise that learning requires active effort on the part of the learner. They discourage a passive approach to learning where, for example, people say 'I've been trained', implying that learning requires no effort on their own part. They recognise that active learning starts at the top. Senior managers embrace an open, active approach rather than portraying HRD as a 'treatment' that costs a lot of money. Reg Revans popularised the formula that, for an organisation to survive, its rate of learning must be equal to or greater than the rate of change in its external environment, which he expressed as $L \geq C$. Companies that acknowledge the importance of this formula invest in their people, empowering them to learn actively. Words like 'learning' and 'development' should be the common language of all employees, not just of those in training departments and management positions.

Achieving the vision

We will now discuss some fresh approaches that will contribute towards creating this new climate and to drawing business and HRD managers together. We suggest three steps to doing this:

1 — Decide, jointly with senior management, 'what we need to be good at'.

2 — Refocus the training function — streamline it and encourage joint working with business managers, to ensure that trainers address business issues.

3 — Increase the pace of learning — use innovative approaches to reduce the inertia usually associated with lengthy programmes of off-site courses.

Step 1 — Decide what we need to be good at

The quest to improve HRD in an organisation should start with the basic question *'What do our people need to be good at?'* A currently popular way of answering this question is to draw up *competency lists*. The term *competency* came out of activity-based research which involved detailed observation, interviewing and analysis of large numbers of managers. A competency can be defined as a capacity in someone which leads to desirable results.

Competency list — Applications

- **HR planning**, eg appraisal counselling, objective setting, development logs (a personal planning and recording tool akin to a personal organiser).
- **Learning**, eg work experience, courses, packages, education, secondments.
- **Evaluation** of HRD activities, eg testing, appraisal, objectives monitoring schemes, targeted research to evaluate specific training outcomes.

To us, the major advantage of the competency approach is that, by involving senior managers in drawing up competency lists, the HRD department can:

- ensure that new HR development agendas fit with strategy;
- gain senior management commitment to and ownership of the new development agenda;
- provide a common language throughout the organisation;
- test existing competencies against the new agenda and join in debate with senior management about strategy;
- start to break down the 'two worlds' polarity by involving HRD in the management of the business.

The competency approach thus offers a chance to involve senior business managers in creating a new architecture, language and set of values for HR development. In our experience almost all senior managers quickly latch onto the concept of competencies and relish the debate. In many cases, we as specialist HRD advisors, and our opposite numbers in our clients' HRD departments, can add value to senior managers' decisions by questioning the substance or speed of the planned changes, using our understanding of the workforce's ability to achieve aspects of the proposed strategy. We can also point out organisational strengths which may have previously gone unnoticed. We would not be able to do this without first involving senior managers in drawing out from their strategy the competencies required by their organisations. Most senior managers realise that 'What do we need to be good at?' is a far from trivial question and are keen to join in workshops or other formats to address it. Such high level events must be supported by detailed data drawn from interviews with a sample of job holders across the organisation and other sources.

A good competency list comes from marrying bottom up observation and top down strategic thinking. The bottom up element provides rich and realistic descriptions of competences while the top down element, often drawn from strategic plans, supplies the vision of how things should be. In this sense, drawing up a new list of competences or revising a current one can offer the HRD department a fresh start.

To illustrate the approach we show, in Figure 4.2, how a large and respected UK firm of architects, engineers and designers, made use of the competency approach. Figure 4.3 shows the competencies that were defined. One of the present authors was involved in this exercise, specifically in running senior level workshops and interviewing individuals across a sample of grades, roles and disciplines. Preparing the competency list, as shown, generated intense debate at all levels, but the process had a unifying effect once the list was finally agreed. The list conveys something of the values and spirit, in addition to the basic abilities required, of the firm's partners and staff.

Also shown, in Figure 4.3, are the higher levels of detail for one particular competency, that of *design*. The most detailed sheet shows how people at all levels, not just senior designers, contribute to good design. It offers a common language to enable HR development to be planned, carried out and evaluated in support of good design. As we discussed earlier it is pointless to have an HR development programme pointing in one direction if other HR processes do not support it or, worse, point in a different direction. Even if the differences are not that great it is essential to have a common language for each of the processes so that a consistent message is given about 'what we need to be good at'. At the time of writing, the firm were working to extend use of the competencies approach into pay and appraisal schemes.

Despite its advantages the competency approach has some dangers, as can be seen from the following:

Dangers of the competency approach

- **Inertia** — when new demands are placed on managers a competency list may become outdated and, if too rigidly adhered to, may become a drag on the organisation rather than a driving force. Review mechanisms are needed, but reviews will be avoided if they involve analysis to the *nth* degree.

  Regular fine tuning with a major overhaul once every two years or so will ensure this does not happen. Also managers must be empowered to request and receive resources for development in competencies not on an existing list. Without this, managers may come to view a competency list as a barrier to effectiveness rather than (as it should be) a help.

- **Pre-occupation with individual deficiency** — some managers, particularly those from an analytical background such as accountancy or engineering, seem to view the competency approach as a way of identifying deficiencies. In this *deficiency model* people are measured or assessed against a list of required skills and are then trained or developed in those skills that they are weakest in. The flaws in this approach are that:

— it is unrealistic to strive for universally competent individuals who excel in all the skills listed

— development activity must focus on an individual's *strengths* as well as weaknesses in helping the employee fully to realise his or her strengths and plan how best to deploy them.

— development must also focus on the combined competence of particular groups, teams or departments — not just on individuals. Individual weaknesses may often be insignificant when mapped against a team's competence or may even become a strength — for example, someone who is overly concerned with fine detail can be a valuable asset to a team as whole

— concentration on *deficiency* can mean that any training or development activity comes to be associated with failure or with poor performance — something that clearly creates the wrong signals in an organisation that wishes to encourage learning

• **Focus on abstract categories** — competencies can be used too rigidly — as when companies attempt to 'measure' competence, relying solely on techniques such as assessment centres involving psychometric tests or observed exercises. Competency measurements so generated take the form of profile data giving qualitative and sometimes numerical scores in relation to a range of categories. This can be misleading. In our experience most senior managers tend to think of people in the round and, moreover, take into account a person's track record of accumulated experience rather than how they 'perform' at a single event or at a moment in time. For example, many senior managers will discuss whether candidates for promotion have managed large projects, led teams, had sales responsibility and they also take into account whether candidates have learnt from successes or mistakes. **Thus competency assessment needs to be based also on experience, via an integrated performance management system designed in conjunction with, and used by, business managers.**

Step 2 — Refocus the training function

In our introduction to this chapter we suggested that attitudes in companies may be changing. Business managers are realising that HRD can be an investment in the future rather than just an overhead. To convince business managers fully, it is necessary to refocus the training function to carry out less repetitive generic course training and make better use of the education sector to provide it, and to do more work jointly with line managers in addressing real business issues.

Carry out less generic training Many companies continue to support training departments that are staffed by HR professionals who design, develop and

Our core abilities are:

8. Communication
— clear and effective communication underpins all of our abilities

1. **Design**
   — we produce a hallmark of design quality

2. **Professional/technical abilities**
   — we strive for excellence

3. **Working with clients**
   — we listen to and understand our clients and we meet and exceed their expectations

4. **Drive**
   — we work hard for design quality, successful projects, development of our abilities and our firm's success

5. **Self management**
   — we deliver: to specification, on time

6. **Working with others**
   — we are one firm: we respect, trust and actively promote own and other professions and seek constantly to understand them better

7. **Organising resources and processes**
   — we work intelligently and efficiently to produce quality and profitability

Figure 4.2 Using competencies: excerpt from a booklet for the staff and partners of a major firm of architects, engineers and designers (a)

1. Design — we produce a hallmark of design quality

In this firm design is not something in the hands of a few. True, some will lead the design process, but all of us contribute to and support that design down to the smallest detail.

Each of us contributes to creating a hallmark of design quality — instantly recognisable by staff, clients and the wider design and construction communities. This hallmark should be more powerful than any logo or glossy brochure.

1. Design — we produce a hallmark of design quality

1.1 Design leadership

Our leaders envision, consult on and gain commitment to excellent designs and follow them through to completion.

1.2 Conceptual design

Following careful analysis we produce aesthetically pleasing outlines and form technical strategies that meet, elegantly, performance, commercial and aesthetic requirements.

1.3 Detailed design

We produce well integrated and high quality design details that practical, cost effective and support the whole.

1.4 Verification

We verify our designs with our colleagues and our customers.

Figure 4.3 Using competencies: excerpt from a booklet for the staff and partners of a major firm of architects, engineers and designers (b)

deliver an eclectic and unfocused range of courses in generic skills that are insufficiently linked to real business needs.

Generic skills training courses are often stimulating and enjoyable to attend and can be popular for this reason, but they are often not useful responses to specific business needs.

The popularity of generic courses arises from a belief that even if training is *not* directly relevant to an agreed business need it is still worth doing in the hope that students will gain something from it. This belief seems, in turn, to derive from an underlying philosophy that certain generic skills or attitudes such as teamwork are always useful. While there may be some validity in this, we maintain that generic training material that is not targeted to meet a specific agreed business need tends to reinforce the view that training is a costly overhead because it is difficult to identify concrete returns on generic training.

Assuming that a business case for generic skills training has been made, development of those skills can be obtained more cost effectively by making better use of the education sector than by employing full-time trainers to run courses. Education programmes, combined with action learning projects (resolving real business problems with training support), will result in practical, business-focused learning.

Case Study — BT South Downs and Erikson

In 1989 British Telecom's South Downs district and Erickson (a telecoms manufacturing company) were each talking separately to Brighton Polytechnic about running in-house DMS Diploma in Management Studies DMS courses. Brighton Polytechnic suggested that both organisations should join forces and offer a consortium DMS programme. Both agreed and a cost effective programme consisting of short residential courses and guided action learning projects was established. The costs involved were comparable to sending the participants on one or two business school courses but the results were much more useful. Senior management were involved in mentoring and sponsoring action learning projects which were of benefit to the organisations as well as the individuals.

On a similar basis, our own firm, Coopers & Lybrand, takes part in a consortium MBA programme, run by Warwick University, with the Metropolitan Police, National Westminster Bank, British Telecom and British Petroleum.

Do more work jointly with line managers In our experience, the belief that a 'course' provided by trainers as the only effective learning medium is being challenged by many organisations.

At a major motor manufacturer we worked with, IT training activities are initiated by a small number of professionals who act as enablers of the learning process rather than as trainers. They work with managers and consultants to achieve results. For example in 1990, the company's British training professionals worked alongside systems and purchasing specialists, senior management and consultants in three countries to provide a programme that would create changes in business processes and management practices within its North American and European operations. Such joint working was far more successful than it would have been had a large IT training department acted in isolation from line managers. It is unlikely that such a department could have reacted quickly enough, or had sufficient know-how or leverage to make the changes happen without the help of line managers.

Where trainers work with line managers directly on business issues the returns on training investment become much clearer. It becomes easier to demonstrate that training is self-financing. We have helped companies to do this through an approach that relies on empowering junior managers to find ways of improving performance in their departments. They are supported and trained jointly by business managers and trainers throughout a ten week period (the duration of the programme) and are given a variety of decision making tools and techniques. Their recommendations for change are vetted by senior managers; those ideas with the greatest potential for improving performance are presented to top management by the junior managers who suggested them. This approach to training and development is practical, action-orientated, and cost effective. A large UK food processing company recently recouped, within a matter of weeks, ten times its investment in a pilot programme; the company repeated the process in all other parts of its business, although asserting that the outstanding return on its investment was not its main reason for doing so. Its real interest lay in empowering junior managers to make informed decisions on how the company's performance could be improved.

Step 3 — Increase the pace of learning

We have found that exclusive use of classroom training will not achieve organisation-wide change. Rather, it creates inertia and resistance to change because of the time required to set up and run large numbers of (usually off-site) training programmes, and the cost of doing so.

We have helped companies speed up learning by developing new learning experiences. An example is an approach that draws together up to 100 people to discuss and decide on the major issues facing their organisation. The purpose of these gatherings is to mobilise everyone's energy in an orchestrated way for the continuous development of better performance. In particular, people who are in direct contact with customers (final or 'internal') are encouraged to learn that they are empowered to develop their part of the business and can influence other parts on which they depend. The process gives managers and staff at all levels an opportunity to learn together and from each other in the light of what their customers demand of them, and to agree actions that immediately improve productivity and start changing their organisation's culture. The following notes elaborate this approach:

The Key Player Seminar — learning for larger numbers at one event

The process involves 10-12 mixed teams (eg managers in a value chain, process owners and their customers, representatives from different sites, representatives from different parts of a production cycle) each totalling between 8 and 12 people. Each group works from colourful A^0 sized posters that stimulate them to think creatively about business issues, challenge each other's assumptions or mindsets, achieve consensus and take action.

The pace is fast, the duration short, and the atmosphere intense but enjoyable. Each A^0 sized poster has a theme to its statements and questions all of which have been generated through interviews with staff at all levels and authorised beforehand by senior management.

Teams work simultaneously using the same posters and record their ideas for improvement on posters. Once a particular poster has been worked through, useful, novel and/or amusing ideas generated by each group are presented to all other groups so reinforcing the value and stimulation of the process.

Part of the success of these gatherings is that the learning experience is so fundamentally different from any previously experienced that participants start behaving differently. They get involved, debate issues, influence sceptics and resolve problems. There are 100 people in the room, working around circular tables without chairs, so there is a lot of noise and movement. It becomes hard to withdraw and say 'I don't want to play this game'.

A final poster contains the theme of action planning. Each team records actions it wishes to implement and, in a final session, presents them to the CEO who empowers them to implement their actions.

External consultants, or a team of internal consultants formed for this purpose, will then follow up with the teams to support them in completing their actions. This might mean bringing together some of the teams or involving other people who have not taken part in the workshops.

An electrical components manufacturer used this approach to boost its total quality programme. The approach was so successful in empowering managers and staff to take action that it was repeated several times and, at the time of writing, was set to become the major instrument in the company's Total Quality Implementation programme. A short programme of such events achieved in a few months what would have taken years if all participants had to wait for a conventional off-site workshop or training course.

Another example of increased pace of learning was where we helped senior managers start a cascade action learning process that flowed quickly down the organisation. The issue we were addressing was how to promote change to a more democratic and empowering management style. Managers, in deciding 'what they needed to be good at', had diagnosed that this was essential to the introduction of flexible cross-functional team working, which was their chosen method of delivering a fast response to customer needs. Sending all managers on an off-site course was ruled out because it would take too long. The following notes elaborate this approach.

An inexpensive but effective learning cascade

We suggested that in order for a clothing manufacturer to change the company wide management style that they should attempt to complete the following process: model the new styles, seek feedback from their subordinates using either a questionnaire or focus group technique and when, but *only* when, the feedback showed significant improvement, direct, mentor, coach and cajole their next reporting levels to carry out a similar exercise. The process was then to be repeated throughout successive tiers in the organisation. The managing director gave the process his full backing. The intervention was inexpensive, involving a briefing for the top team in the overall process and the questionnaire and feedback techniques. Each top team member went away with an 'action kit' including reading materials, reminder cards, video material (or information on access to it) and questionnaires. We had thought that the process would take a long time to take hold, but one board member remarked how it had 'spread like wildfire' with subordinates keen to embark on their stage of the process. Another noted how 'overnight we seemed to feel OK about picking each other up when we got a little autocratic — it was like there was a new highway code and we all became traffic wardens to make it happen'. Another remarked how 'flipcharts were multiplying like rabbits' as all managers were keen to use joint problem-solving techniques.

We foresee training moving in the direction of process interventions using innovative formats such as the two examples described here. They will be especially useful in large, complex organisations that have been slow to respond to environmental change and, as a result, are facing crisis. These and other organisations will realise that conventional learning systems take too long to work their way through their structures and create the cynicism that breeds resistance to change. They will come to understand that enhancing organisational learning through innovative and practical action based approaches is the key to the effective management of change.

CONCLUSION

We began this chapter by lamenting the low level of expenditure on developing people in British industry. We pointed out that managers' attitudes to training and development may be changing. We believe that business managers and HRD professionals owe it to British industry, to their organisations and to each other to work more closely together, not simply to increase the resources being ploughed into HRD but rather because the returns on that investment, if properly approached, will be dramatic. Once business managers start to see those returns, their commitment will rise and their demand for HRD will rise in consequence.

The manager's role is becoming one of continually managing change and renewal. As the pace of change accelerates we foresee a blurring of the boundary between business managers and HRD professionals, as business managers increasingly need HRD skills to survive, adapt and prosper. Soon, in Britain we will learn what our most successful competitors have learnt already — **HRD means business!**

REFERENCES

1. Coopers & Lybrand (1985) *A Challenge to Complacency: Changing Attitudes to Training*, Report to the Manpower Services Commission and the National Economic Development Office, Imprint, Sheffield.
2. Deloitte Haskins & Sells (1989) *Training in Britain: Employers Activities*, Research Report, in cooperation with IFF Research Ltd.

5

MANAGING FOR IMPROVED PERFORMANCE

Lawrie Philpott and Louise Sheppard

Performance management is potentially the area of human resources management which can make the most significant contribution to organisational performance. Performance management is a process which is based on a number of activities; as such it should be designed to improve strategic focus and organisational effectiveness (and hence the financial bottom line) through continuously securing improvements in the performance of individuals and teams. Performance management should provide an enabling framework to integrate performance improvement activities:

- corporate objective setting;
- performance assessment;
- identification of potential;
- training and career development;
- succession planning;
- intrinsic and extrinsic reward.

The system should use performance objectives, measurement, feedback and recognition as means of motivating people to realise their maximum potential.

But why manage performance anyway? Whilst there are many complex reasons there are also a few simple ones. First, there is the old adage 'what gets measured gets done' — and human nature is unlikely to change substantially on this point! Secondly, the relationship between an organisation's strategy and performance management means that the latter can be used to ensure that strategy is translated into action. Thirdly, performance management systems can be used to contribute strongly as a vehicle for encouraging and managing a change in organisational culture. A model which describes the performance management process is shown in Figure 5.1.

The main features of this model are:

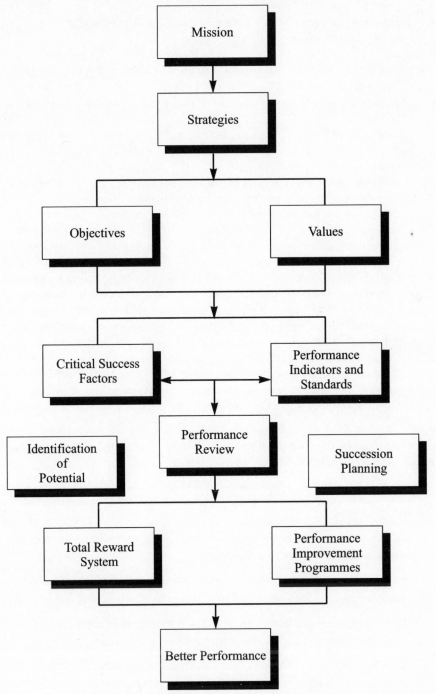

Figure 5.1 The Performance Management Process

- the mission statement, which defines the business the organisation is in (its purpose) and the direction in which it is going;
- strategies — statements of intent which provide explicit guidance on the future behaviour and performance required to achieve the mission of the enterprise;
- objectives — which state in precise terms the performance goals of the organisation;
- values — what is regarded as important by the organisation with regard to how it conducts its affairs (eg performance, teamwork, innovation, the development of people);
- critical success factors — which spell out the factors contributing to successful performance and the standards to be met;
- performance indicators — which are worked out in association with the critical success factors and enable progress towards achieving objectives and implementing values to be monitored and the final results to be evaluated;
- performance review — which reviews individual performance, qualities and competencies against relevant objectives, values, critical success factors and performance indicators; and identifies potential and development needs;
- performance-related pay, which links rewards explicitly to performance and can take the form of merit pay, individual bonuses, group bonuses and other variable payments related to corporate or group performance (eg profit schemes, gainsharing);
- performance improvement programmes — which are concerned with improving motivation and commitment by means other than financial reward (eg training, career development, succession planning and promotion processes, coaching, counselling).

The objectives of two organisations which have established a strong performance management ethic illustrate these points:

PowerGen:

- Ensure PowerGen's culture is characterised as one where striving for continuous improvement is the norm.

- Cascade down the organisation a clear understanding of what has to be achieved by each individual and the manner in which it is to be achieved.

- Facilitate continuous improvement of individual performance against key corporate objectives and leadership practices.

- Devolve performance improvement responsibility and accountability to individual managers (rather than the personnel function).

Ciba Geigy:

- to focus attention on what the business has determined is important;

- to monitor improvement programmes;

- to establish future targets.

Clearly then, leading edge organisations are using performance management to help shape the culture of the enterprise — 'the way we do things round here'. In addition, well managed performance can help to attract, retain and motivate employees.

But what about the costs of *not managing* performance? These are dealt with succinctly in 'Managing Human Assets' by Beer, Spector, Lawrence, Miles and Walton:[1]

> Poor judgements translate into failure for the individual, immediate costs resulting from poor performance, and long range costs associated with missed opportunities to promote employees who have potential. Too many bad personnel decisions can leave an organisation without adequate backup personnel to fill openings created by promotions or retirement. The cumulative impact of poor individual judgements will ultimately impair the ability of the organisation and its sub units to meet their strategic business goals.

For a performance management system to be successful it is vital that support and drive for the system comes from the very top of the organisation. It is also vital to recognise that line management is responsible for performance management — supported by the human resources function — which, to the greatest extent possible, should ensure consistency of application across the organisation. The role of employees in the process should also be crystal clear because it is important that employees 'own' and are comfortable with the process. Organisations which succeed in improving performance are those that keep their sights on the fundamental goal: *Establishing a culture in which individuals and groups take responsibility for the continuous improvement of business processes, and of their own skills and contributions.*

Before designing a performance management system it is essential to ensure that senior managers are fully supportive of the initiative. With this in mind, the primary purpose and any secondary purposes of the performance management system should be clear and agreed at an early stage because they are crucial to the design. The balance of purpose has to be clearly understood between, for example, motivation, reward or skills development. Care has to be taken where the impact of one purpose may impinge on another — and even, perhaps, be mutually exclusive.

In designing the process, it is important that, to the greatest possible extent,

Table 5.1 Performance management systems

Good	Bad
• Tailor-made to fit the particular needs and circum-stances of the organisation • Congruent with the existing culture insofar as they support the achievement of high performance standards, but will help to change or reshape that culture if necessary • Support the achievement of the organisation's mission and the realisation of its values • Define the critical success factors which determine organisational and individual performance • Clarify the principal accountabilities of managers and staff so that they are fully aware of their objectives, the standards of performance expected of them and the quantitative and qualitative key performance indicators which will be used to measure their achievements • Enable systematic review of performance against agreed criteria in order to establish and act on strengths and weaknesses, identify potential, plan and implement career development and training programmes and provide a basis for motivation through intrinsic and extrinsic rewards • Develop PRP systems which provide incentives and rewards as motivators for improved performance • Provide an integrated approach to increasing motivation and commitment, which combines the impact of results-oriented performance appraisal and PRP systems with the actions that management and individual managers can take, such as career development and succession planning programmes to develop attitudes and behaviours which lead to better performance	• Lack of strategic direction, with no clear objectives • Rivalry and territorialism between departments • Persistent failure to meet objectives and deadlines • Lack of clear accountabilities and decision making • Confusion over roles in organisation • Middle managers feel unable to influence events • Absenteeism, sickness and/or overtime out of control • Workforce and middle management resistance to change • High turnover amongst key posts • Staff appraisal lacks credibility • PRP scheme regarded as ineffective • Lack of detailed information on costs and contributions • Poor budgetary control and planning • Outdated or inadequate management information systems • Lack of structural career development and succession planning processes

employees are consulted about the design of the system. As a general rule, performance management systems work better if the process is as open and consultative as possible. The initial design should be piloted amongst a clearly defined group which is representative of different areas of the organisation. As the pilot proceeds, so should evaluation and, where necessary, modification. In our experience, it is important not to rush headlong into performance related pay schemes at the same time as establishing performance management. Ideally, the latter should be in place for at least one year before performance related pay is considered. In this way, the lessons of how to manage performance will be learnt before the organisation embarks on paying for performance.

Whatever the system, it is necessary to recognise that performance management is a continuous process. Figure 5.2 sets out details of the performance management continuum. Most organisations vary between having an annual or bi-annual cycle — this depends largely on the nature and work of the organisation. For example, Coopers & Lybrand's consultancy practice has

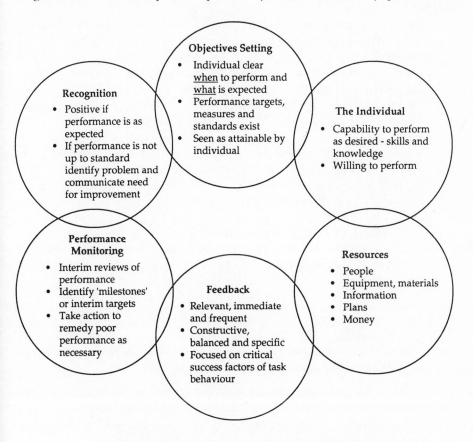

Figure 5.2 The performance management continuum

appraisals after each assignment, supported by an annual performance review (in May) and an annual development review (in November). Other organisations have an annual appraisal, which reflects more closely their business cycle and its needs. The vital thing to recognise is the importance of actually monitoring performance and undertaking regular reviews — either formal or informal.

ELEMENTS OF PERFORMANCE MANAGEMENT

There are many different types of performance management system, ranging from the very simple to the very complex. In designing a system it is essential to consider the factors which will be assessed, the inputs and outputs from the scheme, and effective links to other HR systems. The main factors which can be assessed in a performance management system are:

- **the achievement of objectives** — performance review systems assess performance by reference to agreed objectives and include a performance agreement which spells out objectives for the future. Objectives may be expressed in terms of targets, standards of performance or tasks to be accomplished within a period of time and to an agreed specification;
- **observing core values** — performance management systems are increasingly recognising that performance is not just about achieving objectives. They are also about people behaving in a way which makes the core values of the organisation a reality, not just a string of platitudes;
- **personal qualities** — some performance appraisal schemes still ask managers to assess the personal qualities of staff under such headings as drive, judgement, interpersonal skills and creativity. The argument against assessing personal qualities is that managers are thereby asked to measure abstract personality traits, which they are seldom qualified to do;
- **potential** — performance management systems generally concentrate on the identification of development needs rather than attempting to rate potential. The measurement of potential is increasingly taking place at performance assessment centres where the assessment criteria are related to well researched and clearly defined core competencies which are indicators of successful performance at higher levels in the organisation.

By way of example, PowerGen has established a system which focuses on performance objectives. Each division within PowerGen has developed critical success factors based on PowerGen's corporate objectives. Individual managers must cascade the objective setting process to ensure that:

- every person has a number of clearly defined performance objectives which, if fulfilled, will enable PowerGen's corporate objectives to be met;
- every person knows specifically what they have to do in order to meet desired performance standards;
- individual responsibility and accountability is clearly defined;

- managers will be in a better position to plan their work and monitor progress against clear objectives.

The objective setting process is set out diagrammatically in Figure 5.3 below.

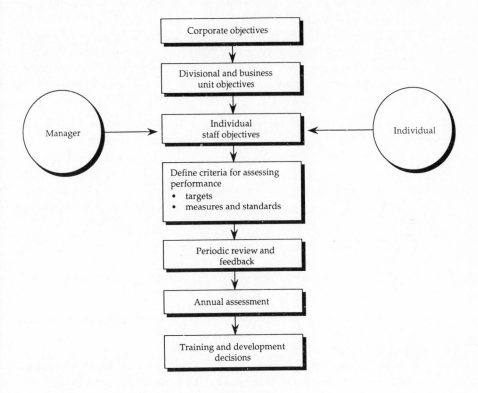

Figure 5.3 The objectives setting process

In order to help managers with the process of objective setting, PowerGen set out the following guidelines:

- Communicate corporate, divisional and business unit objectives to the team.
- Arrange meetings with individual team members to agree objectives and targets for the coming year.
- Set targets for each objective. These should be limited in number.
- Set team objectives to encourage staff to share information and work to a common goal.
- The manager and each team member should retain a copy of agreed objectives, to be reviewed at the annual assessment.
- Ensure that staff progress is monitored regularly against objectives, using 'milestone' targets of performance.

The inputs to the system can consist of all or a selection of the following:

1. statements of accountability or key result areas;
2. definitions of critical success factors and key performance indicators;
3. definitions of the competencies required in particular posts or at different levels in the job hierarchy;
4. objectives or requirements in the form of targets, tasks to be accomplished, standards of performance or corporate values to be upheld. These objectives should distinguish between basic accountabilities (ie continuing objectives) and periodic (usually annual) objectives. Both should be tackled as part of the performance system.

Many organisations are basing their system on key accountabilities and objectives. Prior to the launch of the new performance management system appraisers have meetings with appraisees and agree accountabilities and objectives for the first review period. Whilst the accountabilities are only modified if an appraisee's role changes, the objectives are set on an annual basis at the main appraisal meeting and reviewed during the year as appropriate. For example, in Coopers & Lybrand's consultancy practice reviews are based on self-appraisal performance in main work areas and associated core tasks and the achievement of annual objectives.

Outputs from a performance management system may include any or all of the following:

- a performance improvement plan covering training and any immediate development tasks or experience needed;
- a career development plan;
- a performance rating, followed, where earned, by a performance related reward. There are many issues related to performance management outputs; for example, whether to rate performance or not. If performance is to be rated, how many rating levels should there be? If there are to be rating levels, should there be a forced distribution — for example, limiting the number of people in the organisation who can achieve the highest rating? All of these must be taken into account in the process of design;
- upward assessment — performance management systems are increasingly incorporating upward assessment mechanisms which provide feedback to line managers on their strengths and areas for development. For example, the *BP* scheme is based on questioning each manager's subordinates on their perceptions of their boss and then telling the boss the results. BP Exploration has just completed its first review under the system with 1,200 managers being assessed in the process.

  Coopers & Lybrand's consultancy practice asks reviewees to provide constructive feedback to the line manager. They are encouraged to record on the performance review form at least three examples of what has been handled well by the line manager and what could have been handled better. They then discuss these points with the reviewer at the review meeting.

Many other HR systems are connected to, and are often driven by, the performance management system. For example, succession planning, promotion, employee training development, recruitment, retention, assessment centres and reward may all be linked to a performance management system. It is vital, therefore, to have a clear strategic view of the structure of the overall HR system, the linkages between the various components and balance in terms of the way in which they relate one to the other.

KEY STAGES AND THE SKILLS OF INTRODUCING PERFORMANCE MANAGEMENT

Whilst it is not the intention in this chapter to deal in detail with the methodology of introducing performance management it is important to identify the six classic stages for introducing a system:

1. Establish project;
2. Needs and criteria;
3. Design and pilot;
4. Training and briefing;
5. Implementation;
6. Evaluation and modification.

The content of each of these stages will vary from organisation to organisation. Most importantly, what is required is 'involvement' and 'performance management skills' in order to make the system successful. But what is meant by this?

First, it is vital that senior management, perhaps in the form of a steering group, drives the process forward with the support of specialists from the HR function. Secondly, employees should be involved, perhaps best in the form of a taskforce. This is part of the process of involvement and of building 'ownership' of the system as it develops. If employees have been part of the process of developing the system there is a much stronger chance of spotting potential problems and resolving them before the system goes live; also the employees concerned are likely to have more enthusiasm for the system because of their close association with its design and development.

Consultants are often used in the process of designing and developing performance management systems, and this normally brings a number of benefits:

- extensive experience in designing and implementing performance management systems;
- wide exposure to different systems in different organisations;
- professional assistance in the design and implementation process — assurance that the system is tailor made for the client's needs;
- increased credibility for the process.

High quality training is the real key to the introduction of successful performance management because the effectiveness of a system depends ultimately on the quality of the reviews carried out by managers, and the attitudes of staff to the system. Whilst documentation is important, it is essential to give appraisers practice in setting appraisal criteria (eg accountabilities and objectives), appraisal and counselling skills, use of documentation, etc. The most effective type of training is the use of closed circuit television/video combined with role play.

In PowerGen the skills required by managers for developing improved staff performance are:

- **Objective setting**:

  — identifying critical success factors;
  — setting objectives and targets;
  — prioritising;
  — identifying 'milestones'.

- **Performance assessment skills**:

  — summarising: assimilating a balanced view of the key elements of the individual's performance;
  — evaluating: providing guidance and help by discussing how strengths may be developed and weaknesses overcome;
  — communicating: discussing performance problems and difficulties;
  — judging: assessing current performance and planning training and development needs.

- **Coaching skills**:

  — suggesting or providing instruction on alternative approaches;
  — providing feedback on performance;
  — facilitating performance improvement.

- **Delegating skills**:

  — entrusting individuals with specific tasks or responsibilities;
  — guiding individuals on how they may improve performance;
  — monitoring performance against 'milestones'.

- **Supporting skills**:

  — recognising 'signals' which may indicate the person needs support;
  — interpersonal skills;
  — dealing with emotions and feelings;
  — advising on performance.

- **Communication skills**:

  — listening to people;
  — using discussion to reach consensus;
  — being accessible and available to the team.

- Motivation skills:

  — communicating the process of performance assessment;
  — clarifying key result areas of performance objectives;
  — providing the resources required when the situation changes.

A diagram illustrating the core skills for performance management is set out in Figure 5.4.

Another leading company has established a managers' checklist for performance management, which is set out below.

Performance Management Checklist

- Do you set clearly defined performance objectives for your staff?

- Do the performance objectives you set develop individuals as well as meet the needs of the company?

- Do you plan reasonable objectives for your business unit?

- Do you ensure your staff have the training and development they need to do their job?

- Do you have regular performance 'discussions' with your staff?

- Do you deal with poor performance?

- Do you set a good example to your staff by your behaviour?

- Do you encourage open communications with your staff?

- Do you involve your staff in decisions which affect the way they work?

- Do you communicate company policy and practice to your staff?

- Do you encourage contributions from all your staff?

- Do you encourage your staff to work in teams?

- Do you help your staff to prepare for greater responsibility in the future?

Research by the Huthwaite Research Group[2] has shown that some verbal behaviours are more effective than others in the context of performance management. For example, an examination of 'average' versus 'expert' appraisers is shown in Table 5.2.

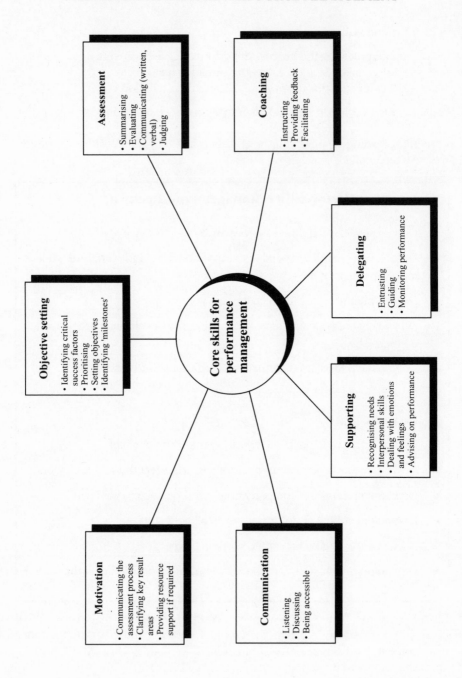

Figure 5.4 Core skills for performance management

Table 5.2 Performance management appraisals — expert v average reviewers

Behaviour category	Behaviour used by 'average' reviewers %	Behaviour used by 'expert' reviewers %
Proposing	16.2	8.1
Building	1.8	4.7
Supporting	8.3	11.7
Disagreeing	6.8	7.2
Defend/attack	1.3	0.2
Testing understanding	3.1	8.3
Summarising	2.3	6.4
Seeking information	12.7	15.1
Seeking proposals	2.0	6.4
Giving information	33.5	17.0
Disclosing	12.0	14.9
Total	100.0	100.0

The data demonstrate a number of important differences between the behaviour of 'expert' and 'average' reviewers. For instance, the average reviewer spends twice as long as the expert *giving information*. Furthermore, by adding *giving information* to *proposing*, it appears that 50 per cent of the average reviewer's behaviour consists of giving opinions and ideas to subordinates. This compares with 25 per cent for the expert. Experts ask more questions. There are three behaviours which involve asking questions — *testing understanding, seeking information* and *seeking proposals*. Added together, the figures for the expert are much higher — 29.8 per cent, compared to 17.8 per cent for the average appraiser.

The balance of questions differs. Of the average reviewer's 17.8 per cent the majority consists of *seeking information*, whilst experts have a much higher proportion of *testing understanding* and *seeking proposals*. This suggests that the experts are interested in what the appraisee 'thinks' and want to check that they have 'understood' what is being said and that average reviewers are more interested in questioning appraisees directly. Experts spend more time clarifying the content of the discussion. They spend 14.7 per cent *testing understanding* and *summarising* against 5.4 per cent for the average reviewer.

Experts also provide more encouragement. They *build* as well as *propose*, and they offer more *support*. The experts' figure for *disagreeing* is slightly higher, confirming that experts are by no means 'soft touches' — when they disagree, they say so.

The figures for *defend/attack* are too small to attach much significance to the difference between them which suggests that all reviewers realise that defend/attack is not a helpful behaviour to use at a review meeting.

The Huthwaite Research Group also researched the amount of time reviewers spend discussing past and future performance, and different levels of performance (eg *below average*, *average* and *above average*), the results of which are shown in Table 5.3.

Table 5.3 Time allocation in performance appraisals

Performance	'Average' reviewer discussion time (%)	'Expert' reviewer discussion time (%)
Past	88	61
Future	12	39
	100	100
Below average	73	33
Average	14	53
Above average	13	14
Total	100	100

Both expert and average reviewers spend the majority of time talking about the past but the proportions vary significantly. In fact, the expert reviewer spends 39 per cent of the time clarifying and providing guidelines for the future whilst the average reviewer spends only 12 per cent of the time doing so.

Experts spend more than half their time focusing on average performance, whilst average reviewers spend the majority of their time reviewing below standard work. In other words, expert reviewers consider that if overall performance is to be improved then the main focus should be on the level of performance which occurs most often, that is, average performance.

The standards set by one leading company for key performance management indicators are set out in Table 5.4.

Table 5.4   Key performance management indicators

More effective	Less effective
Development	
Continually reviews the work of staff, provides honest and realistic feedback, gives the necessary guidance and support through coaching to ensure that all staff develop their skills and knowledge whilst accomplishing tasks.	Reviews the work of staff in a formal manner but does not give the regular support needed to ensure that staff develop their skills and knowledge, and takes no account of personal needs.
Recognition	
Acknowledges and 'rewards' people regularly, based on performance; evaluates achievements fairly and provides timely and constructive feedback.	Gives feedback only when performance is not up to standard and tends to criticise the person rather than their behaviour.
Consideration	
Shows respect, concern and trust for staff as individuals, and understands the differing goals and needs of staff. Fulfils commitments made to them and treats all levels of staff as colleagues.	Treats staff as a homogeneous group. Demonstrates little confidence or trust in them by not giving them responsibility and autonomy. Does not deliver promises made.
Communication	
Promotes open, two-way communications with staff, listens and takes account of their views; keeps them informed about internal developments and runs regular meetings with them.	Does not keep staff informed about what is going on; maintains a 'closed door' policy and is autocratic rather than democratic.
Delegation	
Gives responsibility and autonomy to staff where appropriate; successfully achieves objectives through staff by entrusting them with specific tasks and ensures they have the ability, resources and authority to complete tasks.	Allows staff only limited autonomy in carrying out their tasks, and does not equip them with the requisite ability, resources and authority to get things done.
Organisation and Control	
Arranges and monitors team tasks effectively, defines appropriate roles for team members and organises related tasks together to encourage cooperation.	Deals with team members mainly as individuals; does not pay sufficient attention to issues of coordination and is inconsistent in the way he/she manages.

More effective	Less effective
Motivation Encourages participation in agreeing objectives and targets; encourages informal meetings between groups to resolve problems, discuss ideas etc and provides regular feedback about team progress against objectives.	Tends to dominate the group; does not manage conflict effectively; does not seek group consensus when defining objectives or tasks, or provide regular feedback on progress, and does not deal with poor performance.
Analysis Able to assess situations accurately and involve staff in finding creative solutions.	Makes decisions but does not always get the full facts from the people involved.
Planning Able to develop work plans and set objectives; allows sufficient time to explore problems and their causes, plans reasonable team objectives and distributes workload equitably.	Does not pay sufficient attention to implementing expedient solutions or evaluating alternative courses of action, and to monitoring how effectively decisions are implemented.
Direction Does not shy away from taking tough decisions, is able to act decisively under pressure and assumes ownership for decisions taken.	Tends to avoid dealing with difficult situations and does not always take responsibility for decisions made.

SUMMARY

There are, therefore, a number of key themes which are important to the success of performance management in any organisation:

- First, the system must be linked to the organisation's mission, business strategy, objectives and goals.
- The system must reflect or be used to shape the organisation's culture.
- The system must be managed *proactively* — rather than by default. It is also vital to understand that performance management is a continuous cycle and not just an annual event.
- The system must be 'owned' by top management, line management and the workforce as a whole. Without this, the system will be fragmented and is likely to fail.
- Employees must be involved in the process of design and development of the performance management system as early as possible. It is important to ensure that the system benefits employees as well as the organisation so that they own the process.

- To the greatest extent possible it is beneficial to have a universal approach — that is, the same system should apply to all grades of staff.
- The design team must establish a clear purpose for the performance management system prior to the design stage because the purpose determines the design.
- There must be a clear link between the performance management system and other human resources policies and processes, eg reward, succession planning, and so on.
- Training is key to the success of a performance management system. Documentation is just a means to an end — don't get hung up about it!
- Be patient! Performance management takes time. A new or revised system which represents a major cultural shift may take several years until it is working smoothly. Experience shows that employees can be cynical at first, but will, at the very least, want to give it a try.
- Don't be afraid to modify the system!

REFERENCES

1. Beer, M, Spector, B, Lawrence, P R, Mills, D O, and Walton, R E (1984) Managing Human Assets: The Crowdbreaking, Harvard Business School Program.
2. Huthwaite Research Group – unpublished paper.

6

A NEW APPROACH TO REWARD MANAGEMENT

Denis Crowe

INTRODUCTION

Boards and their advisers recognise the importance of reward policies which are designed in conjunction with an organisation's strategic business objectives in order to provide it with a competitive advantage. Managers recognise also that a reward system can be a key contributor to the effectiveness of an organisation. Reward policies in the 1990s will be more 'flexible', taking account less of internal relativities between jobs and more of individual skills, performance in the job and the external labour market.

As a consultant specialising in reward issues, I am often involved in a review of one particular aspect of an organisation's reward system but I am very rarely asked to consider the reward system as a whole. Perhaps not surprisingly, those responsible for policy within organisations want things done quickly and tend to focus on aspects of the remuneration system which they believe can be changed relatively quickly, for example, the bonus scheme for middle management. Far too often this piecemeal re-engineering will have only a limited effect. If an organisation wishes to change individuals' behaviour through the reward mechanism, it must look both at the components of that system and how those components fit with business objectives and personnel policies, and at the recognition system and the type of behaviour that is being encouraged within the organisation.

Let me start this chapter by examining some of the key reasons why reward policies have failed to meet the challenges of a changing business environment. I shall illustrate the reasons for failure and put forward a series of propositions. I shall then examine how a reward strategy might seek to address some of these failures. Finally, I put forward some suggestions as to where reward policies might go in the 1990s and beyond.

WHY HAVE REWARD POLICIES FAILED?

One of the central reasons why reward policies have failed to live up to expectations is that they have not been able to alter individual behaviour or cope with the increasing demands of changing business strategies and priorities. This situation is not unique to the UK. In the US Rosabeth Moss Kanter, in her book *When Giants Learn To Dance* states that 'traditional pay systems . . . are under attack for being neither cost effective nor motivating people to do more'.[1]

My experience leads me to conclude that the reasons for failure are chiefly as follows:

- **Business strategy** — Failure to design reward systems that underpin and reinforce business strategies resulting in increasing impatience among business leaders who wish to change the strategic direction of their enterprises but are frustrated by traditional pay systems.

  In many cases organisations want to change the behaviour of employees in order to respond to changes in their markets and increased competition. Often, however, there is a lag between changes in business priorities — characterised for instance by an increased focus on core businesses, devolution of accountabilities and the stripping out of management layers - and major reviews of remuneration systems. Although new ideas are available, they are often not given top management commitment or were not designed in sympathy with the enterprise's business objectives.

  For example consider those companies adopting just-in-time (JIT) techniques. Whether applied in a manufacturing or services environment, JIT requires considerable flexibility of working hours and methods. Traditional remuneration systems, based on contracted base time and overtime, are in conflict with JIT objectives. For those companies wishing to introduce JIT techniques, a first step is to design a new reward system.

- **Job evaluation** — The failure of reward systems based on so-called proprietary job evaluation techniques — which are a means of establishing grades within an organisation and associated pay levels — to provide an adequate means of paying for skills and experience development or of rewarding contribution to an organisation.

  One of the most common reasons for losing talented people within large organisations is that promotion and reward systems create structural ceilings. Often the fault lies with the design of the job evaluation system. Companies want to reward key people in a way that recognises their special contribution but they must also be seen to treat people fairly and equitably. Factor comparison job evaluation schemes will analyse jobs by reference to factors such as knowledge and experience, analytical and interpersonal skills and resources controlled. These factors are weighted according to their perceived worth to the organisation and a points score is arrived at for each job. While the job evaluation system provides a means of assigning jobs to a grading structure, it obviously cannot tell the manager how well an individual performs in his or her role.

Proprietary job evaluation and pay systems strive to achieve internal equity, usually by focusing reward on the size of hierarchies controlled by the job holder and on nominal job content, as a proxy for real contribution to, and impact on, the business. An alternative approach is to downplay hierarchical levels and to adopt an egalitarian stance to pay and benefits. Another approach is to introduce parallel career paths so that, for example, individuals can be relatively highly paid by working their way up a technical ladder; they do not have to go on to a management ladder in order to gain higher levels of pay. Marconi has for many years adopted a 'dual ladder' approach to rewards for its electronics technical staff. The 'grading' structure is based on individual capability and qualification criteria, which are openly discussed and well-respected among the employees affected.

- **Market pay data** — The increasing inadequacy of conventional sources of external market pay data.

  Many organisations have well-developed policies that compare pay levels with those in other companies. Some, for example IBM, have a policy of paying salaries which are comparable to those paid among leading companies; this is measured by collecting pay data from organisations with whom they compete for labour. Labour market pressures intensified in the 1980s when companies began to compete within a relatively small pool of highly skilled individuals who were able, in some cases, to set their own terms and conditions. In the 1990s demographic changes will result in shortages of young people entering the labour market.

  This fragmentation of labour markets in the 1980s had important results:

  — Companies are no longer able to rely upon a small number of external pay surveys in order to establish their salary scales.

  — External market forces have tended to put a strain upon the internal job evaluated pay structure which led many personnel departments to manipulate the job evaluation system in order to provide salaries in line with those paid elsewhere.

  — The legal and economic question of equal pay for work of equal value became more pronounced.

- **Incentives** — The failure of many performance-related pay schemes to deliver the expected benefits.

  Many companies introduced incentive pay schemes in the 1980s as a means of making pay reflect contribution, not status, within an organisation. The process was most visible at the top where bonus plans for senior executives became almost universal, but it also extended to levels below the senior management structure with the growth of performance related to pay schemes. These schemes, through which at least some element of pay was linked to an assessment of individual performance measured by means of annual appraisal, were seen as providing a first step in making pay more 'flexible'.

If the aim was more flexibility, why did so many schemes fail to deliver? A principal reason was poor communication. Significant changes in remuneration policy will usually result from a decision by the Board to change the strategic direction of the business. Many companies fail to ensure that their new reward arrangements, underlining the purpose, strategy and often values as set out in a company's mission statement, are given top level commitment and are clearly communicated. Where major cultural change is intended, it is necessary to communicate both the rationale for the changes and the impact that these will have on the staff concerned. Although companies of a certain size may well have written statements on a range of pay-related matters, it is rare to find a document which encapsulates the underlying philosophy that drives the remuneration policy.

- **Value for money** — Increasing recognition by most employees that they are deriving a poor return from the amount spent on their paybills.

Since employment costs represent a major component of most businesses' total costs, many companies have begun to question the true value derived from their current reward structures. In many cases performance-related pay is seen as a way of reducing the fixed cost element of the paybill by breaking the link between the annual pay increase and either the cost of living as measured by the retail prices index or the 'market' movement in salary levels. Performance pay in many different manifestations enables more of the paybill budget to be targeted upon those individuals who are providing a positive benefit to the organisation.

Flexibility in remuneration packages has become a byword. At senior executive levels this has meant individual contracts of employment where the executive specifies the make-up of the package including the balance between basic pay and fringe benefits such as company car, pension contribution, private medical insurance and so on. For those lower down the hierarchy, flexible or cafeteria benefit schemes, whereby an employee can choose from a menu of choices, are beginning to become more common. A principal benefit of such schemes is that they provide a very detailed exposition of the 'value' of both existing benefits and other benefits which can be added to the 'menu' to enable individual employees to choose a remuneration package tailored to suit their particular circumstances.

DEVELOPING A REMUNERATION STRATEGY

If reward policies have been unable to achieve what is expected of them, what steps can an organisation take? The first step is the development of a remuneration strategy aligned closely with an organisation's corporate mission, objectives and goals. Few organisations can claim to have an overall remuneration strategy and most consulting work in the pay arena is concerned with what I referred earlier to as 'piecemeal re-engineering'. For example, this might involve a review of an existing job evaluation scheme or the current performance-related pay arrangements; very rarely will it involve a review of reward strategy in the round. A danger of looking at one element of the reward system is that it may have a dysfunctional effect upon other elements. For example quite often consultants may be asked to review executive bonus arrangements in isolation and once the assignment begins it becomes apparent that base salaries are uncompetitive in the labour market and some form of market pay comparisons is required in order to ensure the right balance between base salary levels and the ceiling for bonus payments.

In the opening chapter of this book, Roger Cooke stated that a reward strategy must be concerned with developing a positive performance orientated culture, underpinning the organisation's values, especially those relating to excellence, performance, teamwork and quality. He also stated that the reward policy must convey a message to prospective high-calibre employees that the organisation will satisfy their reward expectations. That policy must ensure that the right mix and levels of reward are provided in line with the culture of the organisation, the needs of the business, the needs of the employees and the economic, competitive and market environment in which the business operates. An organisation's reward strategy, like its business strategy, must evolve over time; it is a declaration of intent which will seek to define the way in which people are paid in order to attract, retain and motivate the right numbers of people, of the skills and calibre that each business needs.

Components of a remuneration policy

Once a high level decision has been reached on the reward strategy the next step is to develop it into a remuneration policy statement. The policy will need to be related to the company's business strategy if the impact of the pay and benefits system on employees' perception, feeling and behaviour is to reflect the company's real requirements. An assessment will also be required of the type of reward system which might be required in the future. In practice most reward policies will need to strike a balance between a number of influences — some internal and some external.

A policy statement will contain aims and objectives and consideration must be given to how these are to be communicated to staff. It will need to include the basis for rewards, whether pay is to be related to performance, what the organisation's desired market position is, the balance between internal and external equity, whether the organisation intends to adopt a centralised or decentralised policy, and what the mix of reward should be as between base pay, total cash and fringe benefits. Finally, the policy must be capable of being updated and changed in order to respond to external factors: a good example of this is the response to the non-achievement of bonus targets because of a fall in sales.

Design options

It is useful when considering the design options of a reward system to separate the *content* issues from the *process* issues. The content issues are the essential components of a system: the salary structure itself, the performance appraisal forms etc. The process issues include the ways in which the policy is communicated to staff and the decision process parts of the system. One important consideration is the degree of openness with respect to both the design and the administration of the reward system. A useful technique when evaluating an existing reward policy is to conduct an attitude survey. The remuneration manager may be concerned about the value which employees currently place on their existing benefits, the perceived fairness or otherwise of the current performance appraisal process and employee morale following pay increases which may have been restricted for example to around price inflation. However, the content choices will not be influenced solely by the results of an attitude survey; clearly consideration must be given to a number of key structural choices, discussed below, which in turn will lead to process considerations.

PERFORMANCE-RELATED PAY

The emergence of performance-related pay (PRP)[1] schemes in the 1980s has already been noted. For many organisations intent on changing their reward systems, a decision to include such a scheme was a critical first step in the evolution of an overall strategy and one which then enabled other parts of the strategy to fall into place. However, too many schemes have failed because of poor design, communication and implementation.

My approach, when providing advice to clients, is that PRP is not simply a question of pay: for PRP to do any good it must be operated as part of a larger and wider process of performance management. A scheme must have clear objectives for individuals, and these objectives must be related effectively to the objectives of the company and/or business units.

The success of PRP is dependent upon effective performance. When pay is linked to performance, it can help to motivate, attract and retain outstanding performers, but it is equally important that the performance appraisal process is seen to be both credible and fair by staff in general. This is particularly important where a scheme is seen to have 'run out of steam' — see, for example, the Case Study of the work which we conducted at the National Audit Office (see pages 122–3).

There are many different ways in which pay can be related to performance. The design options can vary enormously and will need to fit in with the culture of the organisation.

- The type of payment — this can vary between cash or shares.
- The frequency of payment must be considered.
- The methods of how the payments under the scheme should be related to performance must be decided on — whether that of the individual, the group, the organisation as a whole or some combination thereof or to the performance of the organisation as a whole.

- *What* is to be measured is important: should the measures be quantifiable or subjective, or perhaps a mixture of the two?

Case study — National Audit Office

In 1988 I was a member of a team asked to carry out a review of performance-related pay for qualified audit staff at the National Audit Office and in particular to determine:

- the extent to which the scheme was achieving its objectives.
- whether the scheme had proved to be a satisfactory and fair medium for relating pay to performance.
- whether the incentives provided by the scheme were, or were likely to become, largely exhausted.

The NAO also wished to:

- strengthen staff motivation and encourage performance improvements by more specific and tangible recognition of achieved performance.
- recognise, and reward appropriately, differences in contribution between individuals of the same grade and seniority.
- help solve problems on the recruitment and retention of audit staff to enhance its ability to attract high calibre recruits.

We concluded from our review that the current performance-related pay scheme has fallen significantly short of meeting its objectives as originally defined:

- The high level of negative feeling about the scheme, particularly in relation to the performance assessment process, indicated that staff were not being effectively motivated by the scheme as it now stood, though there was wide acceptance that it had helped to create a strong awareness of performance issues.
- The clustering of assessments within the middle performance categories, the wide range of performance within these categories, the limited pay differentials between categories and the size of merit increases in relation to cost of living rewards, all suggested that the scheme did not recognise and reward appropriately differences in contribution between individuals of the same grade and seniority, and that it had largely 'run out of steam'.
- Staff turnover had increased significantly in the recent past. The available evidence indicated that this was due to reasons other than pay, but the performance pay scheme seemed to have little or no impact on the NAO's ability to retain staff or on its ability to attract high calibre recruits.
- The introduction of the scheme had, however, been successful in moving the NAO away from traditional civil service pay arrangements.

Our principal recommendations, for the most part implemented in full, to improve the performance-related pay scheme were that:

- a process of objective setting should be incorporated into the system;
- performance should be assessed on the basis of achievement against agreed objectives, taking account of their relative priority, and the use of points related to performance factors should be abandoned;
- further use of performance categories should be encouraged to recognise both poor and outstanding performance;
- individuals should be given the opportunity of discussing their performance and contributing their comments before assessments are completed, be fully informed of the contents of the assessment and enabled to add comments if they wish;
- in addition to the full annual appraisal, there should be mandatory performance reviews after four and eight months; all reviews should normally be carried out by the direct line manager;
- adequate training should be provided in counselling and interpersonal skills to support the appraisal process;
- overlapping pay scales should be developed and kept up-to-date in the light of market data;
- Separate cost of living increases should cease and the whole of the annual increases should be determined on the basis of individual performance;
- the performance-related pay scheme should be extended to cover assistant auditors and staff in the general service grades, subject to variations in detail.

Choices will need to be made. For example, a decision will need to be made on whether to base a scheme on the concept of bonuses or to rely solely on the concept of merit pay — that is progression through salary scales or ranges — or on a combination of the two. A scheme might reward only outstanding performers or it might be more widely focused over staff as a whole, with different levels of performance reward linked to different levels of performance, eg from outstanding to satisfactory (or even less than satisfactory).

Schemes which are designed to reward certain types of behaviour will have clear implications for performance and hence will have to be carefully considered in relation to the organisation's strategy. The design of measures will need to be considered in the light of the company's desire to reward short- or long-term performance; whether it wishes to base a scheme purely on profit growth, earnings per share, return on capital employed or some other measure of corporate performance. Whatever measures are chosen, it is important in the development of any scheme to model the potential results so that the costs and benefits can be identified.

It is impractical here to consider all possible design factors and each scheme will need to be assessed in the light of each organisation's objectives. However, it may be useful to evaluate different design features against three criteria:

1. The effectiveness of the scheme in increasing perceptions that pay is related to performance.
2. To what extent does the plan introduce dysfunctional behaviour, eg salesmen not passing on leads because the incentive arrangements are geared solely to individual achievement and not group performance.
3. The extent to which the plan encourages cooperation between employees.

The empirical evidence as to the success of PRP schemes is fairly limited, but clearly those organisations which do not have PRP forego a potentially important means of motivating employees provided the scheme is carefully thought through and designed to promote the right kind of behaviour. It is also clear that the correct starting point must be performance management and that giving line management, ie those who will actually implement the scheme, ownership of it is critical to its success.

Importance of market position

Most remuneration managers will have a view as to how the pay levels of their firms should compare with pay levels in other companies. It is also important to define what it is that is being compared with other organisations: for example, some companies will wish to compare on the basis of basic salary alone; others will wish to compare on the basis of total cash, that is, including the value of bonus payments; yet others will wish to include total compensation comprising a value for all fringe benefits included in the pay package.

Non-pay factors can be equally as important in attracting and retaining the most skilled individuals. Those individuals choosing to work within the Civil Service or the academic world may be more concerned with factors such as the ability to influence government policy or with research budgets than with pay rates. Furthermore, since pay rates in the public sector are constrained by cash limits, they tend to be lower than in the market-driven private sector. Pay levels are also influenced by the fact that civil servants operate in what might be called a 'closed' employment market — many will have joined direct from university and will remain within the Civil Service for the entirety of their careers. They will, therefore, be particularly concerned with 'internal' relativities. In the private sector, many individuals will expect to change employers several times, and on each occasion they will have an opportunity to gauge their external market worth — most people will not voluntarily change jobs to progress their careers unless they receive at least a 10 to 15 per cent increase in their current pay.

The pay equity challenge

Equity or fairness is a central principle which cannot be ignored in any reward system. It can embrace many different issues including:

- pay differences caused by external competition or market pressures;
- the legal and economic question of equal pay for work of equal value;
- the fairness of individual wage rates for people doing the same job;
- individual employees' views of their value relative to their pay.

Pay equity poses an important challenge for most employers: the need to reconcile the company's *ability* to pay (financial resources), *desire* to pay (values, culture and image), and its *need* to pay (labour market) with the employees' perception of *fairness* (equity).

How employees perceive fairness is, of course, different from an employer's view of fairness. Most companies will, when developing their remuneration strategy, compare their employees' pay with the remuneration received by those who work for other firms. There are several reasons why organisations will lay stress on external equity: first, the belief that a failure to match other companies' salaries will lead to decline in employee morale and productivity; second, belief that below average wages will hinder a company's ability to attract and retain good people; third, a view that management is psychologically committed to paying prevailing rates, and that an inability to do so is an admission of managerial failure.

When asked about the many things that influence an employee's perception of equity, employees will rank job security, working conditions, progression opportunities, flexibility of hours and so on, above pay. Of course job security is linked to stability of income, and it is possible that employees are reticent in talking about pay and that pay, is in fact, more important than studies show. Even where employees believe that pay inequalities exist, they may not be able to move to other employers since their skills may not be readily transferable, or they may be constrained by the expense of moving geographically unless the cost is borne by their new employer.

When comparing their pay structures with those of the external labour market, companies will focus on a number of key variables including the competitive sector in which it competes for labour, the industry sector, organisation size, company image and geographic location.

Market pricing

One difficulty with a focus on external equity is the reliance on external market pay surveys. Market pricing can be fraught with perils for the uninformed or uninitiated. Most salary surveys rely upon information which is voluntarily provided by firms, so a survey's validity is dependent upon the numbers of firms which can be persuaded to join in and the reliability of the information given. However, the general premise is that some information is better than no information at all. A second major difficulty concerns job matching. Most surveys will collect only a limited amount of information about the jobs to be compared and therefore there is a very real danger that apples will be compared with pears.

If the focus of attention is to be the external market, then it is critical that the remuneration manager has access to reliable market data. If a firm wishes to be seen as an above average payer (however defined), this policy will contribute towards the feeling that the organisation is prepared to pay to attract only the best who will want to work within an elite environment. Some organisations will also seek to compete for labour by offering above average pay packages which lay stress upon non-cash factors in order to attract and retain the best talent. This might include interesting and challenging work, geographic location, support services available and so on.

Because external and internal equity operate independently, the wage or salary suggested by the external market can be significantly different from that suggested by an internal job ranking. Lawler, a US pay specialist, says:

In most cases, it makes sense to focus on external pay comparisons as the major criteria for determining total compensation levels. Both internal and external equity have serious consequences for the organisation. However, the consequences of external equity ... are the most severe for the organisation and are the ones that deserve primary attention.[2]

NEW APPROACHES TO REWARD MANAGEMENT

For many organisations wishing to introduce new and innovative approaches to reward management — in order to survive the challenges of the 1990s — the first task will be to integrate performance management and performance related pay with the business strategy. For some this process of change has been radical while for others, where the pay system was already fairly well developed, the changes are less so. British Rail, for example, has moved away from a traditional pay system, and the introduction of a merit pay scheme for managers was a key plank in its human resource strategy; for others, notably subsidiaries of US firms, the concept of merit pay is relatively old hat. Although the move to effective performance management represents an important cultural change that organisations are likely to want to make in order to affect the behaviour of their employees significantly, there are a number of other innovative approaches which can be adopted and these are addressed below.

Flexible compensation

There are essentially two types of approach to flexible compensation: a total remuneration package approach, whereby the employer places a ceiling on the cash cost of a total package which the employee can receive: the employee is then free to choose either to take the whole amount in cash or to take part of the total in fringe benefits; or a 'cafeteria' approach where a base salary is set but the employee is free to choose from a menu of fringe benefit choices up to an agreed cash ceiling.

Employees are thus free to make up their own reward packages to fit their needs and desires. Although the concept of total remuneration packages is quite common, particularly for senior executives, the cafeteria approach is as yet not particularly widespread in the UK, although it is more popular in the US. One possibility for employees below executive level is to retain the provision of 'core' benefits such as pension, life assurance, paid sick leave etc, but to introduce a degree of choice over others eg, personal financial counselling, child care support, free petrol for private use, career counselling and so on.

The advantage of paying employees in cash is that its value in the eyes of the recipient is universally high, whereas it is often the case that employees may underestimate the true 'value' of fringe benefits, either because they are ignorant of the actual benefits provision which is available or they are simply unable to place a monetary value against known benefits. In 1979 the new Conservative government reduced the top marginal rate of tax from 83 per cent to 60 per cent; the 1988 budget went further, abolishing the top bands and replacing them with a single top tax rate of 40 per cent. The impact of these changes, apart from dramatically increasing the after tax income of the higher paid, was to diminish — but by no means to eliminate altogether — the attractions of what are usually referred to as tax-efficient fringe benefits.

Many employees will find an attraction in certain status symbols such as the company car, which may actually outweigh the actual cost to the organisation of providing them. Although cash is attractive, one advantage of the cafeteria or total remuneration approach is that it helps to focus attention on the 'value' of providing benefits. It also assists in the design of reward packages which meet the demands of an increasingly diverse workforce which typically include both married and single parents, dual-career families, or individuals who may simply wish to place a different emphasis on the types of reward which they wish to receive.

The choice of the form of rewards needs to be driven by the aims and objectives of the remuneration strategy. For example, a flexible remuneration approach may be appropriate for a participative open organisation which wishes to give its employees as much choice as possible, but it will be less so for other more bureaucratic organisations which continue to lay stress on status benefits such as the company car.

Paying for skills

The majority of reward systems are based on the types of job that people do. Often jobs are assessed in a hierarchy by job evaluation techniques which can range from the simpler non-analytical methods of ranking and classification to the more elaborate methods of points rating and factor comparison. The latter method is based on an assumption that an organisation can measure job worth and it can form the basis of pay comparisons with other organisations that employ similar sorts of people doing similar jobs.

An alternative approach is to pay people for their skills. The potential advantage of skill or competency-based pay is that it can significantly affect the reward culture within an organisation so that individuals will no longer be paid simply for moving up a job hierarchy but will be paid for the skills they acquire and for developing themselves.

Pay progression curves

Pay progression curves allow managers to compare where an individual is in terms of pay and where he or she might be expected to be taking into account skills acquisition and job performance. Once again the emphasis is on what an individual does or does not contribute on the job. A role can be expressed as a series of broad accountabilities and competences that an individual requires in order to fulfil his or her responsibilities.

Salaries are determined by reference to a series of pay curves on the basis of an assessment of an individual's competences, how effectively he or she uses those competences (performance), and the value of those competences in the labour market.

A system of pay curves is shown conceptually in Figure 6.1.

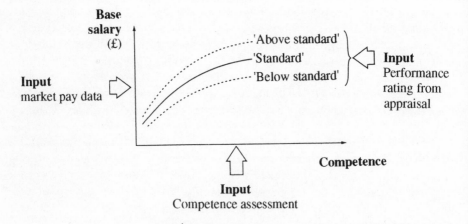

Figure 6.1 Pay curves system

Such a system allows considerable flexibility and decisions need to be taken on the following factors:

- **Function or skill group curves** — It is possible to have a set or series of curves which apply to a function or skill group, eg finance, computing, engineering, or to a skill group which cuts across functions, eg management.
- **Shape of the curve** — The shape of the curves can be adapted to include differential progression for different skills and pay budgets.
- **Curves in a set** — The number of curves is directly related to the number of appraisal ratings considered necessary to account for differences in

performance levels. Three are shown in Figure 6.1 but organisations will want to adapt the number, shape and classification of each curve in order to suit the particular circumstances of the business.

- **Actual salary** —In addition to personal skills and performance levels, the actual salary paid will depend upon individual circumstances eg, what the starting salary was, an individual's long-term potential, market pressures for individuals in this particular skill group.
- **Market data** — There will still be a need for reliable market data in order to assess pay market movement and to set basic salaries and progression curves.

There are several distinct advantages to such a system: the first is that it encourages individuals to extend their skills and, should they choose to do so, these will be reflected in higher pay. Secondly, it should mean that individuals will not be paid more simply for moving up the hierarchy. Lastly, it should encourage the use of previously underused skills and competences.

Two potential difficulties arise:

1. The measurement of a unit of skill which is worth a pay increase: in a typical job-based pay system, different rates of pay are tied to different jobs.
2. Such an arrangement may be more difficult to administer since a company must decide how much a different skill block is worth in the outside market place.

CONCLUSION: REWARD MANAGEMENT IN THE 1990S

The go go days of the 1980s enabled many organisations to avoid facing the consequences of inherently weak pay structures and practices because staff turnover, rapid rates of market pay movement and economic growth enabled them to offer employees plenty of headroom and progression.

Many organisations in the 1990s are facing quite different circumstances. Confronted with little if any business growth and very low rates of staff turnover, their pay régimes are coming under increasing pressure from staff who, not unnaturally, expect to receive material pay progression.

In this situation, employers may need to manage their staff turnover upwards by moving people out of their structures in a supportable and humane way, in order to create opportunities for others and they will also need to examine their reward arrangements against a more demanding culture. The key question is whether remuneration systems will meet the challenges of the 1990s. Undoubtedly the continuing development of performance management and performance related pay schemes will be a major theme of the 1990s. There is an increasing recognition that people really do make a difference, and that if an organisation wants to change strategic direction then it must change the way individuals behave. The reward system must ensure that this process of change can happen and that the implementation of reward systems do not work against business objectives.

To be effective reward management must begin with an assessment of strategic business needs in the context of the organisation's products and services, its structure, technology etc. It must then assess the organisation's values and culture, and the kinds of behaviour it wishes to promote in the future. The gap between the kinds of behaviour currently being emphasised and those which the firm wants to encourage will provide the basis for developing alternative systems of reward.

Although I have discussed the various components of the reward system as independent factors, I have also stressed the underlying importance of reward system *congruence*. In other words the components of the reward system are not stand-alone items. Once a business has established its priorities it must assess what elements of rewards should be changed and assess them against the business needs, the priorities for change and the realities of the external labour market.

Congruence is not limited to just the elements of the system itself. Any new arrangements must fit the other features of human resource management systems — these will include manpower and skill requirements, career patterns, needs for staff mobility and so forth. Some organisations, for example, have embarked on the path of setting individual objectives as the basis for performance management only to find that the underlying strategic objectives of the business were not sufficiently clear or robust to allow the system to operate credibly.

Having decided on the priorities for change, an assessment will need to be made of the options for change, each of which will have advantages and disadvantages. Whatever options are chosen — and there are a variety of tools and techniques for assessing such options — a number of critical success factors will apply:

- Any change must be seen and believed to have top level commitment.
- There must be full involvement and commitment from middle managers who will be key to any implementation programme.
- The changes must be communicated so that both managers and other employees will play a vital part in reinforcing the messages to be communicated and in ensuring that they are fully understood.
- Each individual component of the reward management programme must fit in with the overall remuneration and other human resource strategies.

By adopting a logical review of their reward management needs, organisations will be able to decide on the direction for change and will be able to adapt and respond to changing economic circumstances in order to compete in an increasingly competitive world.

NOTES

1. *The abbreviation PRP is sometimes used to refer to profit-related pay. In this chapter, however, it refers to performance-related pay.*

REFERENCES

1. Moss Kanter (1989) *When Giants Learn to Dance*, Simon & Schuster, Hemel Hempstead.
2. Lawler (1981) *Pay and Organisational Development*, Addison-Wesley, Wokingham.

7

EMPLOYEE RELATIONS: A NEW FRAMEWORK

Alan Cave

INTRODUCTION

Traditionally the term 'employee relations' has been synonymous with the more formal aspects of the relationship between the organisation and those whom it employs. The term is often used almost interchangeably with 'industrial relations' and, indeed, is often associated with the conduct of relations with employees collectively: especially where trade unions or staff associations are recognised as representing employees.

Typical concerns of employee relations departments within organisations have therefore included:

- **negotiation** with trade unions on terms and conditions of employment;
- **interpretation** of collective agreements;
- **representation** of the organisation in matters of individual or collective grievance concerning the employment relationship.

In recent years there has been a move in many organisations against the use of the term 'employee relations'. This has coincided with increased use of the language of human resource management. Indeed in many instances this has not been a coincidence. 'Employee relations' became seen as having somewhat negative connotations: a preoccupation with firefighting and compromise; a loyalty to the provisions of collective agreements, sometimes, apparently, at the expense of business priorities; and the appearance of putting relations with employees — and in particular with their collective representatives — above other considerations.

All of this can be made to seem to run counter to the increasing stress on individuals and with the precepts of strategic human resource management, in which all questions of policy in the field of employment flow from business priorities rather than being a motor force in their own right.

EMPLOYEE RELATIONS AND HUMAN RESOURCE MANAGEMENT: THE RELATIONSHIP

The tendency, therefore, has been to pose 'human resource management' and 'employee relations' as opposing — and indeed excluding — concepts. This reflects a parallel debate between two concepts often used in the literature of industrial relations: *pluralist* and *unitarist* relations. The former sees employees and employers as two separate forces with interests that are essentially in conflict but which can, through a variety of institutional and ideological mechanisms, be brought together in a negotiated relationship in order to make a particular factory or office work. In this model 'employee relations' is about policing that relationship and keeping the rather unstable show on the road.

The unitarist school of thought sees the world differently. In place of two legitimately separate constituencies there is really only one interest: that of the organisation as a whole — one which is led and articulated primarily by those at the top of the organisation. In this model, 'human resource management' is about communicating and winning commitment to the goals and policies of the organisation and about ensuring that the individuals who work within it have the skills, motivation and attitudes necessary for the achievement of those goals.

The central theme of this chapter is about whether the growing use of human resource management techniques and precepts is, by definition, at the expense of the concepts and values (such as negotiation, mediation from outside and compromise) traditionally associated with employee relations. Is human resource management, in other words, founded exclusively on unitarist principles or, conversely, does it admit of the continuing existence of an employment relationship that requires regulation through a variety of methods — including negotiation with the representatives of employees?

In examining this theme, the chapter's starting point is an apparent paradox. The decade of the 1980s saw an unprecedented onslaught on the component aspects of traditional employee relations:

- The proportion of employees in trade unions fell to the point where less than one in three private sector employees now belong to them. Employment has continued to grow fastest in non-union sectors whilst two million jobs have disappeared from the union heartland of manufacturing.
- Industry-wide collective agreements diminished in importance and in many cases disappeared.
- The law now intervenes much more directly and many previous practices, such as the closed shop and secondary industrial action against employers not directly involved in a dispute have been effectively outlawed.
- Employers are freer from official regulation of wages and thus more able to offer the terms and conditions they believe best suit them.
- Management prerogative in decision-making has grown. Management strategies have placed a greater emphasis on devolution of responsibility to

operating levels, on dealing with individual employees and with the flexible utilisation of labour.

Taken together this represents a formidable list and yet the real scope of this transformation appears to be in doubt. ACAS, the government-sponsored conciliation and arbitration body, included in its 1990 report the following observation: *'Collective bargaining still remains, directly or indirectly, the prime determinant of the terms and conditions of employment for the majority of people at work'*.

THE FORCES SHAPING CHANGE

In order to explore this apparent paradox the remaining sections of this chapter look in turn at the four principal sources of pressure which, together, shape the pattern of employee relations. These are:

1. Corporate strategy.
2. The legislative framework.
3. Economic influences.
4. European developments.

It is the changes in each of these areas — and the interaction between them — that have shaped developments in the field of employee relations in the 1980s. The result is a subtle series of shifts, rather than a 'big bang' change from one model to another. Indeed, at present the field of employee relations is clearly in a state of transition: one in which statements of intention are easier to find than concrete examples of change and in which in any case the final destination of change is still open to question. To illustrate this, consider some of the concrete examples of change which are available:

- Two 'blue chip' companies withdrawing from industry-wide collective agreements; one proceeding to cut down radically on the areas over which it bargained with unions, the other continuing to maintain its existing industrial relations arrangements in their entirety.
- Two foreign-owned electronics companies setting up new plants in Wales; one (a Japanese company) recognising a trade union and negotiating a single union 'no strike' agreement with it, the other (US owned) conducting its employee relations through an in-house non-union 'consultative committee'.
- Two parts of the civil service; one a central government department still covered by national 'Whitley' arrangements but introducing performance related pay for all staff, the other becoming a Next Steps Agency and introducing (in consultation with trade unions) a more radical package of human resource practices and cutting its link with nationally negotiated arrangements.

The common theme is greater variety in arrangements and a greater choice facing organisations in their approach towards employee relations. What factors will govern the operation of this choice in the 1990s? To shed light on this question we now look in turn at each of the four areas of pressure shaping the development of employee relations. For each area we look at the key influences on organisations in the last decade and some of the significant changes in employee relations that have come about as a result; and the key factors that will shape developments over the next decade and thus determine the choices available to organisations.

Corporate strategy

Discussions of industrial relations and employee relations usually focus on trade union policy and actions rather than those of employers. Yet corporate strategy is the logical starting point. It was, after all, corporate strategy that produced the network of industry-wide national agreements — designed initially to limit competition between employers over wage levels and reduce the influence of trade unions in the workplace — that was the pre-eminent feature of the British industrial relations scene for two generations. In just the same way it was employers' policy in Sweden that, until very recently, upheld the highly centralised national regulation of wages and conditions, and in Germany it is employers' policy that upholds the policy of 'mitbestimmung' or joint determination involving, as it does, strong enterprise works councils and board level worker representation.

In the last decade the most important development in the industrial relations sphere has been what might be called the *internalisation* of employee relations. Organisations that were previously happy to import wage levels, job structures and procedural arrangements that were negotiated between trade unions and national employers' organisations have moved decisively in favour of arrangements tailored to their particular organisational needs.

The roots of this shift lie to a large extent in developments in corporate strategy. The key features of this have been:

- the devolution of profit responsibility to operating units, profit centres and strategic business units;
- the redefinition of the role of the centre to focus more on monitoring bottom line performance of profit centres and on taking decisions concerning long-term capital allocation rather than with detailed operational intervention;
- growth through diversification and merger leading to corporate profiles that cover a multiplicity of industrial sectors and which reinforce the devolution of decisions and performance measurement to subsidiary businesses.

All these are developments that were visible before the 1980s but which accelerated sharply in the last decade. Not surprisingly the result was a collision with employee relations systems that were designed to produce firm-wide conformity with agreements which assumed that the firm 'belonged' to one industrial sector rather than another. This point has been expressed in the following terms by John Purcell[1]:

> Strategic business units have tougher requirements to meet in terms of performance but are freer to choose the policies they require to meet performance targets . . . profit responsible unit managers have exerted pressure on corporate offices to be given bargaining freedom.

In another study of nine companies which decentralised collective bargaining in the mid- to late 1980s, Purcell also concluded that:

> Without exception, motivations for changing bargaining levels derived from changes in a wider business structure/style and not for industrial relations reasons . . . the stated aim has been to tie industrial relations and bargaining outcomes to the business performance of the operating units.

How has the shift in strategy been manifested?

The most visible manifestation of this development has been the withdrawal of organisations from multi-employer industrial relations arrangements — in private and public sectors alike — and in some cases the ending of these agreements altogether.

Examples of the latter include:

- engineering;
- independent television;
- newspaper printing and distribution;
- cement manufacturing;
- the ports (following the abolition of the Dock Labour Scheme);
- clearing banks.

Examples of major companies withdrawing from national agreements include multiple food retailing (the withdrawal of the ten largest supermarkets in 1988) and clothing and textiles (the withdrawal of Coates, Viyella and Tootal in 1988).

Examples of decentralisation of bargaining *within* corporations are too numerous to chronicle. Suffice it to say that the most frequently cited example of a company standing out against this trend and retaining corporate-wide bargaining — ICI — is now reported to be considering actively a measure of decentralisation.

The examples quoted above are drawn from the private sector but a closely parallel development can be seen in the public sector, with cash limits, the Financial Management Initiative and structural change (notably the advent of Executive Agencies) producing a similar pattern of decentralisation and localisation. Public sector manifestations of this trend have included:

- the introduction of greater local variation in local authority pay;

- the complete breakaway of some local authorities from the national agreement;
- the break up of national pay bargaining in the railway industry.

The key attributes of this trend then are:

- the tailoring of terms and conditions to local circumstances and priorities; and
- the pulling away from arrangements that gave national or regional trade union officials a say in the regulation of employment relationships within the firm.

Relations with trade unions

This trend has also produced a redefinition of relations with trade unions. Interestingly it has *not* manifested itself in any significant push to exclude trade unions where they have been previously recognised. This contrasts sharply with the experience of the U S where similar changes in corporate strategy led to a concerted campaign by employers to remove recognition from trade unions.

Instances of derecognition have been rare. Much more frequent have been moves to:

- reduce the range of subjects and decisions covered by joint determination;
- concentrate attention on relations with in-house employee representatives rather than with 'external' union officials;
- reverse the trend towards unionisation of more senior employees;
- ensure that trade unions do not enjoy a monopoly over communications with the workforce;
- rationalise the number of agreements and unions with whom negotiations take place.

The situation is very different in new workplaces, especially those on greenfield sites. Here the choice for employers is widest and the indications are that union recognition is now less likely to be granted than in the past. Where it *is* granted it is rarely, if ever, given to multiple union structures; hence the rise of the 'single union deal'.

Although covering, by some estimates, still under 100,000 employees, these employee relations arrangements have attracted a great deal of attention, partly because of the controversy they have generated between unions, partly because they represent a genuinely new strand in the patchwork quilt of British industrial relations — one which draws heavily on Japanese industrial practice.

Philip Bassett who, as Labour Editor of the Financial Times, was the pioneering analyst of these arrangements described their key characteristics:

- Single union representation.
- Flexible use of labour across traditional demarcation lines.
- Single status: harmonisation of conditions between managers and staff.
- Participation — usually by means of a company council.

- Pendulum arbitration as a means of final resolution of disputes, linked to a 'no strike' provision.

One might add that the other key characteristic lies in the way in which these deals are struck. In a reversal of past practice unions are invited to present themselves in a competitive 'beauty contest', laying stress on the contribution which they can make to the company's success, before, typically, the first employee has been recruited.

This process is illustrated in the following Case Study. This summarises the draft agreement which Toyota drew up for its new UK manufacturing plant in the UK and which it then circulated to a number of trade unions, in effect inviting

---

Case Study: Toyota recognition agreement: key features

Principles:	The agreement is based on an explicitly unitarist principle: that the interests of union members will best be put by supporting the company's objectives and in particular the 'Kaizen' programme of continuous process improvement.
Basis of representation:	The company's workforce will be represented through a Toyota's Members Advisory Board comprising elected representatives (union and non-union) and senior executives. This body will be a forum for information and consultation as well as for reviewing terms and conditions.
Areas of responsibility:	The draft agreement states that the union accepts the company's exclusive might over decisions such as manpower planning and production scheduling, establishing standards of conduct, training and transfer of staff, communication with members, and establishing terms and conditions in line with the agreement's procedure.
Resolution of disagreements:	These are termed 'concerns' rather than disputes. The procedure to be followed is entirely based on the principle of continuity of production at all times.
	Union officials come in at a very last stage and the final recourse lies in a reference to ACAS.

---

to present for inspection so that the company could decide which union was most likely to make the agreement work in the way the company wished.

The significance of this development has certainly been recognised by individual trade unions which have invested much time and money into the search for a winning beauty contest formula, and also the TUC which has talked about putting forward 'single table' bargains in existing workplaces and about coordinating the approach of unions towards single union deals (albeit so far inconclusively).

Finally, this redefinition (and reduction) in the relationship with trade unions has had significant implications for decision making and the exercise of authority within the workplace. The underlying industrial relations strategy of the 1960s and 1970s was described by Eric Batstone[2] as 'giving up control in order to regain control'.[1] In other words, managers recognised that the power of shop stewards had become strong and institutionalised and, rather than trying to confront that power and roll it back they sought to incorporate local union representatives into the decision making process — hoping along the way, by stealth, to persuade them to adopt a positive, perhaps even a unitarist, view of the organisation's needs.

The 1980s has seen, almost universally, the abandonment of this approach and a reassertion, often in quite combative terms, of the notion of managerial prerogative.

Signposts for the future

If we look ahead towards the year 2000 there is no reason to expect that the developments in corporate strategy that have been recorded here will change in their impact on industrial relations. If anything we must expect an intensification of the central drivers for industrial change:

- A growing emphasis on flexibility of production methods.
- An increasing search for ways of reducing the time involved in developing new products and bringing them to market.
- A continuing drive to devolve bottom-line profit responsibility to lower and lower units of operation.
- A recognition that speed of response and the ability to change direction is the key to survival.

All of these pressures will increase the resistance of organisations to any industrial relations obstacle to progress. The key question, therefore, is what range of employee relations arrangements will be compatible with this continuing thrust of corporate strategy: what, in other words, will be the area of optimum choice for organisations? Here are some projections:

- There will be no interest in the traditional style of multi-union industrial relations linked to extra-organisational agreements. Those who still have such arrangements will progressively rid themselves of them, those drawing up new arrangements will not give them a moment's consideration.

- There will be instances of de-unionisation, going beyond the spectacular but unrepresentative previous examples of Wapping and one or two large manufacturing plants on Humberside.
- Newly established firms and workplaces will continue to be less likely to be unionised than their predecessors.

However, this will leave large swathes of the economy in which the decision whether to conduct employee relations on the basis of recognising trade unions or not will be finely balanced and, further, the question of which unions to recognise will be a very open one. Key considerations in making these decisions will include:

- The overall stance of the TUC — will it, for example, continue to encourage individual unions to participate in the rationalisation of bargaining arrangements (through, for example, the concept of the single bargaining table)?
- The success of individual unions in presenting themselves as positive partners in the development of the enterprise, stressing their commitment to peaceful problem resolution, skill development, product quality and so on. Initiatives such as those taken recently by the GMB general union in defining a new bargaining agenda, focusing very much on these sorts of issues, are important pointers in this regard.
- The ability of employee relations departments and practitioners within firms to shift the emphasis away from the firefighting, crisis management mentality of the past towards a positive employee relations agenda of their own — one that at least matches that being prepared in the more progressive trade unions.

Looking beyond this, however, the actual choices made by organisations about the future pattern of employee relations will, crucially, be affected by the legislative framework and by economic developments: the focus for the following two sections of this chapter.

THE LEGISLATIVE FRAMEWORK

Throughout the 1960s and 1970s a great deal of political heat — and occasionally light — was generated about the legal underpinning of British industrial relations. Until the 1980s, however, such change as took place was either limited in importance or so controversial as to invite immediate reversal by the next government.

The key shift of the 1980s has been the replacement of a legislative regime that has been variously described as 'voluntarist' or 'abstentionist' by one which is highly interventionist.

Throughout the preceding decades of the post-war period the law on industrial relations was founded on a murky fudge, but one which tallied broadly with a widespread consensus of opinion. Common law had traditionally held no legitimate place for trade unions: based as it was on the individual and on

140

contract law, it could only see such organisations as unlawful conspiracies against the public interest.

As public sentiment recognised that the economic power of an employer made him or her an unequal individual participant in a contract and that the logical counterbalance was a combination of employees, the legal system came, through a rather erratic zig-zagging series of judgements to grant various 'immunities' to trade unions from action against them for the breach of contract that would otherwise inevitably be involved in organising industrial action.

In this rather ragged way the law on industrial relations came to reflect a consensus that mirrors the 'pluralist' position described in the introduction to this chapter: seeking to achieve a rough even-handedness between employers and trade unions but — crucially — without any positive rights ever being ascribed to the latter. Instead the basic stance was that the law should keep out of industrial relations, holding the ring and allowing the participants to reach voluntary deals. This essentially unstable arrangement was put under increasing strain in the 1970s as the area of industrial relations 'immune' from common law torts was first restricted and then expanded significantly.

The hallmark of the 1980s has been the replacement of this 'voluntarist' legislative framework with one which intervened directly and sharply, redrawing the map of allowable and illegitimate industrial relations practices in four important respects:

1. Reducing the statutory immunities for trade union action.
2. Attacking the legislative basis of trade union organisation and collective bargaining.
3. Increasing the legal rights of members against their unions.
4. Reducing the statutory rights of individual employees.

The key changes have been:

- Lawful trade disputes have been redefined to apply only to disputes between employees and their own employers — effectively outlawing 'solidarity' and 'sympathy' action. Immunities have been withdrawn for picketing other than at the place of work and the number of pickets has been limited.
- Immunity from tort for industrial action has been made conditional on carefully specified ballots of members.
- A union may now be held liable for unofficial industrial action unless it specifically repudiates that action.
- Unions are required to conduct postal ballots every five years for the election of executive committees and general secretaries.
- The individual taking strike action is now subject to selective dismissal, without the right to reinstatement at the end of a dispute.
- The closed shop has been effectively outlawed by giving job applicants a right of legal redress if their services are refused on grounds of non-member-ship of a union.

In addition a series of other legislative changes have removed regulations that impinged directly on the determination of wages and conditions. Included here are:

- the abolition of the procedures under which trade unions could seek to enforce recognition for collective bargaining;
- ending the ability of unions to extend the provisions of collective agreements to employment contracts in other organisations, even where they were not recognised;
- the weakening of individual employment rights — especially in small firms — in areas such as unfair dismissal, maternity provision, health and safety protection and so on.

There has been a certain amount of disagreement concerning the extent to which the fall in union membership and in the level of strike activity in the 1980s can be attributed to these legislative changes. Some writers have seen it as a prime and direct determinant, others have argued that the economic changes described in the following section have been much more influential.

Nonetheless the list of changes recorded above represents an unprecedented rewriting of the industrial relations rulebook. It is, moreover, a rewriting that is entirely consistent with the developments in corporate policy described in the previous section. Professor Lord Wedderburn, one of the leading authorities on labour law, has described the underlying thrust of the 1980s legislation as 'the doctrine of enterprise confinement'[3] — a perfect echo of the thrust towards the internalisation of employee relations regulation and its alignment with business unit organisation described earlier.

Pointers to the future

Perhaps the true significance of the legislative changes of the 1980s lies not so much in their radical scope but in the fact that they look set to endure: the pendulum pattern of previous decades seems to have been broken. The Conservative election victory in 1992 and the changes in TUC and Labour Party policy over the last three years mean that in the 1990s no fundamental changes are anticipated in the law concerning the scope of allowable industrial action (with one exception mentioned below), picketing, balloting before industrial action, the closed shop and elections within trade unions.

The one exception is that if Labour does form a government in the latter half of the 1990s it may extend slightly the scope of 'immune' industrial action to allow limited secondary action in support of workers in another part of an organisation which has been 'artificially' divided in order primarily to take advantage of the limitations on secondary action.

What then would be the differences in the legal framework for employee relations laws as between the Conservative view and that of the more 'union friendly' Labour line?

Most of the Conservative agenda on industrial law has now been completed: very little change concerning the conduct of industrial relations seems therefore to be on the cards. The one area in which further changes might be introduced concerns the position of trade unions themselves. Further detailed intervention in trade union internal organisation, finance and rulebooks is likely. The biggest possible change, however, would be the regulation of union subscriptions and, in particular, restrictions on the 'check-off' — deduction of union subscriptions at source by employers.

Check-off arrangements cover the vast majority of trade union members and this has led to a view that union membership is therefore, in effect, largely sponsored by employers. Interference with the check-off has long been dreaded by many union officials who fear that if union members are required to make regular positive re-commitments to their union through, for example, being asked to give their agreement on a periodic basis to the continuation of deductions (as proposed by the Conservatives in 1991), then many members would leave the union.

The second main area of change would be, effectively, to remove the power of the TUC to regulate inter-union membership demarcation (the so-called Bridlington rules) and thereby open up a freer market place — allowing individual unions more choice in which unions they join. Some employers may find this a less than comfortable arrangement if the results conflict, say, with their own choice of the union which they wish their workers to join — as in the case of single-union deals.

The Labour agenda on the other hand includes changes in the following main areas:

- Procedures for facilitating the recognition of trade unions in one form or another.
- A considerable strengthening of individual employment rights and the introduction of a minimum wage.
- Rights to information disclosure and consultation for workforce representatives.

This combination would favour a rather new form of employee relations. Unions would be more likely to be a keystone of the system than under current arrangements. Their profile would be different than that of the past, however; less concerned with the exercise of collective bargaining power through industrial action and much more concerned to be the champions and enforcers of a new set of individual employment rights. Individualisation, in other words, will even touch the area previously described in purely collective terms.

ECONOMIC INFLUENCES

Economic forces influence the employee relations scene in two ways. First, they help determine the structure of employee relations: what proportion of the workforce will belong to trade unions, how widespread is collective bargaining, what is the 'mark up' on wages from union bargaining — these are the sorts of questions covered. Secondly, within the area of the economy in which the employment relationship is jointly regulated in some form, economic pressures determine the style and content of that regulation.

Economic structure

The rapid changes in industrial structure that have characterised the 1980s have cut a jagged line through the pattern of the employee relations system. Industries (and indeed regions) characterised by high levels of union membership and formal industrial relations machinery (typically the heavy end of manufacturing) have seen the loss of millions of jobs. On the other hand employment has grown rapidly in the service areas and in occupations where formalised, union-based employee relations is a rarity.

In rather crude terms, the middle-aged male manual worker from a large manufacturing plant north of Watford — the stalwart of trade union membership — has been the chief employment casualty of the 1980s, while the part-time, female service industry employee (whom unions tended traditionally to see as not doing 'proper' jobs) has become far more commonplace.

Arguments continue amongst researchers as to whether economic structural changes or legislative changes are the more powerful 'explainers' of union membership decline. The question of workplace size is also sometimes underplayed. There is evidence to suggest that above a certain size threshold (perhaps 2-3,000 employees) union based industrial relations was virtually the norm — below that size its incidence dropped away sharply. The reduction in production unit size has, of course, been one of the salient features of the 1980s industrial scene.

Looking to the future, Professor David Metcalf[4] of the LSE recently questioned the rather mechanical view that changes in industrial structure (which are likely to continue in the 1990s) will automatically presage the withering away of trade unions in the workplace. He said:

> The trend towards smaller workplaces, the service sector, part-time jobs, non-manual occupations, and location in Southern Britain were all apparent in the 1970s when union membership and density rose. Composition effects neglect the attitudes and policies of the main actors — employers and unions. They beg the key question: why have unions not been able to organise and recruit in expanding areas of employment in the 1980s?

Gradually, haltingly, the major unions have come to address this question and have set about various forms of expansion strategy aimed at establishing themselves with a natural presence in the new areas of employment. Typically these efforts include the provision of new services for union members reorganisation to give more internal political clout to new occupational groups and a serious attempt to update and improve the image of the union. These efforts will increase through the 1990s, although, as Professor Metcalf concludes: 'the fate of unions — at least as far as membership goes — to the end of the decade rests mainly with employers and the state'.

Pressures from the marketplace

Turning now to the impact of economic influences on the style and content on industrial relations we can see three sources of pressure at work: the product market, the labour market and the macroeconomic regime. Let us look at these in turn.

The product market

The key product market has made itself felt on the employee relations scene in the following main ways:

- Ever-increasing pressure for more flexible methods of production and utilisation of labour — a growing emphasis on multi-skilling, developing, organisationally-based skills and competencies, rather than importing externally defined occupational structures.
- The pre-eminence of quality as the determinant of competitive advantage and the corresponding emphasis on performance — and therefore on differentiation between individuals in terms and conditions of employment.
- The elevation of (in Charles Handy's words) the 'smart' process and worker with a consequential challenge to more hierarchical and authoritarian systems of decision making.

All of these factors move with the grain of business-specific and locally determined employee relations patterns discussed earlier in this chapter. They point to a continuing emphasis on the individual and on flexibility. They also, however, reveal a need which has been imperfectly handled in many organisations: managing the performance of the many as well as the few — ensuring, in other words, that the emphasis on quality, flexibility and performance is managed in a consistent and productive way through all levels of the organisation and not just in the top tiers.

The labour market

If the product market is a source of pressure for the insulation of employee relations from the outside world, the labour market tends to act in the opposite direction. Underneath the current recession the basic weaknesses in UK labour supply are still evident:

- An overall shortfall in the educational and vocational skill levels of the working population as compared with those obtained in major competitor countries such as Germany and Japan.

- The continuing existence of major shortages in specific skill shortages, particularly in the high technology end of industry.
- An underlying demographic shortfall of new labour market entrants, temporarily suppressed by the recession.

Taken together these factors cut across the attempts of organisations to customise and insulate their employee relations arrangements. The small cogwheel of a specific skill shortage meshes with progressively bigger cogs and drives up the wages structure across a swathe of the economy. The individual firm does not find it cost-effective to launch a major training programme and, faced with under-resourced public training programmes, falls back on 'poaching' skilled labour and thereby importing an occupational structure at odds with its home-grown variant.

More widely we find ourselves looking at a potentially rather unstable mix. In effect, employers drive towards fragmenting the labour market by internalising employee relations and destroying cross-industry structures and mechanisms that no longer fit their business strategy requirements. Yet due to deficiencies in the labour market they still face what economists call 'externalities' — costs and issues which they cannot resolve by themselves — for example skill levels and stubborn wage inflation pressures.

This, therefore, brings us to the third area of pressure.

Macroeconomic policy

In past decades the response to what was described above as an unstable mix would have been a shift in macroeconomic policy; most probably some form of devaluation which sought to reduce the temperature of the externalities facing all employing organisations. Some form of incomes policy would probably accompany the devaluation.

The advent of the Exchange Rate Mechanism (ERM) of the European Monetary System has changed all that, however. The ERM re-writes the rules of the wage fixing business. If the aggregate impact of wage bargaining is a level of wages that is uncompetitive in world market terms, the 'hit' will be taken not on the exchange rate but on the level of employment. The near universal declaration of the political impossibility of incomes policy therefore means that we face the prospect of a fragmented and localised employee relations and bargaining system which rubs up abrasively against a macroeconomic regime that takes a stern and unforgiving stance towards the aggregate outcomes produced by that system and offers no cushioning or support.

Looking ahead it seems hard to avoid the conclusion that, within the ERM, there are only two possible ways of living with this combination of pressures:

- **Either** the UK economy will continue to operate at a constantly higher level of unemployment than its competitors — or than it has been accustomed to — pending some major strengthening of the supply side of the labour market (something which in the past has always been the grudging product of labour market tightness rather than of slackness).

- **Or** political pressure will steadily remount — irrespective of the party in power — for some form of intervention in the wage determination process to create a more acceptable macroeconomic outcome from fragmented wage fixing.

Synchronised bargaining, in which the wage round is re-ordered and rationalised, seems the most likely candidate for such a change.

EUROPEAN DEVELOPMENTS

We live in a transitional period. Within five years it will seem ludicrous to pose 'European developments' as a separate category from 'legislative changes' and 'economic influences'. Closer economic and political union will mean that the latter areas are as much 'European' as 'domestic'.

Writing now, however, it is possible to discern a limited but distinct impact on the development of UK employee relations emanating from the European Community — one that cuts somewhat against the domestic grain in important respects. Three areas demonstrate this clearly:

1. **Equal pay** — The introduction of the equal pay for work of equal value regulations stemmed from a decision by the European Court. At the heart of the regulations is a principle that runs counter to the market-based and individualising current of UK policy in the 1980s.
2. **The social charter** — In some form or other, the charter of employment measures drawn up as the 'social dimension' to the single European Market will come into effect in all the EEC countries except the United Kingdom in the 1990s. The Conservative Government is opposed to the Social Charter although it has been warmly embraced by the Labour and Liberal Democrat Parties. If and when it does apply it will put a limit on the process of internalising and localising the regulation of the employment relationship which this chapter has charted. It will, in effect, fill the gap in the employee relations system left by the demise of industry-wide collective agreements. It will prescribe minimum standards in many of the important areas of the employment contract and therefore define the limits to differentiation and employer choice.
3. **Industrial participation** — Since the Bullock report of 1977 the sole source of pressure towards extending industrial participation, information and consultation rights in the UK has been the EC. That pressure will increase and the main vehicle may be the European Company Statute. With the move to qualified majority voting in the community the introduction of this measure, in some form, now seems more likely. It will mean that companies above a specific size operating in more than one EC country will

have to adopt clearly specified measures to involve workers representatives in consultation and decision making.

At a time when UK public policy has stressed the unitarist employee relations philosophy described at the outset of this chapter, the European Community has been (and will continue to be) a consistent source of countervailing pluralist pressure.

CONCLUSION

This chapter began with an observation and a question. The observation was that after a decade of radical change, employers now have a wider choice in the way in which they conduct their dealings with their employees than at any time in the last two generations.

The question was whether, as employers make their choices, the emerging pattern will be a highly individualistic and 'unitarist' form of human resource management with little room for traditional 'employee relations' concepts, or whether there will continue to be a strong pluralist and collective flavour to the regulation of employment — albeit in different forms.

The implications of the chapter suggest a tension. On the one hand the product market and corporate business strategy will continue to push towards the greatest possible degree of individual differentiation and freedom from joint regulation of employment. At the same time pressures from the labour market and from European legislation will point towards a more regulated and organised approach towards employee relations.

The exercise of political influence by the Government will be significant: it will determine on which side of this balance the weight of public policy and domestic legislation is placed.

At the outset of this chapter an apparent contradiction was highlighted. On the one hand we see the concerted and mutually reinforcing steps to undermine the employee relations *status quo*. On the other hand there is the obstinate continuity of many long-standing features of the traditional scene — notably the extensive influence of collective bargaining on the determination of wages. This has led some commentators to suggest a gap between the stated intentions of employers in this field and their actual actions.

Perhaps it is more helpful to see the current period as one of transition. Certainly we have witnessed the end of what might be termed the 'Donovan' era (after the Royal Commission of the 1960s). This was characterised by the search for industrial relations peace by way of formalising the (often very informal) employee relations arrangements, recognising the legitimacy of trade union organisation, maintaining the voluntarist approach towards legislative regulation and emphasising instead the primacy of collective bargaining, and of conciliation and mediation as the methods to resolve disputes.

But if the Donovan era has passed it is by no means clear that there is a straightforward replacement for its model of employee relations. Several models have emerged, driven as we have seen by consistent strategic and economic pressures but taking different form according to the culture, traditions and precise circumstances of the organisations concerned. This breaking of the mould leaves us at present without a dominant model of industrial relations but, instead, will offer a very wide range of options available to employing organisations. To conclude therefore, here is a set of the key questions that organisations should ask themselves in making that choice:

- How far can the process of decentralisation be taken: will it conflict with the search for stability in wage costs and higher standards of skill?
- To what extent can employee relations be managed on an individualistic basis? Will the growing need to raise the performance of the many, be manageable on an individualistic basis or will more collective structures and approaches be necessary?
- What benefits might accrue from recognising a trade union (almost certainly in the singular)? What contribution will it make to the competitive success of the organisation, on what basis should the choice between unions be made?

The balance sheet at the moment shows that the development of human resource management techniques in the UK has been compatible with a continuing prevalence of collective bargaining and with the collective representation of a substantial minority of the working population. It is hard, looking ahead, to see any reason for a drastic change in that position.

REFERENCES

1. Purcell, J (1991) 'The rediscovery of management prerogative: the management of labour relations in the 1980s', in K Mayhew (ed) *Labour Markets – Oxford Review of Economic Policy*, vol 7, no 1, Spring.
2. Batstone, E (1988) *Reform of Workplace Industrial Relations*, Clarendon Press, Oxford.
3. Wedderburn, W 'Freedom of Association and Philosophy of Labour Law', *Industrial Law Journal*, 18 March 1989.
4. Metcalf, D (1991) 'British unions: Dissolution or Resurgence? in K Mayhew (ed) *Labour Markets – Oxford Review of Economic Policy*, vol 7, no 1, Spring.

8

EMPLOYEE COMMUNICATIONS AND EFFECTIVE INVOLVEMENT

Martina Platts and Anne-Marie Southall

WHY COMMUNICATE?

Military geniuses from Julius Caesar to 'Stormin' Norman Schwarzkopf have stressed the importance of clear direction, good information and open lines of communication. Communications are just as critical to all aspects of business success — not least the management of people. Organisations need complete, coherent and efficient communications systems in which essential information is channelled upwards, downwards and laterally between managers and employees, as well as outwards to customers, suppliers and shareholders.

Fundamentally, organisations are simply collections of different groups of people. The groups may be departments, divisions or levels in a hierarchy. Left to their own devices, each group tends to develop its own culture — its own set of beliefs, attitudes and values — and its own understanding of what the organisation's objectives are and the best route for achieving them.

Communications provide the link between these different groups, helping to ensure that common beliefs, attitudes and values are held, and that there is a common understanding of the organisation's goals. Good employee communications can be a major tool for both line and human resource managers in enabling, progressing and supporting business goals and objectives.

Giving information to employees should not be a burden, but an opportunity. Good communications are likely to increase performance and results as well as the individual's sense of self-fulfilment and commitment to the organisation. If properly handled, such programmes can contribute to releasing energy, ambitions and ideas which might otherwise lie dormant. Whether one-to-one, in teams or organisation-wide, communications should be designed, therefore, to meet the particular needs of a business with an emphasis on supporting business and individual results and performance, building corporate culture and values and developing people.

The link to strategy and change

A focus on these three issues will provide a natural link to the overall HR strategy of the business. An HR strategy is about ensuring that the culture, style and structure of the organisation and the quality, motivation and commitment of employees contribute fully to the achievement of business objectives. It should help employees understand what their role is in the overall business, building mutuality of purpose through a common interest in business success.

The communications strategy and policies of an organisation should support the HR and business strategy, enabling each person to do their job more effectively by providing information that contributes to the quality of judgement and decision making. Effective communications should provide the means for gaining an understanding of the organisations' overall objectives and plans, and of the thinking behind them.

In recent years too, many organisations have recognised the critical importance of good communications in managing change. The need for employees to find opportunities rather than threats in new ideas, new ways of thinking and operating is a central challenge for managers. Clear, constant and consistent information provided to employees in a range of media can be an enormous help to managers in convincing employees to accept change. This is illustrated in the following short case study of H&R Johnson, a medium sized manufacturing business, facing up to the need for change when we advised on the development of an employee relations and communications strategy.

GETTING IT WRONG

So if good communications are so important why do things so often go wrong? There are as many opportunities for things to go wrong as there are employees . . . probably an exponential relationship. A list of some of the organisational communication issues that we have encountered illustrates the potential for misjudgment:

- Communications climate and corporate culture.
- Communication content and clarity .
- Accuracy of identification of employee groups and horizons of interest.
- Which communication channels?

    — face to face communication; one-to-one or in groups;
    — written communication; letters, memos, reports, notices;
    — audio-visual communication.

- Frequency of communication
- Degree of openness.
- Communication patterns between, and information needs of, individuals, sections and departments.

Case Study: H & R Johnson

H&R Johnson, a ceramic tile manufacturer based in Stoke on Trent, employs around 1500 people. The company is part of the Norcros group, having been taken over in 1982, but its origins stem from a series of mergers between small family-based firms in the Stoke area dating back to the mid-eighteenth century.

H&R Johnson began to invest in increased mechanisation to improve productivity from the mid-1980s, but changes in shop floor working practices were slow to materialise. A new top management team, including a new managing director, started to tackle some fundamental problems during early 1990. Key changes were discussed with employees in the areas of working practices, terms and conditions and internal management systems. A first priority was to reduce overmanning, resulting in 300 redundancies in September 1990.

The new managing director's natural approach to communication was based on openness. He used a range of methods to get messages across including addressing the workforce face to face, both in groups and during unscheduled visits to the shop floor, and through the written word. The focus of communication was the future needs of the business, stressing that changes were aimed at supporting the long-term job security of remaining employees. This was a continuing theme in 'roadshow' presentations carried out for all sites by the production director and the personnel director. The announcement of a three year investment programme, worth £6 million, reinforced this commitment.

But to achieve long-term changes to working practices and to productivity, a different degree of cooperation was required. For this reason, senior management developed a long-term employee relations and communications strategy geared to building union participation and to increasing commitment at all levels. This culminated in a working document which provided a new basis for managing employee relations within the company — the Johnson Accord. After much discussion this document provided both the detail of the annual wage negotiation and a vehicle for continuing changes in working practices in the longer term. In June 1991, a copy of the Accord was sent to each member of the workforce, with a recommendation from the union negotiation team for acceptance. This was subsequently accepted by a majority vote.

Overall, the experience of H&R Johnson demonstrates the importance of open and consistent communication in employee relations, and of senior management and unions seizing a need for rationalisation as a real opportunity for fundamental change.

- Middle management: lack of sufficient information, commitment and skill.
- The impact of informal communication and the grapevine.
- The effects of inconsistent messages sent by other corporate policies.

- The human and organisational aspects of using information technology such as electronic mail and voice messaging to communicate.

Common problems

A common management mistake is simply to think 'who do we want to talk with — and why — about what?' The more difficult, and much more searching question is 'who wants to talk with us — why — and about what?' The sooner we learn to listen as much as we talk, the better we can focus on key issues and avoid potential information overkill. Talking down to employees from management levels is inefficient and outdated. Communication is not a one-way process and should work to support the flatter, minimal bureaucracy organisation of the 1990s.

Another dilemma, particularly in a production environment, can be the perception of time spent communicating as lost output, which adversely affects delivery schedules and production efficiency. The reverse of the coin is to see human resources as assets, not costs, and to generate effective employee communications supporting continuous improvements in quality, efficiency and cost reduction.

The most difficult aspect lies in deciding how much to say, when, and to whom. Channels and media should be selected in the light of the content and the audience.

There may also be a number of barriers and blockages to communication which need to be identified before communication can be effective. Some of these are illustrated in the following:

- Distance: There is an inverse relationship between physical distance and effectiveness of communication
- Skill: Poor communication skills
- Serial transmission: Cascaded information may be coloured, distorted, omitted, or denied at each relay
- Process: What is obvious to the sender is often obscure to the recipient
- Predisposition: People only hear what they expect or want to hear
- Trust: May be lacking between sender and recipient
- Status: Individuals with low status are inhibited in communicating with those of higher status.

Trade unions can be a major blockage or a major enabler in employee communications. An effectively managed company must control quick, effective and consistent two-way channels of communication. A well-run trade union will counterbalance with its own channels. Genuine, constructive dialogue with a well-informed workforce and a well-informed trade union can produce radical improvements in performance — as H & R Johnson found.

CHARACTERISTICS OF EFFECTIVE COMMUNICATION

Getting employee communications right is not easy but there are some readily identifiable common characteristics in those organisations which communicate well. Here is a simple checklist of the principles of effective communication:

- Top management commitment.
- Planned and deliberate.
- Systematic.
- Relevant.
- Reliable.
- Upwards, downwards, sideways.
- Supported by training.
- Agreed objectives.
- Open and honest.
- Interesting, significant content.
- Two-way.

- Sufficient time and money.
- Understandable (for all!).
- Regular and well timed.
- Right amount.
- Flexible.
- Supportive attitudes.
- Support in preparation.
- Think message then medium.
- Within recipients' horizons.
- Constantly reinforced.

The Glaxo Case Study illustrates how one successful organisation has applied these principles in practice:

Open management, candour and building trust help management to build goodwill with employees. If you give people information, they will often want more. But if the general rule is to tell as much as possible, then people will more willingly understand and accept those occasions when only a minimum can be said. Being secretive is normally unnecessary and potentially harmful. If there are particular (unusual) considerations of confidentiality that prevent you saying more than a limited amount say so and say why not. If it is a good reason, well-informed employees will understand.

Audiences: horizons of interest

The audience for a communication may range from all employees to a particular sub-group or individual. A sub-group will often be a department or a level in the hierarchy, but may also be a cross-departmental or cross-hierarchy group. For each potential audience, their horizon of interest should be established. This is best done by asking employees, but particular levels in the hierarchy tend to have a horizon one or two layers out from themselves. Thus the layer of management below board level may look upwards and outwards and beyond board issues to the wider economic environment, and downwards to first line supervision on the shop/office floor. This is why middle management are critical enablers or blockers in communications processes.

One particularly important sub-group — and the most difficult to identify and communicate with — is opinion formers, people at all levels, in all departments, who take an interest in what the company is doing (positively or negatively), absorb information like sponges, and express opinions readily and/or vocifer- ously. Union representatives are often in this group, but some anti-union or non-union, people may also be members. Often the only way to reach opinion

Case Study: Glaxo Holdings

Glaxo is one of the world's leading, fastest growing pharmaceutical companies with sales of over £3 billion. Glaxo medicines are sold in about 150 countries throughout the world and the group employs nearly 38,000 people based in over 50 countries.

Glaxo Holdings, the company headquarters, acts as the central coordinator and information provider for employee communications throughout the Glaxo group; and organises local communications for Holdings staff based at three UK locations.

Glaxo sees the purpose of employee communications as being to help stimulate and motivate staff. Glaxo wants its employees to be as well informed as possible about what the group is achieving throughout all of its companies. It wants people to understand the importance of new product development, and understand the contribution of individual parts of Glaxo to the successful launch of new products. Glaxo also want to ensure that staff worldwide understand the company's position on possible contentious public issues such as the use of animals in testing drugs, and be in a position to make an informed response.

Holdings Communications department coordinates the supply of information around the group so that staff in all countries can receive the same information, but does not impose communications on local companies.

The media produced centrally by Glaxo's Communications department include:

Glaxo World	— A glossy magazine providing worldwide business information and profiles of key people.
Staff Report	— A publication designed to enlarge on the annual report, for staff.
Videos	— On the annual report, and a recording of a studio discussion between senior and middle managers.
Video Conferences	— Used by senior managers to hold worldwide meetings.
Other Publications	— For example, a leaflet to explain the company's policy on caring for the environment.
Key Facts	— A booklet produced annually and circulated to all staff giving key facts about the group. This is also used for marketing purposes.

Local communications

Each site and business unit has its own communications arrangements. In Holdings headquarters local communications are used to build links between different departments who, in the normal course of business, have little opportunity to work together, and include:

Focus	— A bi-monthly newspaper issued to all staff. This contains articles of interest about Holdings' business activity and more personal articles - about individual members of staff.
Conference	— From time to time (two in three years) all Holdings staff are invited to a business conference in an attractive United Kingdom location.

formers is to communicate to everyone, knowing that you are really addressing the opinion formers. This may mean that you include more data in a communication than most employees might want: this is particularly so when seeking to get a rational decision made about an industrial relation issues, in the face of union opposition.

Reinforcement

Whatever subjects are addressed, to whatever audiences, through whatever media, they need to be repeated and reinforced. A message important to the sender but not to the recipient may be ignored if sent only once. Receiving information is very much like the process of learning: it depends on the level of interest and previous knowledge of the recipient. Repetition, varied levels of detail, and varied language are thus also important.

Messages and information need to be disseminated several times in a variety of forms. Some employees like to read, others to listen, others to watch, still others to gossip. So newspapers, telephone newslines, video and the grapevine all have a role to play.

But there are no easy answers. So do not worry if employee communications are hard to get right — expect them to be, and learn from things which do not work.

COMMUNICATION SYSTEMS . . . OLD AND NEW

Face-to-face communication

What communications methods should form part of an overall system? Classic wisdom is that communications systems should draw on a number of different methods, producing a series of interlocking channels as the basis of a communication network. But face-to-face communication, where it is a component of organised line management communication, has the greatest impact and is generally the most popular method of receiving information. Face-to-face is the most likely method of ensuring that messages are clear and sustained. The biggest potential barrier to face to face communication, however, is usually middle management. Their training and the provision of good senior management support are therefore essential components of a communications strategy.

Team briefing

The classic technique for face-to-face communication in British industry has become the Industrial Society's team briefing process. This aims, through regular meetings involving 'boss' and 'subordinate' teams, to pass management

156

information down the organisation to all employees. This should be understandable by recipients at all levels by being relevant to their needs, thus forming the basis for future action. It is often achieved through a 'core' brief of common company information, supplemented by local information specific to each team's own operation. Team briefing used well can also support upward and lateral communication.

Whilst team briefing has served many organisations extremely well, like any other communications technique, it is not a panacea. Our experience in introducing team briefing in firms like Book Club Associates shows that it will only work if it has continued top management backing and belief, if briefers are well supplied with timely relevant information, well trained and confident in their delivery, and if logical teams are identified. Devoting at least a part-time facilitator to the process, to help in preparation of briefs, take follow-up actions, arranging for questions to be answered and monitoring how the process is working, supports continued success.

Internal mass media

Methods such as employee newspapers, reports, conferences and audio-visual techniques have a more supportive role. A by no means exhaustive checklist of such communications methods is included overleaf; it may prompt some useful ideas.

Employee groups

Developments in direct or task participation such as quality circles, or improvement groups, became popular in the UK in the 1980s. Defining 'success' and 'failure' in the case of employee groups, such as quality circles, is not an easy task. Quality circles have intangible benefits which can be greater than immediate cost savings. Typical benefits cited by circle members are increased job satisfaction, an opportunity to become involved in the organisation, making a contribution to solving real problems, and better teamwork within the department. Benefits for managers include the resolution of problems at shop floor level and the enhancement of the leadership role of supervisors. The organisation benefits by tapping the knowledge and experience of its employees at all levels resulting in increased involvement, better communications, and improvements in quality and productivity.

Europe

In the UK, the participation of employees has been associated historically with indirect or representative participation such as joint consultation or collective bargaining. In Europe the debate on worker participation has been going on for a long time and attempts are still being made through various directives on

Communication Methods Checklist

- Staff meetings, lunches or dinners
- Company conferences
- Committees
- Breakfast with the boss

- 'Open' house — company wide or department basis
- Team briefing/briefing groups
- Employee directors
- Union-management meetings
- Joint consultative committees
- Ad-hoc groups; project teams; working parties
- Task forces
- Skunk groups
- Focus groups
- Face to face interviews
- Speak-up schemes
- Quality circles
- Suggestion schemes

- Social audit
- Staff publications/newspapers/journals
- Exhibitions — eg for a new investment programme, a relocation

- Leaflets
- Notice boards
- Direct mail
- Employee reports — Annual/Quarterly

- Audiovisual programmes — slides and tape
- Video
- Teleconferencing
- Closed circuit TV or radio
- Interactive video
- Audio-cassette tapes

- Electronic mail
- Electronic voice messaging
- Dial-the-boss
- Telephone newsline/hotline
- Recruitment literature
- Induction programmes
- Contributions to leisure time activities

- Attitude surveys
- Training
- Employee appraisal systems

information, consultation and participation from the European Commission to arrive at common rules.

EC legislation and participation

The debate on worker participation has been going on for some twenty or more years in the EC countries. The European Commission, through various initiatives and directives on information , consultation and participation, has developed an action programme to arrive at common rules. These initiatives, including the

Social Charter, have not generally been seen as a major issue for human resource management in the UK and Europe. But they are a reality which cannot be ignored, and which perhaps do not pose such a threat as some managers, and the CBI, have thought.

What is the current position? The controversial Vredeling proposals, named after the Dutch Commissioner who originally introduced them in 1980, were most recently redrafted in 1983. The proposals, under repeated attack, have been watered down but currently call for an undertaking with complex structures (ie major national and trans-national companies), and over 1,000 employees to:

- inform workers fully about the company they work for, its tactics, prospects and strategies by furnishing them with all corporate information not considered private;
- give workers' representatives at least once a year, a detailed account of company structure, employment and investment intentions;
- give workers 30 days notice and complete information about possible closures, moves, reductions or significant changes in output or activities;
  - agreements with other firms;
  - major organisational changes, working methods or manufacturing techniques;
  - new technology to be introduced;
  - changes which might affect health and safety.

Discussions were vetoed in 1986 until 1989 — but no discussions have taken place since then; the proposals are therefore dormant and could be withdrawn.

The draft fifth directive (which would require a qualified majority vote) was first proposed in 1972. A revised directive was proposed in 1983. This draft allows for both employee director representation on single-tier or two-tier board structures, or alternatively a works council or system arranged by collective agreement giving specific information and consultation rights. It covers only companies with more than 1,000 employees. Council working groups are currently meeting to try to negotiate a text which would achieve sufficient agreement for the Council of Ministers to reach a 'common position'.

The European Company Statute (first proposed in 1970) is a single package of company law which companies operating in more than one EC country could choose to adopt, thereby avoiding the complications of operating under a number of conflicting national systems and gaining additional benefits such as being able to offset losses in one country against profits in another. A revised version was published in August 1989 in two parts: a regulation which deals with the company law aspects of forming a 'European Company', and a directive which sets out the employee involvement procedures that companies choosing to adopt European company status would be obliged to set up. These are aimed at ensuring employee participation 'in the supervision and strategic development of the company' in largely the same way as the fifth directive.

Neither the draft fifth directive nor the European Company Statute would mean that UK companies would have to have workers on the board. Both provide for several options, including the option of a system developed through collective agreement. Some companies might choose to have worker directors, but none would be obliged to do so (a new possibility being canvassed by the UK is 'equity option', which would treat employee share option schemes as a valid method of employee participation). Both will need a substantial amount of amendment to achieve the required number of votes in the Council of Ministers, as several member states have expressed their reservations on the proposals. It will be some time before a harmonised framework for employee involvement can be agreed.

Electronic communications methods

A look at some of the methods using recent and emerging technology gives pointers for new directions and initiatives in the 1990s.

New techniques which will become commonplace as we progress to the year 2000 include telephone newslines, voice messaging, teleconferencing and the improved use of electronic mail. Used 'smartly' they can support flatter, integrated, customer focused (both internal and external) organisations and start to break down some of the traditional middle management layers. Some of these have already been used to great advantage in some complex organisations — essentially using electronic networks to support internal organisational networks.

Voice messaging

Voice messaging enables a caller to leave a spoken message for a user when the latter is away from the telephone, with guaranteed delivery and receipt. The message (as long as necessary) is stored on digital exchange equipment and the addressee can call up his 'mailbox' from any telephone, worldwide, to hear the message. If the original caller is also on the voice messaging system a reply can be sent by keying just three digits. The same message can be sent to groups of people according to need and/or organisational layer. Messages can be stored for reference to be dealt with at a later time or forwarded to other users. This is an extremely effective, personalised and relatively cheap communications system for employees who are not generally office based, and therefore can be difficult to get hold of.

Teleconferencing

The first two weeks of the 1991 Gulf War led to a 60 per cent increase in the use of international videoconferencing. But even this will be eclipsed when the 'videophone' develops from a working prototype to become a commonplace accessory using the Integrated Services Digital Network (ISDN). Videoconferencing is appropriate for larger groups of people, whilst the videophone is restricted to one or two persons at each end of a videophone. Recent psychological research has shown that more than half of ordinary conversation is triggered by visual clues — all of which are lacking on the ordinary telephone. Videoconferencing and videophones will allow a more natural dialogue, including time to think!

Videoconferencing can be used to call top people together quickly, reduce decision making times and overcome travel and time problems. High quality pictures can be sent down ordinary telephone lines, putting a videoconference call at only roughly double the price of an ordinary telephone call. The development of visual communications, including videophones, is likely therefore to be similar to that of mobile communications over the past 10 years. As the network develops, attracting more users, equipment costs will fall as a direct result of increased popularity and further breakthroughs in technology.

BUILDING INVOLVEMENT . . . A PLAN

The technological imperatives of continuous innovation, improvement and implementation demand ongoing and increased levels of employee involvement. Competition over quality, price and timely delivery continue to promote technological innovation and the necessity to keep communication networks open, flexible and active. Opportunities exist to exploit major new electronic telecommunications developments in the employee communications field. Generating and maintaining high employee involvement must not, however, sacrifice productivity in the process. A tested pattern for building involvement in this way includes the steps below. Figure 8.1 sets out these and some other key actions and issues.

1. **Begin with employee input before any recommendations are considered.**
   This can be through an attitude survey, focus groups, meetings of horizontal or vertical groupings, an audit or suggestion schemes. Understand what employees want to hear and consider this against what management want to communicate and how open you are prepared to be.
2. **Develop a mechanism whereby the issues can be held in focus.**
   This could be a communications task force (consisting of representatives from all levels) or a communications manager. A board member with specified responsibility for employee communications should also be nominated. The mechanism should help to clarify and resolve, segregating potentially overlapping activities and integrating those that otherwise may stand alone.
3. **Demonstrate commitment.**
   At a strategic level, the employee communications strategy should be written to form part of the organisation's overall communications and public relations strategy, and be visibly supportive of the corporate strategy itself.
   For example, organisation wide team meetings can act as tangible indicators that management are both prepared to relay information and are

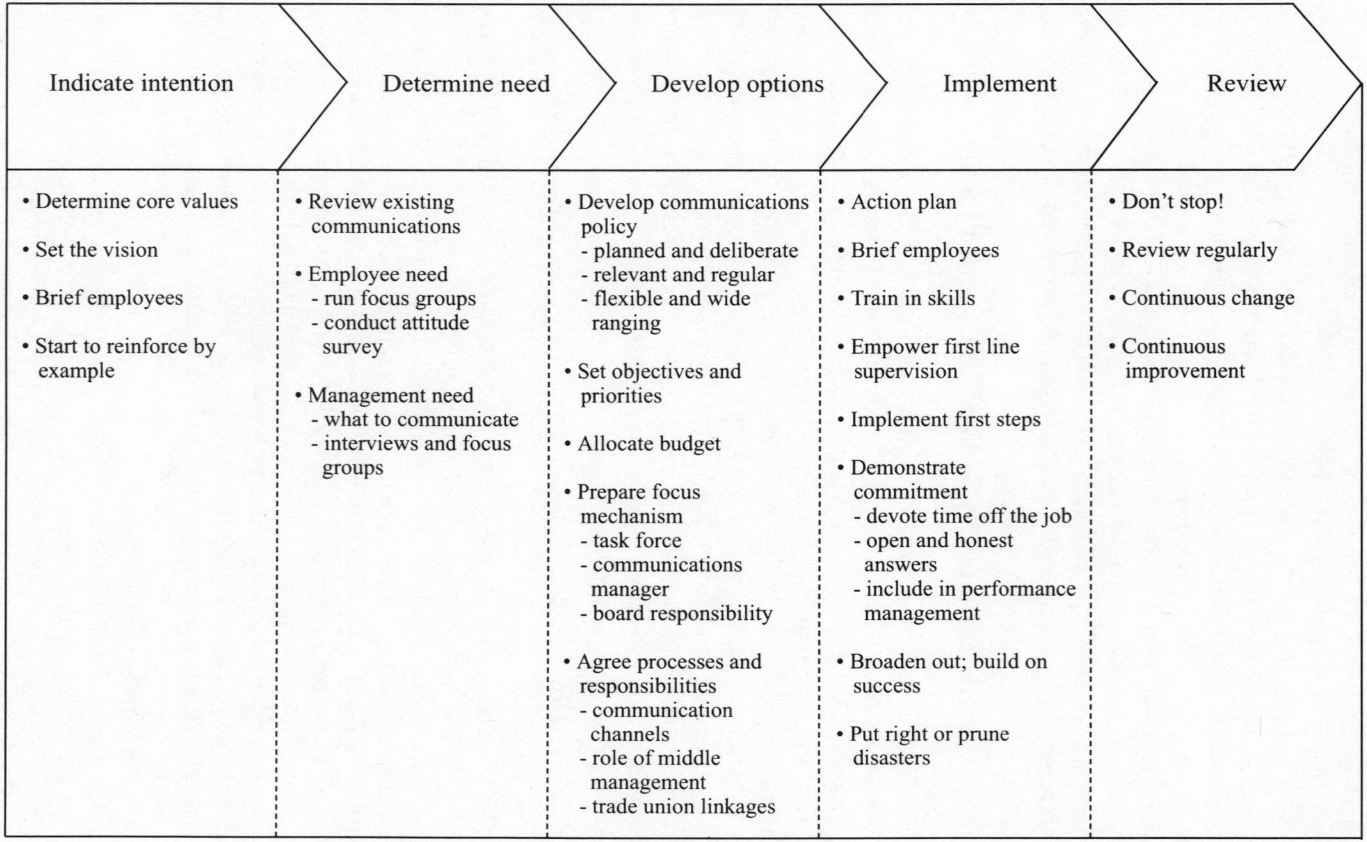

Indicate intention	Determine need	Develop options	Implement	Review
• Determine core values	• Review existing communications	• Develop communications policy - planned and deliberate - relevant and regular - flexible and wide ranging	• Action plan	• Don't stop!
• Set the vision	• Employee need - run focus groups - conduct attitude survey	• Set objectives and priorities	• Brief employees	• Review regularly
• Brief employees		• Allocate budget	• Train in skills	• Continuous change
• Start to reinforce by example	• Management need - what to communicate - interviews and focus groups	• Prepare focus mechanism - task force - communications manager - board responsibility	• Empower first line supervision	• Continuous improvement
		• Agree processes and responsibilities - communication channels - role of middle management - trade union linkages	• Implement first steps	
			• Demonstrate commitment - devote time off the job - open and honest answers - include in performance management	
			• Broaden out; build on success	
			• Put right or prune disasters	

Figure 8.1: Employee communications: developing a policy

seeking it. Employees must be encouraged to ask questions and be given responsible, well-informed answers whenever possible.

4. **Ensure that the management structure supports, or at least does not directly interfere with, communication activities**.
   As organisations become flatter and managers and supervisors have wider spans of control, team meetings and guidance by team leaders become essential. Senior managers will find it impossible to monitor day-to-day activities closely, requiring empowerment of team leaders.

5. **Provide training to assist and support communication activities**.
   All parties must become competent in communications skills. Simply providing the mechanisms for communication will produce little more than frustration without training to enhance skills.

6. **Provide support to allow a variety of differences to be accommodated**.
   Differences in the capacities of various subsystems to learn new skills and be motivated to use them can vary tremendously. Enough support must exist to absorb such differences and potential conflict, possibly through providing a variety of communications devices.

ASSESSING THE QUALITY OF COMMUNICATION

Not necessarily the last element in communications planning, but one which should continually recur on a regular basis, is assessing the quality of communication.

A number of methods exist for looking at the quality of communication in business organisations; probably the two most common are communications audits (popular in the late 1970s and early 1980s) and employee attitude surveys. Asking questions like these may also help you on the right track:

- Are the staff well motivated and actively engaged in the company's business? Or are there any sub-groups that do not seem to be aware of, or reasonably supportive of, the aims and long-range objectives of the company?
- Are there undue tensions between various groups of employees, tensions that create negative effects on job results and performance?
- Do the employees at various levels know and believe that they have access to management, directly or through a well-established procedure, when they want to convey ideas, ask questions or make suggestions for change?
- Is attrition higher than desirable in any section, plant, age group or job category?
- Do grievances or complaints occur without management knowing about it or 'feeling it in the air' well in advance?
- Do you have a well established system through which your employees can suggest improvements in methods or work procedures and get credit for it?

Netmap

A technique which many organisations have used successfully with a number of clients to improve communications and organisational effectiveness, is Network Mapping (Netmap). All organisations rely for their successful operation upon the effectiveness of both their formal structure and their informal networks. It is usually easy to identify the formal structures through published organisation charts. It is more difficult to identify and evaluate the informal networks which employees develop in order to carry out their specific roles within an organisation. Yet it is often these complex informal relationships which contribute most to the organisation's success or failure, and which are the real communications networks.

Netmap is a computer-based system which charts and analyses these critical informal networks. From data collected from individuals within the organisation, informal networks are charted within and between departments, identifying key players as well as those who are not contributing, and showing the teams of people who interact on various important aspects of an organisation's operation. Data on frequency and importance of communication is included.

CONCLUSION

Communications and involvement are becoming more, not less, important to managing and motivating a workforce. They are a major tool for line and human resource managers in enabling, progressing and supporting business objectives. As technology progresses and organisations become flatter, wider and more geographically spread the challenge will be to use new technology to develop and empower whilst still maintaining the essential personal touch.

9

TOTAL QUALITY: THE ROLE OF HUMAN RESOURCES

Ron Collard

THE SIGNIFICANCE OF TOTAL QUALITY

Quality management continues to have a high profile. Most chief executives confirm that to survive in the 1990s quality of product and service should be an integral part of the strategic direction of an organisation.

As we face the 1990s we find an environment where trade barriers will no longer protect us as we move to closer economic union with Europe, where survival will depend on competitiveness and meeting customer and client needs and where our strongest competitors — the US and the Japanese companies — are now firmly established within Europe. The Japanese view of our position can be summed up by that famous quote 'it would take you ten years to get to where we are now and by that time we will be even further ahead. And besides we know you won't do it'. That was said before the major Japanese companies had a foothold in Europe and particularly in the UK.

In the public sector too we face major challenges. The public sector is under pressure to provide better services with tight budgets as well as getting and keeping the best people.

Total quality is seen as a major ingredient in the strategic response to these challenges. It is defined as a 'systematic way of guaranteeing that all activities within an organisation happen the way they have been planned in order to meet the defined needs and requirements of customers and clients'. In other words it is designed to match internal systems to external requirements.

Total quality (TQ) and BS5750

Within the context of TQ, the quality assurance standard BS5750 has become such a buzz-word that there is a risk it is used as an alternative to total quality. BS5750 lays down the requirements for a cost effective quality management system and provides a structured approach on which to base that system. It is not a product standard or specification and does not attempt to establish a level of quality for a product. In short, BS5750 sets out how an organisation can establish and maintain an effective quality system which will demonstrate to customers and clients that the organisation is committed to quality and is able to meet their quality needs. It provides a framework for management action in establishing quality standards. It is not a recipe for TQ management since it does not in itself gain the commitment of everybody in an organisation to a quality programme.

Total quality and the human resource function

It is the contention of this chapter that the human resource function can make a major contribution to the development and maintenance of TQ initiatives. But before exploring the strategic and operational roles of the function it is necessary to consider:

- how the concept of TQ has evolved;
- what TQ means;
- customer care programmes as an important aspect of TQ;
- why companies embark on TQ;
- the challenges they face.

THE EVOLUTION OF TOTAL QUALITY

Total quality has its origins in the United States of America where, during the Second World War, the armaments industry utilised the techniques of two of the leading gurus of TQ, Deming and Juran, in the production process. After the war, however, their principles of quality were ignored as the mass consumer market expanded and quantity of output became the driving force.

Deming and Juran did, however, find a receptive audience in Japan which at that time had the reputation of being able to mass produce cheap products but of poor quality. The Japanese turned to Deming and Juran to help them offer products that could challenge the best whilst continuing to be cheap to produce. The Japanese success story is well known and it is sufficient to say here that by the mid-1970s there had been a dramatic improvement in the quality of a wide range of Japanese products without increased costs. Thus western companies found themselves competing with, and losing out to, high quality inexpensive Japanese products. One example of this is Rank Xerox who had enjoyed a virtual monopoly of the copier markets from the early 1960s. In the mid-1970s when their patents ran out the Japanese aggressively entered the market with products that were not only of a very high quality but were also significantly cheaper to the extent that, in one case, a Japanese competitor was able to sell a product at a price that was approximately equivalent to what it was costing Xerox to build their comparable product.

It was at this time that western companies were forced to review their whole way of operating and looked to Japan and the methods used by Japanese companies for guidance. As a result of this the profile of the approaches, tools and techniques of the advocates of the TQ approach was raised and, particularly in manufacturing, came to be applied outside of Japan.

At the same time a number of other 'gurus' had broadened the scope of TQ to stress the importance of people in quality and the need for employees at all levels in the organisation to play an active role in continuously improving the quality of products and services. Two key exponents of this element of TQ were Ishikawa, who introduced quality circles in Japan and Phil Crosby in America, who stressed the need for every member of an organisation to 'do it right first time'.

The most recent development in TQ is the move to apply it outside manufacturing. A wide range of service organisations have taken the basic principles and concepts of TQ and applied them to their operations in order to achieve improved quality of service without an increase in costs.

THE CONCEPT OF TOTAL QUALITY

To explain the concept of TQ it is first necessary to define quality in terms of customer satisfaction, bearing in mind that this refers both to external and internal customers. The significance of the word 'total' can then be considered. Finally, it is necessary to examine the cost implications of TQ.

Customer satisfaction

The only real measure of the quality of a product and service is whether it delivers customer satisfaction. If you take the example of a car, there are a number of elements which will affect the perceived quality (see Figure 9.1) including performance, features, reliability, serviceability, durability, conformance and aesthetics. For every customer the relative importance of these elements will vary depending on his requirements so, for example, for one customer the speed and acceleration of the car will be critical whilst for another knowing that the car is reliable and will not break down is far more important. This raises the meaning of the word satisfaction, which in this context can be defined as 'when all customer's wants, needs and expectations whether expressed or not are met'.

In order to achieve satisfaction, then, the supplier has to understand clearly these wants, needs and expectations and work with customers to agree a set of requirements that can be met. It is important to note here that some wants, needs and expectations will not be articulated. If we again use the example of buying a car there are a number of things that the customer will expect but will not be in any written agreement or even expressed. For example, as a customer I would expect the garage staff to be polite, the car to be clean when I take delivery and

167

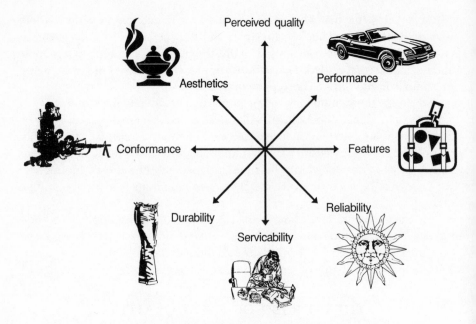

Figure 9.1 What is quality?

for there to be sufficient fuel in the tank for me to get home. If any of these elements were missing, I would not be satisfied.

The significance of the internal customer

So far, in discussing quality in terms of customer satisfaction we have considered the customer's requirement from the viewpoint of a customer purchasing a product or service. A further key concept in TQ is that of the *internal* customer. This extends the importance of meeting customers' requirements to within the working environment so that we consider anyone to whom we pass information or material as a customer and treat them accordingly (Figure 9.2). The concept of the 'internal customer' is vital to improving the effectiveness of an organisation's processes in that it ensures that what we provide to our colleagues meets their requirements and enables the activity or operation to progress smoothly through the organisation. For example, when a personnel manager is asked to recruit someone, a line manager may pass information on the type of person required. In this situation the personnel manager becomes the customer. When the personnel manager has turned this information into a person specification and passed this to the line manager, the latter in turn becomes the customer. This is an important distinction from the classic understanding of who is the customer. A line manager may not consider treating the personnel manager as a customer, but by trying to satisfy the needs of the personnel manager in ensuring he or she receives all the pertinent information required, the line manager should be assured of more effective service.

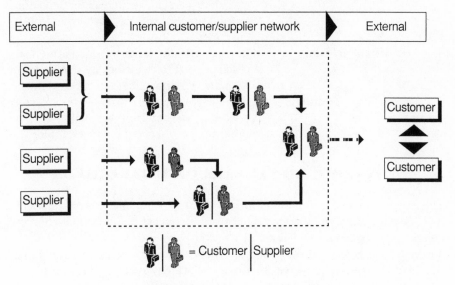

Figure 9.2 Who is my customer?

TOTAL QUALITY

So, if quality is defined as customer satisfaction what is the implication of the word 'total'? In simple terms this indicates the requirement for *all* employees in an organisation to be involved *all* of the time in meeting *all* customer requirements. A culture is developed within an organisation in which continuous improvement is integrated into all activities as everyone strives to meet their customer's requirements.

The cost of total quality

Concern is sometimes expressed that the pursuit of TQ costs more money than it saves. However this contention is controlled by the evidence from Japan and those western organisations which have successfully implemented TQ. In real terms, the cost of quality is the cost incurred in not getting things right first time.

The costs of quality are a key element in understanding where existing processes are failing and if identified can help organisations to focus their efforts to ensure noticeable improvements. The costs of quality are typically identified under the following five headings:

1. Cost of prevention: the cost of an action to prevent or reduce defects and failures.

2. Cost of appraisal: the cost of assessing the quality achieved.

3. Cost of internal failure: the costs arising within the organisation due to failure to achieve the quality specified before the transfer of ownership to the customer.

4. Cost of external failure: the costs arising outside the organisation due to failure to achieve the quality specified after the transfer of ownership to the customer.

5. Cost of lost opportunity: if we lose customers through poor quality products or services we will lose the opportunity to sell to them in the future.

WHY COMPANIES EMBARK ON TOTAL QUALITY

The key reason for any organisation to embark on a TQ initiative is survival. In the 1990s service and manufacturing organisations are being faced with major competitive challenges which are increased by deregulation, globalisation and advanced technology. These have had a noticeable impact on what companies need to do not only to grow but also to survive in today's market place. To survive in today's business environment companies are realising that they have not only to meet their customers' requirements both in terms of product and service, but must also be sufficiently flexible and adaptable to continue to meet those requirements as they grow and develop in the future.

To achieve this, companies are being forced to address many of the traditional beliefs and methods, considering and changing such fundamental factors as their structure, business processes and culture in order to foster teamwork and a real sense of responsibility in all their employees for the quality of what they do and for continually looking for methods to improve the work process. They have recognised that without this they will not be able to deliver a product or service of a consistent quality in a timely manner and which meets their customers' requirements. Fierce competition in the market place has forced the issue since even when a company has found a way to meet customer expectations it runs the risk of its competitors finding and achieving an equally high level of customer satisfaction more effectively, at a lower cost.

The Challenges

Implementing any major initiative is always difficult however much senior management recognise its value. TQ is potentially one of the most difficult to implement effectively. So what are the challenges that companies face? First, as with any initiative, the potential conflict of time. The need to put considerable amounts of time aside, particularly in the early days of a total quality initiative, for agreeing aims and objectives, defining an implementation plan, training, carrying out analysis and monitoring progress is vital. It is too easy to become enthusiastic about the concepts of TQ without facing up to the demands on time that its implementation requires.

Secondly, and equally challenging, is the need to recognise that there are significant short-term costs while the payback is long term. TQ initiatives will fail unless an initial investment is made which enables all members of an organisation to gain an understanding of TQ and to learn new skills and techniques.

A third challenge is the resistance from middle management often experienced by companies introducing TQ. Unless great care is taken they regard it as an imposition from above which involves criticism of the ways in which they have been running their department.

A further challenge sometimes develops when an organisation spends time and effort to communicate their plans for a TQ initiative and then, from the employee's point of view, nothing happens. For example, one organisation made a video describing what it meant by total quality and its intention to become a quality company. This was shown to all employees, but then many months passed before the more junior members of the organisation heard any more about it or saw any visible action from above. In reality much preparation work was taking place but expectations and interest had been raised and no follow through had been seen.

Probably the greatest challenge facing any organisation implementing TQ is that of continuation and integration. For total quality to be successful it has to be seen as a permanent and fundamental part of everyday working. Many organisations have, in the short term, achieved measurable success as a result of training and the application of problem solving techniques to address immediately identified areas for improvement. In the longer term, however, the culture of their organisation has not moved towards one of continuous improvement; the 'project' has ended and the original attitudes and behaviours that encouraged reactive firefighting and acceptance of errors have prevailed. TQ will only succeed if, from the outset, the issue of integration is addressed and planned for.

THE CONTRIBUTION OF THE HUMAN RESOURCE FUNCTION

TQ may put people at the heart of the business process but does it follow that it puts human resources at the heart of the business? It is certainly an opportunity, but is the human resource function capable of grasping that opportunity? It should be. It should have the expertise required to develop and implement means of influencing the behaviour and attitudes of employers and to manage the cultural changes involved. TQ initiatives should be based on the research and analysis of present behaviours, attitudes, beliefs and competencies which lead to the design and organisation of education, training, communication, involvement and performance management programmes. All these are within the remit of the human resource function.

The potential for making a major contribution would seem to rest at three levels, strategic, operational and within the human resource and personnel function itself. These are considered below.

Strategic

Total quality represents a significant strategic change in the way an organisation is managed. It is likely to result in changes in the organisation, changes in management style and changes in key processes. A decision to undertake a TQ programme is likely to be based primarily on market and competitive pressures and the need to protect the organisation's position in the wider environment. But the impact of this decision has such a profound effect on the internal processes of the organisation that it requires an understanding of:

- the existing culture and climate within the organisation including attitudes to change;
- the hierarchial structures and key elements of organisational design;
- the underlying skill base;
- current approaches to employee communications and, more importantly, their effectiveness;
- detailed knowledge of the impact and effectiveness of the people processes such as recruitment, reward systems, appraisal systems and training and development issues.

To be at the core of the change process the human resource specialist needs to contribute at the strategic level on the impact of introducing TQ on those human resource processes and how existing systems and procedures can be shaped to support the TQ programme. There is also a requirement to understand the barriers to change both generally within the organisation and specifically within the HR systems and procedures.

Total quality in itself also gives strategic importance to the policies and processes traditionally associated with human resource and personnel management. It raises their level of importance to the extent that the HR and personnel professional must be able to consider a series of operational responses within the wider strategic concept.

Operations

Once the strategic decision to introduce TQ has been made, there is an operational impact on human resource and personnel policies and procedures which requires an operational response from the function. Broadly this response falls into two categories:

1. The potential direct involvement in the TQ process by the human resource and personnel specialist, primarily through the education and training process involved in the TQ programme. The key features of such a

programme require extensive education and training in team working, problem solving techniques, facilitator skills and quality awareness.

If the human resource function is at the heart of the training and education within the organisation — and it ought to be if it is providing a major contribution — then total quality provides an opportunity for using training and development as the engine room for change and the heart of the total quality programme.

2. The design of policies and processes which support the TQ initiative, for instance;

   — *reviewing the remuneration system to ensure that it supports the strategic objectives of the total quality programme.* If the reward system is essentially a production driven individual based reward system, it is likely to conflict with a quality driven teamwork approach.

   — *evaluating the performance appraisal system to ensure that performance management objectives reflect the objectives of the total quality programme* — for instance, do team working, networking, quality standards feature in the performance management system?

   — *reviewing skill needs for all levels within the organisation and ensuring that the recruitment, training and development processes reflect the likely new skill needs required of a total quality programme* — for instance, if TQ ultimately depends on the self responsibility for quality it may require a different type of employee with different educational and training levels to meet these skills.

   — *changing the management development process in a situation where an organisation is moving towards a learning, self-development, continuous improvement culture.* This changes the role of management from coordinating and supervising to 'enabling' which requires a different set of skills for management. Authority is no longer based on role and status but on ability to help others.

Additionally, where trade unions exist within organisations, there is a key role to play in winning the commitment of trade unions to the TQ programme. Trade union representatives are likely to be extremely suspicious of a TQ programme, particularly since it may appear potentially to undermine the role of the local trade union representative.

PUTTING YOUR OWN HOUSE IN ORDER

Total quality does provide an opportunity for a significant contribution at both the strategic level and operational level within a TQ organisation. Additionally, if the human resource function is to play a key role it needs to establish itself as a role model within the organisation in applying TQ to itself. This provides a challenge, perhaps unprecedented, to the human resource function in that it is not only required to provide service and support to others but it also needs to apply the higher standards it preaches to others to itself. A feature which, like the cobblers' children, has never been strong in many human resource functions.

A good starting point is some of the disciplines provided by BS5750 as applied to the human resource function. The specific requirements of BS5750 and the human resource response could include the following:

- **The senior manager with the necessary authority must clearly be responsible for quality with the task of coordinating and monitoring the quality system and seeing that prompt and effective action is taken to ensure that the requirements of BS5750 are met** — who is responsible within HR for ensuring that the recruitment procedures are properly followed by line management? Who is responsible for ensuring that training standards and requirements are met?

- **The nature and degree of organisation structure, resources responsibilities, procedures and processes affecting quality must be documented** — is it clear to all concerned who is responsible for what in relation to human resources whether it be line management or support personnel management? Is it clearly written down? What is the organisation structure of human resources and how does it relate to the line management structure?

- **The quality system must be planned and developed to take account of all other functions** — do the procedures which apply for payment systems in one area of the organisation fit the needs of a different area of the organisation? How is overall quality control maintained on performance review systems in different parts of the organisation?

- **Control in writing of purchased product services, purchasing data and inspection and verification of the purchased product** — what systems and procedures do the HR function have in place for ensuring a quality of service from suppliers such as recruitment agencies, external consultants and others. Are processes in place to evaluate performance? All these require to be written down.

- **The establishment of procedures and work instructions including all customer specifications in the simple form** — are there clear instructions on how to complete performance review forms? Do reviewers understand their role and is it clearly documented? Is it clear, where there are several interviews, who is responsible for what part of the interview process and what questions do they need to cover, again all in writing?

- **Written control procedures in order to establish quickly at all times when a product has been inspected and approved, has not been inspected, or has been inspected and rejected** — are there clear competencies for each job and is it possible to measure performance against these competencies in a way that action can be taken for those who are performing well or not performing?

- **Detailed records that customer quality requirements are being met including data such as audit reports, quality assurance systems** —

careful records should be kept on individual files covering performance, discipline and all other aspects to ensure that a fair and equitable system applies within an organisation.

The above represents just a small sample of the sort of guidelines provided by BS5750. They provide as indicated a disciplined framework for the human resource function to ensure that internal systems match its external customer requirements.

BS5750 merely provides a framework within which an organisation can develop a management action programme: The framework does not in itself ensure a quality of service to the customers and clients. This leads to an important and indeed essential part of TQ: defining customers and clients and their requirements. Applying TQ processes to the human resource function requires a clear definition of who the customers or clients are. Are they the senior line managers to whom the human resource function may report and provide a support service? Are they the functional leaders within the organisation who set the framework for quality standards within the HR function, such as the personnel or human resource directors? Or, are they the employees who will often seek help and guidance or support from the human resource professionals? It is almost impossible to generalise on the most appropriate answer and it may be that more than one customer or client exists.

If the human resource function is to operate at the strategic level, then it is likely that the key customer or client will be the chief executive or the senior line person to whom the human resource specialist provides an overall service. Their requirements should, in this scenario, be paramount. However, in meeting their needs and delivering an outstanding service they would also have to provide a similar level of service to what I will call the 'sub customers'. Let us illustrate this by an example. An organisation is faced by a difficult redundancy situation where a number of individuals will have to leave because of business needs. The driving force from the human resource function is to serve the customer — the chief executive or senior line person — who on behalf of the organisation requires the redundancies. To meet their requirements there is a need to ensure that proper procedures are followed, that the 'right people are selected' and that the individuals who are counselled leave the organisation, given the difficult circumstances, in the most positive frame of mind possible. Meeting these objectives will in turn meet the customer requirements. But in achieving these objectives a number of other customers or sub customers will be involved, for instance, the departmental managers of those staff who are being made redundant and of course the staff or employees themselves. They will therefore have needs which will be different from the main customer needs but in order to achieve the objectives these needs will still have to be met.

The lesson is that you need to define exactly who your customers or clients are and what their requirements are. Once this has been done, within a total quality framework you can develop your strategy and operational plans.

CONCLUSION

We do not see TQ as some others do, as either a 'win' or 'lose' situation for the human resource function. With people at the heart of TQ it provides the human resource function with an opportunity:

- not to seek power but to make a useful contribution to running the business;
- to use the change management skills which ought to be part of the skills of human resource specialists;
- to serve customers and clients both within and outside the organisation.

A successful contribution to the TQ programme should be no less and no more than using the skills that human resource specialists have, adding value to their customers and clients and thus meeting the objectives of the TQ process.

10

HUMAN RESOURCE INFORMATION: A STRATEGIC TOOL

Jan Morgan

I have become a fanatic about quantifying — but a new sort of quantifying.I insist upon quantifying the 'soft stuff'— quality, service, customer linkups, innovation, organisational structure, people involvement . . .

Tom Peters

INTRODUCTION

After decades of stating that 'people are our most important asset' organisations are now beginning to believe it. People are invariably an organisation's single most expensive asset, with payroll costs typically running at between 40 and 60 per cent of total expenditure. There is an increasing realisation that better use of these human resources, and more attention to the structure and culture in which they work, can give an organisation a competitive edge. Yet despite this increased awareness, and despite the unquestioned assumption that managers at all levels, and particularly at the strategic level, need information on which to make decisions, the systematic definition and provision of human resource information is rarely addressed in human resource management. This chapter outlines the type of information that is currently available to HR professionals, then presents a framework for analysing and identifying the sort of information that should be available for strategic HR management purposes, and finally gives a brief review of the ability of computerised HR systems to provide that information.

First, a definition of what we mean by strategic human resource information. It is any information which will enable the HR strategist to better understand:

- the contribution that the HR strategy can make to the overall business strategy (how can we make more effective use of our human resources to give us a competitive edge?);

- the impact of the business strategy on the organisation's human resources (what does the strategy mean in terms of the type of people we want?).

The information needed to address these points can be 'hard', or factual — relating to costs, numbers, percentages, ratios; or 'soft', or qualitative — relating to structure, culture, morale and motivation, skills, personal qualities and potential. As suggested by Peters, there should be ways of measuring these soft items, not in order to get precise measures which ignore the subjective (and possibly value-laden) nature of these factors, but rather to provide indicators which can be monitored over time, or between different divisions, or even between different organisations.

HUMAN RESOURCE INFORMATION — THE CURRENT PICTURE

As any harassed personnel manager will confirm, there are usually plenty of data about the people the organisation currently employs, used to employ, or is thinking about employing. Even personnel departments without a computerised personnel information system (CPIS) will almost certainly have personnel files with application forms, references, offer letters, other copies of contractual information, performance appraisals, history of salary and career progression, training courses attended, sickness records, warning letters and a host of miscellaneous correspondence. Furthermore, some of the data will almost certainly be duplicated, in the line manager's files, in the payroll department and, depending on the size and nature of the organisation, in a corporate personnel office, industrial relations office, occupational health section and so on. One large, well-known organisation in the UK completes seven copies of a form setting up a new employee, each copy going to a different department.

Of course, the critical point here is that there may be a lot of data around, but this is not the same as information, which requires some form of manipulation of data. The information in turn needs to be analysed and interpreted to provide something that is more meaningful and useful to decision makers and planners.

The amount of information available about an organisation's human resources will vary according to the sophistication of the personnel department, the size, nature and complexity of the business, the types of HR issues it faces, and so on. There is a hierarchy of complexity. For example, most organisations will know their headcount, although it is common to find two different figures provided, from the personnel and payroll departments respectively. The personnel department usually can provide information on number of starters and leavers in a period, and may express them as labour turnover rates. More sophisticated personnel functions will look at turnover rates for different occupational groups, and may also do stability indices and cohort analyses. Large, complex organisations, such as the Royal Navy, will go further and use the information as input into manpower planning.

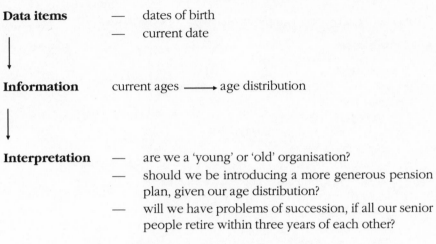

The difference between data, information and interpretation

Data items — dates of birth
— current date

Information current ages ⟶ age distribution

Interpretation — are we a 'young' or 'old' organisation?
— should we be introducing a more generous pension plan, given our age distribution?
— will we have problems of succession, if all our senior people retire within three years of each other?

Figure 10.1 Data and information

Similarly, most organisations collect data on sickness absence, if only for statatory sick pay purposes, or to monitor when entitlement is due to expire. Increasingly, and particularly with computerisation, line managers use absence information to 'manage' (ie control) their staff better, looking for patterns of absence and cautioning staff who have more than a certain number of spells of absence over a defined period. More sophisticated organisations will use absence data as input to labour availability and productivity measures. Few personnel managers use absenteeism as an indicator for morale, or monitor the organisation's absenteeism rates and how they change in response to new policies, or attempt to cost the effects of absence in terms of lost production or service, increased overtime, etc.

Cost information is one area about which, in our experience, HR managers are ambivalent. They will be responsible for setting, implementing and administering salary policy, and are almost obsessive in the way they monitor external salary information, but often do not know, or see it as their responsibility to know, total employment costs for their organisation. Instead, they see it as a responsibility of the finance department. Only a few have an accurate idea of the proportion of total expenditure which is made up by employment costs. Yet, as noted above, the payroll is typically 40-60 per cent of an organisation's total expenditure, by far and away the largest single item of cost. Once employment related costs are added, such as recruitment and training, it is even more bemusing that HR practitioners do not see themselves as able to play a major role in helping the organisation to be more cost-effective through tighter scrutiny of the use of its major, most expensive resource.

Components of employment costs

What does it really cost to employ your staff?

- **Direct costs**:
  — basic salary;
  — bonuses, commission, incentive payments;
  — overtime;
  — employer's NI;
  — employer's pension contribution;
  — employee benefits:
    — *health, life assurance*
    — *cars, running costs. petrol, parking, etc*
    — *uniforms*
    — *subsidised meals, luncheon vouchers;*
  — relocation costs;
  — recruitment costs;
  — training costs (training budget, accommodation, travel, etc.);
  — HR department's budget (salaries, equipment accommodation travel, etc.);
  — welfare services, occupational health;
  — payroll department's costs.

- **Indirect costs**:
  Opportunity costs (loss of production, sales, income, etc.)

  — absence on holiday;
  — absence through sickness;
  — absence on training course;
  — vacancies.

A CONCEPTUAL MODEL OF HR INFORMATION

A simple way to analyse the types of human resource information is to use the familiar pyramid (Figure 10.2) of strategic, tactical (or decision-support) and operational (or administrative) levels. This model is useful for analysing the human resource information which is typically provided and used in personnel departments, and the information which, we shall argue, ought to be used at a strategic level. It is also useful for understanding the capabilities and limitations of software packages for computerised human resource systems.

The distinction between the levels is not completely clear cut and may well vary in different organisations according to their size, complexity and sophistication of their personnel function. However, the framework provides a useful starting point for gaining a better understanding of what is truly strategic and what is merely tactical or managerial. Some examples are given in Table 10.1, page 184.

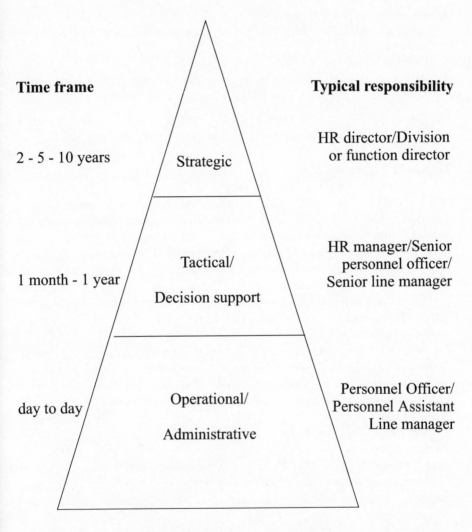

Time frame		Typical responsibility
2 - 5 - 10 years	Strategic	HR director/Division or function director
1 month - 1 year	Tactical/ Decision support	HR manager/Senior personnel officer/ Senior line manager
day to day	Operational/ Administrative	Personnel Officer/ Personnel Assistant Line manager

Figure 10.2 The managerial pyramid

Operational information

Starting at the lowest level, personnel departments are generally very good at providing and using information for normal day to day operations. Computerised personnel information systems are particularly useful at this level, and unquestionably have had major benefits in reducing tedious clerical work, producing better quality letters and listings and reducing the chance of errors. The type of information used at the operational level includes, for example:

- individual records to show a person's salary progression;
- job history or training records;
- 'diary prompts' that an employee is due a performance appraisal or a salary increment;
- listings showing people due for a long service award;
- lists of employees with the skills or qualifications to be considered for a vacancy.

In general, operational information makes the job of the personnel assistant easier, and that of the personnel officer more productive.

Tactical information

The information needed by HR managers for tactical or decision support purposes is not so universally defined or provided. Those managers who are still in reactive mode, responding to vacancies, salary reviews or industrial relations issues as they arise, probably do not need very much information beyond an awareness of which papers or professional journals to advertise in, or the going rate for cost of living increases in the area. They probably hold a lot of subjective, judgmental and intuitive information about the thought processes, power bases and hidden agendas of union officials, but such information is not of direct relevance here.

Proactive HR managers will have a greater need for information. For example, they will want to know the effectiveness of a particular recruitment campaign, in terms of the costs of using different media for advertising or different methods of selection, and their outcomes. Some of the information can be collected easily, and a good CPIS will provide information on costs of, and number of respondents to, different media.

Other information, particularly qualitative and judgmental data, such as how 'good' were the candidates chosen, can only be collated after looking at performance appraisals, promotion record, length of service with the organisation, and so on. Usually such information is not collected or analysed in a systematic way.

Another example of decision-support information is that used for salary modelling purposes, to provide the answers to 'what if?' questions such as 'what happens to total salary costs if we implement a basic increase of x per cent and performance increases ranging from y to z per cent?' Recently, such financial modelling has increasingly been used for costing redundancy packages: 'what should be the structure of the redundancy package given the service and salary distributions of the employees likely to be made redundant?'

Computer systems are getting better at providing information at this level, and it is not uncommon for a CPIS to provide links to a standard spreadsheet package for modelling purposes. A few systems offer help at annual salary review although only in the form of providing 'bulk update' facilities, which is useful for administrative purposes but not for decision support.

Strategic information

The third level of information, the strategic level, is one which is hardly addressed or understood by HR practitioners, let alone by the suppliers of computerised HR systems. Yet this is the level which has greatest potential benefit to an organisation. By operating at a strategic level, with relevant information to support the arguments, the HR director can make a full contribution to the setting of strategic direction for the business.

At present, strategic HR information is either not recognised as important, or is seen only in terms of manpower planning. For example, Peter Wickens, Director of Personnel and Information Systems at Nissan Motor Manufacturing UK, claims that computerised information, at least, has never assisted him in making a strategic decision. This may be a direct criticism of computerised systems, but implicit in his statement is that there are no systematic, or objective, or hard factual data which he needs in order to formulate personnel strategy and thus business strategy.

As Peter Wickens noted in the same paper, most standard personnel management textbooks do not mention human resource information or else give it barely a passing acknowledgement. Books on strategic human resource management, as well as general books on strategic planning, also fail to make mention of the need for good information on one of the major resources the strategy is concerned to deploy. Even Tom Peters, a self-avowed measurement fanatic, includes only four measures directly related to human resources in his list of performance measures in 'Thriving on Chaos'.[1]

Thus the information required at the strategic level is, in general, unrecognised and undefined. The following section, therefore, attempts to redress this omission.

Table 10.1   The different levels of information

Some examples of the three levels of information requirements for different HR functions

Recruitment	Appraisal/Performance management

Operational

• Who has applied for the vacancy?	• Who is due to be appraised?
• Which current employees have skills for the vacancy?	• Whose performance rating has gone down since last time?

Tactical

• How effective was this campaign?	• What is the performance distribution across the departments?
• Who are the internal candidates from the succession plan?	• How has this division performed?

Strategic

• Should we be recruiting or reducing numbers?	• How have we performed in our management of human resources compared with other companies?
• How can we ensure we have sufficient managers long-term?	

Training and Development	Reward

Operational

• What training has this employee had?	• What is the salary history of this person?
• Who is due to attend this training course?	• Who is due an increase?

Tactical

• How many courses do we need to run next year?	• What should the performance increases be, given the distribution of ratings and our salary budget?
• How effective is training?	• How can we structure a self-funding bonus scheme?

Strategic

• What level of investment should we make in training and development?	• How effective is our remuneration policy in supporting our business objectives?
• Will our development programme provide us with sufficient high calibre future managers?	• Is our reward policy consistent with other HR policies?

IDENTIFYING STRATEGIC HUMAN RESOURCE INFORMATION

The relationship between business strategy and human resource strategy is still subject to considerable debate and a wide range of views. For the purpose of this book and of this chapter, we regard the two as separate but interlinked and influencing each other.

As mentioned in Chapter 1 (pp. 25–44), an assessment of the organisation's human resources and the internal and external factors influencing them is, or should be, a vital ingredient to formulating the business strategy options, which are then assessed for their impact on the organisation's human and other resources, and modified as necessary. The finalised business strategy will then provide the basis for formulating the HR strategy, along with the assessments previously carried out of the current human resources and influences on them. Figure 10.3 (next page and on p 34), summarises the relationship between business strategy, the external environment ('inner context'), the internal organisational and the HR environments ('outer context and 'HRM' context').

The final part of the process is implementing the HR strategy through translating it into specific objectives and identifying and monitoring the critical success factors and performance indicators which determine how well the strategy is achieved.

Because of the iterative and interlinked nature of the model it is difficult to be prescriptive about the precise sequence of the activities, but for convenience they may be grouped together:

- business strategy formulation (Business Strategy Content, influenced by HRM Context, and Outer Context including the HR implications);
- human resource strategy formulation (HRM Context and Content, influenced by Business Strategy Content, with strategic HR objectives attached to each element);
- human resource strategy implementation (which depends on establishing critical success factors and performance indicators for the key HRM Context and Content objectives)

Each of the elements of the HRM Context and Content can be translated into a series of activities and described as a number of questions to be asked. Information in a wide range of forms is needed in order to provide answers to the questions.

Business strategy formulation

In the past, business strategies have been formulated without sufficient attention to the human resource implications:

- A survey in the US in 1981 of human resource executives and strategic

185

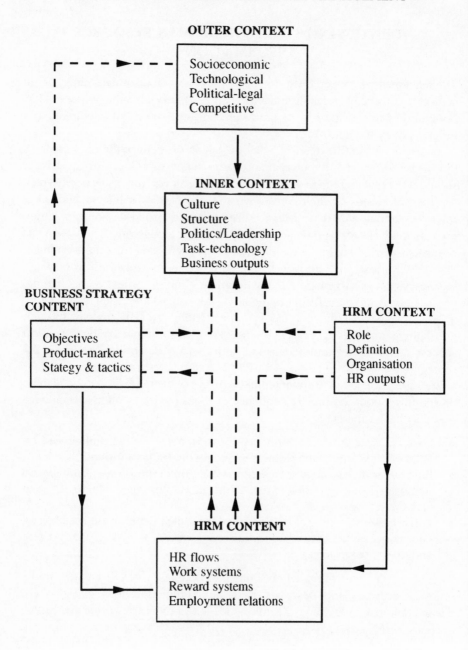

OUTER CONTEXT

Socioeconomic
Technological
Political-legal
Competitive

INNER CONTEXT

Culture
Structure
Politics/Leadership
Task-technology
Business outputs

BUSINESS STRATEGY CONTENT

Objectives
Product-market
Stategy & tactics

HRM CONTEXT

Role
Definition
Organisation
HR outputs

HRM CONTENT

HR flows
Work systems
Reward systems
Employment relations

Figure 10.3 Model of strategic change and human resource management

planners found that 53 per cent said that human resource considerations had a 'less than moderate' effect on strategy formulation.

- It is estimated that 70 per cent of acquisitions do not realise the expected benefits, a major reason being the relatively small number of human resource audits that are made of the firm to be acquired prior to acquisition.
- Revisions were needed to British Airways' strategic decisions on Shuttle and Tristar once the industrial relations implications became apparent.
- A large insurance company tried valiantly for two years to recruit sufficient school leavers for its head office, without realising that its requirement exceeded the total number of school leavers produced by schools in the area.

Business strategists are beginning to learn from their past mistakes and are now including an assessment of the implications for the organisation's human resources when formulating their strategies. The HR director can take an even more proactive part, by providing insights to the following questions:

1. What sort of people, in terms of numbers, skills and capabilities, do we currently have?
2. What are the dynamics currently affecting those people, in terms of recruitment, promotion and turnover rates?
3. What are our current organisation structure, culture and values: do they support our business mission or are they dysfunctional?
4. What changes are taking place in the external environment which will affect our current and future staff?

To answer these questions there must be good, reliable and relevant information about the human resources within and outside the organisation which in turn can be analysed and interpreted, and judgments applied. The ability to interpret the information will depend on the abilities of the strategists. However, we can give guidance on the type of information to be provided.

Current stock

With regard to the current stock of human resources, an assessment of quantity, quality and potential of existing staff needs more than simply the headcount figures in broad occupational groupings. Yet a comprehensive skills inventory could be a major undertaking, fraught with problems of defining skills, assessing the level at which they are held by individuals, ensuring the information is kept up to date, and so on. Many organisations make a token effort, by holding data on secondary and tertiary qualifications of their staff, apparently unaware of the fact that up to 80 per cent of graduates end up working in occupations not directly related to their degree subject — or they hold records of training courses attended and assume that that is an indication of skills acquired and still retained.

Given the trends in the work environment, of an ever-increasing amount of change, the need for multi-skilling, increased customer and service focus, total quality and continuous improvement, empowerment of employees and increased delegation of decision making, perhaps some new measures of qualities need to be developed. For example, the new measures could focus on flexibility, versatility, openness to change, problem-solving abilities, courtesy and genuine liking of other people, preparedness to accept responsibility, and so on.

If this approach seems a little too radical, another approach could be to focus on those skills and abilities which are perceived as critical to the business. There is an immediate problem of definition and timing, as to whether they should relate to the business as it is now or as it will be in the future. At this stage of collecting information on the present situation as input to business strategy formulation, it is probably necessary to collect both — which means the HR director may need to 'second guess' what the likely future strategy will be in order to collect the relevant data and identify any constraints, through skills shortages, to future strategic options.

Whatever other skills are needed for the present and future business strategy, management skills will be essential so an assessment of the current managerial capabilities will be needed. Some writers go so far as to claim that management ability is the only strategic human resource. Exxon regard this resource as so vital to their business that a small senior management team, headed by the CEO, meets weekly to review the performance and development of the top 250 managers.[2]

Clearly it is important to identify whether managerial capability is sufficient for, or could act as a constraint on, the business strategy. For example, if there are plans to expand and diversify the business then information about the present capability, as well as the number of people coming through the system who will be able to hold senior management positions, is very important.

The proliferation of software packages dedicated to succession planning, is an indication, perhaps, of the recognition of the importance of keeping track of current and future managers. However, the question remains as to whether the information is used as input to business strategy formulation, or used only when the HR director starts assessing the implications of the strategy and realises there is a gap to be filled by external recruitment or a very fast development programme.

Current dynamics

The assessment of current human resource stocks is only half the picture. It is important to know how they are changing. At what rates are staff:

- recruited externally;
- promoted;
- transferred;
- leaving;
- retiring;

and how do these rates differ for different occupational groups, ages, and lengths of service? A further dimension is the external environment — are the organisation's turnover rates particularly sensitive to recessions and high growth times?

There is potentially an enormous amount of data to be collected in this area, and thus the danger of 'information overload'. The real skill of the organisation's manpower planner is in ensuring that the data are collected by groupings which are meaningful, that they can be regrouped and reanalysed if necessary, and that the key information is presented in a succinct and imaginative way for the HR director and other strategists to be able to focus on the key implications.

At this stage a preliminary analysis should be done, bringing together the information on current stocks and dynamics to determine what will happen to current stocks in five or ten years time if (a) current dynamics are applied; or (b) there are changes in labour turnover rates or in the mix of internal promotion and external recruitment.

This is the real value of manpower planning. The Institute of Manpower Studies in the UK has transformed the image of manpower planning from one of ivory tower planners who inevitably 'get it wrong', to one of modelling and sensitivity analysis, and understanding the dynamics of the organisation in terms of the rates of promotion and labour turnover for different ages, occupational groupings and lengths of service.

The importance of such an understanding cannot be emphasised too strongly. There are more than a few firms in the UK which, if they had thought about, for example, the impact of a recession on labour turnover rates, would have cut back on their recruitment programmes and saved themselves the pain and expense of redundancies one or two years later.

Unlike the packages on career and succession planning, software packages are not particularly sophisticated in providing the information needed to study the organisation's dynamics. There are a few dedicated manpower planning packages available, but they tend to be complex to use. General HR information systems are usually limited in the extent to which changes can be traced back over time. A pragmatic approach would be to use a mixture of computer produced data, manually analysed and held for future reference.

Structure, culture, values

Today there is widespread recognition of the importance of culture and values to give an organisation a competitive edge, thanks largely to *In Search of Excellence*[3] and the plethora of books which followed it. Interestingly, Tom Peters now admits that in that book the authors did not give as much attention to the importance of structure as they should have. Given that culture, values and structure — the 'soft stuff' — are now as critical to the success or failure of a business, who is better placed than the HR director to be the custodian of these soft 'resources'?

However, how to assess them and whether they help or hinder the current business, let alone assess whether and how they should be changed in line with a new business strategy, is no easy task. Very large discrepancies — for example, the long hierarchical chain of command with an over-bureaucratic culture in an organisation needing to become more business orientated and faster in its response to customers — are fairly easy to spot. But a less superficial analysis which gets to the subtleties and which can also identify the good and not so good aspects of both the structure and the culture, is not at all easy to undertake. After all, 'the way we do things around here' is a recognisable description of culture precisely because it is so difficult to list all the nebulous values, norms and mores that make up the social unit which is the organisation.

Let us suggest a practical example. An organisation which has never previously consciously studied its structure and culture as a strategic resource should collect as much data as it can as a starting exercise. The data could include the more straight forward facts and figures, as well as more subjective items:

- **Factual and/or objective data**:

  - rationale for current structure (functional, geographical, product, or market focused, etc);
  - number of managerial levels;
  - smallest, widest and average spans of control;
  - formal meeting and communication structures;
  - number of ad hoc cross-functional work teams;
  - measures of morale such as labour turnover and absenteeism.

- **Subjective data**:

  - informal communication patterns;
  - attitudes of staff through attitude surveys and focus group interviews;
  - attitudes of staff who left through an analysis of exit interviews;
  - 'internal customer' survey to assess internal service levels.

Subjective information will be more difficult to get and it may be advisable to use external consultants who will be seen by the staff as independent. Consultants are also more likely to have standard tools and techniques for collecting the information. For example, Coopers & Lybrand use a software package, *Netmap*, to collect and analyse data on informal communication patterns. They also use a variety of attitude survey questionnaires, including the Organisational Assessment Process which has been validated internationally on over 300,000 employees as a means of assessing various factors, including the organisation's readiness to change.

Once the data are collected a very broad picture can be drawn up showing the features of the organisation structure and a description of its culture. It may be possible at this stage, knowing 'what is', to identify the critical features that particularly help or hinder the organisation to achieve its business mission. More likely, it will take a year of monitoring, reassessing and reinterpreting to decide what are the critical pieces of information, the touchstones which in future years can be used as the barometers of effectiveness of changes to HR policy that help or hinder achievement of business strategy. The main point is to start wide, then narrow down.

Conventional computerised human resource systems are unlikely to prove much help. Individual data from attitude surveys needs to be kept confidential so should not be held on the CPIS. Furthermore, the data require dedicated questionnaire software to analyse it.

External assessment

In one sense, formulating business strategy is all about external assessments. Drucker considers the first and crucial question should always be 'who is the customer' before asking 'what is our business?', and 'what should our business be?'. The most successful business strategists have always considered demographics when developing and changing their businesses. Sears, Roebuck first focused on isolated farmers, then changed its business with the change to motorisation in farming and the growing suburban population. Sydney Bernstein chose Manchester as the location for his TV franchise bid for his newly formed company, Granada, on the grounds of maximising both population density and rainfall.

Human resource professionals have not traditionally undertaken systematic assessments of the external environment. If they had, the 'demographic time bomb' would have not appeared out of the blue — after all, there is a 15 year lead time in producing school leavers.

Tony Attew's paper at the 1989 CIP Conference provides a good overview of sources and adequacy of data on labour market trends, although he concludes that overall they are not very adequate, particularly at the level of travel to work area. The Institute of Manpower Studies publishes very good papers on labour markets. However, the systematic analysis of demographic and labour market trends as input to a human resource strategy, as opposed to a marketing strategy, seems to be rare. At best, data on the labour markets of different areas might be collected when an organisation is thinking of relocating.

One systematic approach to analysing external factors as they impact on an organisation's human resources is to hold a brainstorming session, possibly with external advisors, and with a cross-section of employees including the newest graduates. The STEEP framework could be used; ie what are the likely changes under the headings of:

- **S**ocio-legal;
- **T**echnological;
- **E**conomic;
- **E**nvironmental;
- **P**olitical;

and what are the implications of these changes for the full range of human resource functions from organisation and job design, recruitment, selection, reward, motivation, training and development, performance management, communications, industrial relations, career management, and so on?

Population and education projections in countries with low levels of immigration and emigration are, barring major calamities, very reliable. However, much of the other information which comes out of a STEEP analysis will be conjectural and subjective. We gave earlier our views about the likely changes in work patterns and expectations; they are based on our interpretation of the likely effects of 'hard' facts such as the increasing levels of education among the workforce and the continuing technological advances, and partly on our interpretation of trends, particularly the 'new ideas' which are still around 10 years later such as total quality and customer focus.

One final word on the external information gathering process — computerised HR packages are unlikely to be of much help, except, possibly, in organisations large enough to be able to use data on their staff to check out trends for themselves. Perhaps there is an argument for holding data such as educational qualifications after all, although it seems somewhat tenuous.

Human resource strategy formulation

So far we have only identified the HR information requirements to enable the HR director to have some input into the business strategy. Fortunately, this information is also needed for developing the HR strategy. But it is not sufficient on its own; there needs to be further analysis in light of the agreed business strategy to determine the answers to the following questions:

1.   What sort of people, in terms of numbers, skills and capabilities, do we need in the future?
2.   What organisation structure, culture and values do we need in order to support our business strategy?
3.   In the light of the assessment of our present situation (current stock and dynamics, structure, culture, values) and the external factors influencing us (external assessment), what changes do we need to get the people, structure and culture identified in answers to questions 1 and 2?

Compared with question 3, getting the answers to questions 1 and 2 are relatively straightforward.

What people do we need

Organisations that have well-established manpower planning processes will have no problems answering this question; they will already have systems in place for setting establishments for different divisions and occupational groupings for five or ten years' time and under a variety of growth scenarios, including negative growth.

Human resource directors who have not done such an exercise before will quickly realise they need input from line managers; indeed there is probably, in another part of the organisation, a group already studying labour productivity, job measurement, standard times and so on. If there is, their results can be used as a starting point.

The role of the HR function in this process is challenging line managers to think more radically — 'upside down' thinking as Handy[4] calls it — to look for opportunities, for example, for multi-skilling, or questioning the need for certain educational or skills qualifications. In this way the broad direction given in the business strategy is translated into the human resource requirements. The HR function also has another role, that of identifying new skills and qualities as well as redundant skills that will no longer be needed in the new strategy.

Computerised HR systems show their administrative strength in this area, particularly those which are built on positions and jobs and hierarchical organisation structures, as opposed to using individual employees as the basic building block. Such systems usually hold detailed information on skills and qualifications needed for each job or position. Unfortunately, these systems are not flexible enough to cater easily for changes in skill requirements, multi-skilling or job sharing, let alone organisational structure changes.

What structure and culture do we need

The earlier analysis carried out for structure, culture and values will provide some pointers in this area. Structure is such a fundamental part of the business that structural options may have already been considered as part of the business strategy. If it has not, then there is little guidance, in the form of straight information, that we can offer to help the HR director decide on the most appropriate structure; it is more a matter of keeping abreast of articles and books on the subject, learning from other organisations and using the advice of external consultants.

On the type of culture the organisation needs to meet its business mission, it is also a matter of analytical thought, using the material gathered from the earlier survey, teasing out whether and how the different elements need to change in light of the strategy, and thinking through the impact on culture that a changed organisation structure might have.

What changes are needed

The identification of the changes that are needed is an analytical process, rather than one requiring any new information. It involves a comparison between, on the one hand, the human resources the organisation currently has and is likely to have if current dynamics continue, and the current structure, culture and values; and on the other hand, which resources, structure, culture and values the organisation needs in order to meet its business objectives. Incorporated into this is the assessment of the external changes likely to affect the workforce.

As this chapter is about the information required to formulate the strategy, rather than the analytical process of developing the strategy or the likely outcomes, there is no further contribution that we can make to this stage of strategy formulation. The systematic collection and assessment of relevant data and information will not in itself provide the answers, but it should provide a very sound base on which to carry out the challenging task of thinking through the changes. The vision of what is needed, and the changes in HR objectives and policies to achieve the vision of the human resources, culture, structure and values, is the subject matter of the HR strategy.

HUMAN RESOURCE STRATEGY IMPLEMENTATION

Strategy implementation has two aspects:

1. translating the strategy into specific HR objectives and policies;
2. identifying critical success factors and their associated performance indicators to monitor the success of the objectives and policies in meeting the HR strategy, and in fulfilling the business strategy.

The first aspect involves another analytical, brainpower exercise, thinking through the implications of the strategy, and what existing policies might need to be changed. Most importantly, it involves developing an action plan for implementing the changes. The only information requirements of this might be a review of previous change management activities to learn lessons (good and bad) from them.

The second aspect, of identifying the critical success factors and setting up systems for monitoring them, is equally important but is in danger of being ignored by the HR function. Few organisations consciously monitor the effects of their HR policies in terms of meeting the objectives they are meant to achieve.

Monitoring, feedback and amendment go on to some extent — consider the regular adjustments that are made to performance appraisal systems, or the annual changes to salary structures and benefits packages. But we suspect that the former changes are usually reacting to yet another set of criticisms from the users or 'victims' of the performance appraisal system, while the latter are often a reaction to external market forces plus whatever is fashionable in reward structures that year. It is very rare for HR directors, to assess consciously the impact of their HR policies in terms of what they were meant to do, and make adjustments accordingly. At best, they will be reactive — 'our labour turnover rates are too high; therefore we must pay higher salaries/give service payments/provide more training courses'. Such a piecemeal, reactive approach is likely to lead to the commonly found situation of different HR policies giving conflicting messages to staff and working against each other in promoting the business strategy.

The one exception to the lack of policy monitoring is in equal employment opportunity. Legislation in the US has forced organisations to set up such monitoring. In the UK, despite the proclamation at the bottom of many recruitment advertisements that 'we are an equal opportunity employer' only a few enlightened organisations have set up monitoring practices beyond keeping application forms for six months in case of a tribunal claim.

Are your HR policies consistent?

The results of piecemeal development of HR policies can be inconsistency of messages to staff.

Case Study 1

Organisations want to give their managers sufficient authority and encouragement to foster initiative and innovation, but they often have a reward policy which punishes risk-taking if it results in failure, as is common with so many performance-based systems.

Case Study 2

Staff handbooks often have an opening statement that: 'Our employees are our most valued asset' but the rest of the book contains detailed rules and regulations which have an underlying assumption that employees need to be controlled and are not really to be trusted.

There is a very obvious way to assess the success or failure of past HR policies. The existing staff, who have lengths of service ranging from a few months to twenty, thirty or more years, are a reflection of past recruitment, retention, training and development policies, as well as the lasting elements of the organisational culture. It may not be so easy to identify cause and effect of specific policies, although if the objectives of the policies were stated at the time they were first introduced, it may be possible to make judgments about the extent to which the objectives were met.

With increasing emphasis on performance, it is perhaps surprising that the HR function has escaped scrutiny for so long. The very crude measures of headcount and payroll costs have often served as the only key performance indicators for human resource management. It is not surprising that an organisation's reaction during an economic downturn is to reduce the headcount, in any way and at whatever cost, usually starting with a freeze on recruitment, then early retirement and finally redundancy. The consequences of these actions are rarely studied so lessons are not learned and the whole demoralising process is repeated in the next recession.

So how can a forward-thinking HR function set up a performance monitoring system? There are two opposing schools of thought: one is to identify the 'key' performance indicators, or the 'critical' success factors, the implication being that there only need be a few measures for the CEO (or the HR director) to be certain the business is on course. The ultimate single measure is the 'bottom line'. Such an approach is laudable in its attempt to keep things simple and avoid information overload, but does not provide much guidance when starting from scratch.

The opposite view, espoused by Tom Peters, is to measure everything that can be measured, the basis being 'what gets measured gets done'. There is, however, the risk that the task of collecting data, manipulating them and interpreting the results will be costly and time-consuming, and will result in confusion and no clear overall picture. Again we suggest a pragmatic approach similar to the one outlined above for collecting information on culture and structure. Start with identifying as many measures as possible, at least in the human resource areas of greatest concern. Eliminate those measures where the expense of collecting or analysing the data seems out of proportion to the possible benefits. Set up systems for regularly collecting the information, preferably devolved to the sub-functions within HR where possible, and make a commitment to spend time on understanding the information and what it is saying about the performance of the HR strategy.

After two or three years, which is the minimum time for many HR policies to have an effect, it may be possible to reduce the number of measures, eliminating those which only confirm the results of other measures. There are software packages which can help to do this. They generate a series of random business results on selected performance indicators, then from the judgments of the CEO as to what each of the sets means in terms of how well the business is doing, they can identify a subset of performance indicators to which the CEO is unconsciously giving more weight.

Another approach to monitoring the success or otherwise of the HR strategy is to identify the critical success factors associated with each policy developed to implement the strategy. This has an obvious logic to it — if objectives have been defined then there should be associated measures developed at the same time, and it may well reduce the number of measures and thus the effort in collecting and analysing the data. However, this approach runs the risk of being too superficial. It is not enough to know that a policy has succeeded to a greater or lesser extent; to be of real benefit there must be enough information to understand why, and incorporate the lessons learned.

A third approach to performance monitoring, and one which is gaining popularity, is through benchmarking, ie comparing selected performance indicators from different organisations, typically from the same industry but also with organisations which are judged to be 'best in class'. Salary and benefits surveys are a form of benchmarking, but it is rare for HR departments to go beyond this, partly because of the problems of common definitions as well as reluctance of companies to give out sensitive information. However, it can be done: one successful company in the information industry monitors sales per employee of its own and competitor organisations, using data published in the companies' annual reports.

We expect to see an increase in interest from HR professionals in benchmarking,

Key HR performance indicators

Examples of Performance Indicators for assessing human resource management effectiveness, through comparisons over time, between divisions, or between organisations.

Recruitment/promotion

- Proportion of vacancies to total headcount
- Cost of recruitment per vacancy
- Average length of time to fill a vacancy
- Proportion of vacancies filled internally
- Average number of promotions per employee

Training and development

- Number of trainee days per employee per annum
- Investment in training per employee per annum
- Training budget: total payroll

Reward structure

- Average salary per employee
- Basic salary: total remuneration
- Compa ratio
- Total bonus pay: increase in revenue
- Number of regradings per annum

Structure

- Number of management levels
- Average span of control
- Number of ad hoc working groups

Culture and values

- Labour turnover per annum
- Stability index
- Rate of absenteeism
- Number of short spells of absence per annum
- Attitude survey information

Overall HR performance

- Productivity ratios (output, sales, etc. per employee)
- HR staff: total staff
- Actual costs against budget
- Actual headcount against budget
- Employment costs: total expenditure (See page 180)

using consultants as independent 'honest brokers' to collect and analyse the information. As benchmarking becomes more common it may be possible to develop standard definitions and agreed performance indicators, similar to the standardisation of financial performance measures such as return on capital employed, gearing ratios, etc. However, this may take some considerable time.

Meanwhile, there is still a need to develop performance indicators for internal monitoring, including comparisons between divisions. The type and mix of measures of use to a particular organisation will vary according to its business, complexity and diversity, problem areas, thrust of its HR objectives and so on. For example, if an objective is to ensure a high level of retention of key staff then information will be needed not only on turnover rates, but also on relative salary levels, training, promotion rates, and so on.

Another example might be a strategic objective of creating a more commercial approach, something which is close to the hearts of organisations going through privatisation in the UK, or 'corporatisation' in Australia. Specific HR measures could include, for example, before and after measures of number of management layers, internal customer service levels, success rates in attracting recruits (particularly at senior levels) from the private sector, number and size of regular meetings, number of task forces or project teams and average life of such teams, percentage of time spent on internal administrative matters, and so on.

Finally, the emphasis throughout this chapter has been on 'measurable' information, in the form of hard, factual numbers or costs, or surrogate measures of the more soft qualitative aspects. There is, of course, room for the information that cannot be quantified, the instinctive assessments, judgments, intuition and 'feel' that something is right or wrong. Scientists now believe that such intuitive behaviour is based on past experiences, with the brain subconsciously recognising patterns and similarities which the conscious mind does not.

BELIEFS QUOTE

Reality is what we take to be
True

What we take to be true is what we
Believe

What we believe is based on our
Perceptions

What we perceive depends upon what we
Look for

What we look for depends upon what we
Think

And what we think depends upon what we

Percieve

What we perceive determines what we
Believe

What we believe determines what we
Take to be true

What we take to be true is our
Reality

'The Dancing Wu Li Masters'
Gary Zukav

There is little point in trying to identify or understand the more objective factors which may have led to these intuitive reactions and hunches. If the hard evidence supports the instincts, there is no problem; where there is a conflict it might be useful to analyse whether it really is an intuitive feeling, or just an unwarranted prejudice. Having the 'hard' data will be a check against sorting out prejudices from instincts, if only after the event. But at least this is the basis for experiential learning.

POSTSCRIPT — COMPUTERISED HUMAN RESOURCE INFORMATION SYSTEMS

Throughout this chapter we have made reference to computerised systems and the extent to which they can or cannot be used to help provide strategic information. This section provides a brief summary.

Despite the wide range of differences in HR functions in organisations, most HR professionals want two requirements of a CPIS, apart from basic functionality. They want flexibility, and they want user friendliness. Unfortunately, despite the incredible advances in computer technology, and in spite of the claims made by software sales staff, there is, as yet, no ideal package. One solution to the lack of a good, comprehensive, flexible and user-friendly all-purpose system is to have a number of packages, ideally linked together as in the boxed example.

Most of the leading systems are excellent at handling the administrative aspects, and are reasonably good at providing decision support information. However, they fall down on providing good strategic information. Perhaps this is a reflection of the nature of such information; it is complex, and it needs to answer a wide range of questions which will change over time.

However, much of the strategic information which is built on characteristics of the staff (as opposed to attitudes and values) can be obtained by extracting from and manipulating the 'raw data' entered for administrative purposes; start and leave dates are the raw material for length of service distributions and labour turnover analysed by length of service. Entering details of an individual promotion can build up to promotion patterns, average lengths of time in a job, and so on.

Standard CPIS — basic record keeping, administration, and provision of decision-support information.

Plus

Application	Level
Wordprocessing	Administrative
Recruitment administration	Administrative and tactical
Succession planning	Administrative and tactical
Manpower planning	Tactical and strategic
Job evaluation	Administrative
Training administration	Administrative and tactical
Salary modelling/spreadsheet	Tactical
Time and attendance	Administrative and tactical
Report writer	Tactical, possibly strategic
Executive information system	Tactical and strategic

At present there are two major obstacles in using the data in this way. The first is a computer design problem — with one or two exceptions most software packages are not designed to allow access to past data in a meaningful way, to trace individual career paths and build them up to a picture of career patterns. The second is a user problem, that of creating robust coding structures, particularly for jobs and/or skills. All too often the coding structure becomes over-detailed and does not allow sufficiently for change. The purpose of a coding structure is usually seen as a mechanism for helping clerks carry out data entry rather than for analysis purposes.

Thus the administration requirements end up driving the provision of information which could be used for strategic purposes. Perhaps this is symptomatic of the whole problem; the CPIS is being asked to satisfy quite different needs of speeding up the administration, providing management information and now, providing strategic human resource information. Just as executive information systems (EIS) have developed partly as a response to the incompatibility of financial, production and marketing systems to do both the processing and satisfy strategic decision making needs, perhaps there is a need for a different type of human resource information system which extracts aggregate data from the traditional CPIS, and which can then be used to provide some of the information the HR director needs for strategic human resource management. Possibly a more imaginative use of an EIS could provide the answer.

The key to designing more effective computerised personnel information systems, however, lies in the hands of the information users. By more clearly thinking through the information they are likely to need for strategic purposes rather than for decision-support and administrative purposes, they can then give a clearer specification to the software suppliers. An increasing awareness of the value of strategic human resource management information, in terms of contribution to an organisation's competitive advantage, can only help to increase demand, and thus stimulate provision of good computer systems which improve the effectiveness of the HR function.

REFERENCES

1. Peters, T (1987) *Thriving on Choas*, Harper & Row, New York.
2. Fombrun, C, Tichy, N and Devanna MA (1984) *Strategic Human Resource Management*, John Wiley & Sons, Chichester, p 30.
3. Peters T, and Waterman, R (1982) *In Search of Excellence*, Harper & Row, New York.
4. Handy, C (1989) *The Age of Unreason*, Century Hutchinson, London.

11

PUBLIC SECTOR HUMAN RESOURCE MANAGEMENT: AN AGENDA FOR CHANGE

Peninah Thomson

INTRODUCTION

Policy initiatives enacted by government in the last decade have created a radically changed management environment in the public sector. The privatisation of many services, the creation of NHS self-governing trusts, the translation of discrete units of government work into Executive Agencies under the Next Steps initiative, the introduction of compulsory competitive tendering in local government, the production of a Citizen's Charter and other changes are gradually stimulating a radical overhaul of practice in the management of people — human resource management — in the public sector.

The purpose of this chapter is to identify those changes in human resource management practice that are taking place in the public sector now and also to identify some commonalities of approach between the public and private sectors.

The chapter is divided into four sections. The first sets the context, placing in review the major themes of government policy since 1979 and the way in which those themes have been the stimulus for particular policy initiatives. The second section examines the broad implications of some of those initiatives for the way people in the public sector manage and are themselves managed. (Not every initiative is examined: for example the implications of trade union reform are not reviewed. This is not because such implications are unimportant but because the focus of this chapter is upon the management of human resources by employers.) The final sections consider specific implications and identify those human resource management issues that must be addressed if the changes in the public sector are to be harnessed to the benefit of those who work in it and therefore — ultimately — to the benefit of the public itself.

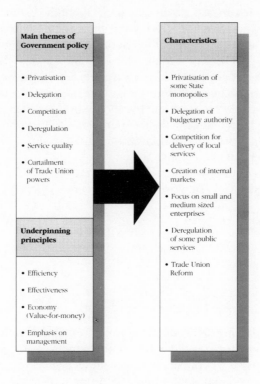

Figure 11.1 Main themes of Government Policy 1979–1992, and their characteristics

CONTEXT

All governments are committed to change. They take office with the intention of pursuing certain political objectives through a programme of legislation and in this sense the Conservative government of the last thirteen years is no different from the Labour government that preceded it. What does differentiate it is the radical nature of its legislative programmes; fundamentally different both from those of the preceding Labour government (which was to be expected) and from those of earlier Conservative governments (which was not so axiomatic).

For the past thirteen years therefore Britain has had a radical government, committed to change and reform and powered by the wish to 'roll back the frontiers of the State'[1]. Regardless of individual perceptions of the merit of the changes that have taken place during the period — an essentially political judgement — there can be little disagreement about the extent to which public sector institutions have been affected by the impact of thirteen years of sustained reform. There is scarcely an area of the public domain that remains untouched: central and local government, health, education and training, the professions — all have been affected, to a greater or a lesser degree, by the interventions of an administration determined to change things. The purpose of this section is not to evaluate the appropriateness or otherwise of individual interventions because, again, this is a political judgement. The purpose is to map the main themes of government policy over the period and consider their impact upon human resource management in the public sector.

The main themes of government policy since 1979, and their characteristics, are shown in Figure 11.1. They are, broadly, seven:

1. privatisation;
2. delegation;
3. competition;
4. enterprise;
5. deregulation;
6. service quality;
7. curtailment of Trade Union powers.

The themes overlap in places; some have received more emphasis than others. But taken together they constitute the overall framework for much of what has happened in public life in Britain in the last thirteen years.

The themes have been underpinned by three principles: the principles of efficiency, effectiveness and economy (together comprising value-for-money). These have been yardsticks against which systems, processes and services can be evaluated, and throughout the thirteen years there has been a sustained critical appraisal of the way in which they are being achieved in the various policy initiatives. This appraisal has been exercised in central government through the Financial Management Initiative (FMI) launched in May 1982, and in local government, health and central government quangos through the studies and advice of the Audit Commission and the National Audit Office.

The 'givens'; the governing assumptions from which both the seven policy themes and the underpinning principles derive, were two-fold. First there was the belief that Britain was under-performing in economic terms, and that this fundamental lack of competitiveness was due not simply to particular economic and fiscal policies but also to the way in which the State had in the past managed those bits of the economy for which it was directly responsible, from nationalised industries to the education system.

The second governing assumption driving government policies was the perceived failure of collectivism, or corporatism. The Government that came to power in 1979 was committed to the power of the market, and it is that

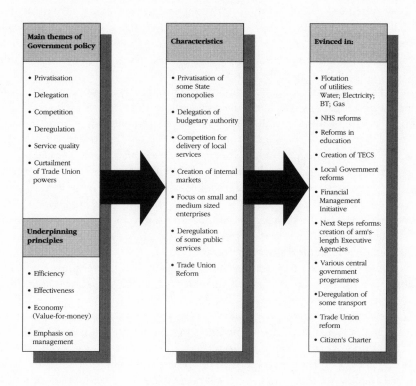

Figure 11.2 Main themes of Government Policy 1979–1992; as evinced in particular legislation or activity

commitment that has driven its policies, both towards the economy and towards the management of the public sector.

The whole programme of radical legislation over the past thirteen years has therefore been predicated upon two hypotheses: first, that the ideological purpose of rolling back the frontiers of the State, moving toward a more market-based economy, was a desirable end in itself and second, that Britain's competitive position was worsening and that radical measures were therefore necessary to halt the decline.

Whether or not the hypotheses were correct, radical measures have, manifestly, been enacted in the public sector. Figure 11.2 shows how the main themes of government policy have been translated into particular reforms and initiatives: how, for example, improvements in the quality of service delivery have been sought by shifting the locus of budgetary authority and managerial responsibility from the (policy) centre to a point closer to the delivery of the service. This particular theme — the delegation of managerial responsibility — is evinced in the Local Management of Schools reform, in the reforms in the National Health Service, in the creation of the Next Steps Agencies and in the preceding Financial Management Initiative in central government. Similarly, the themes of deregulation and competition have been enacted in the deregulation of some public transport services and in the introduction of compulsory competitive tendering in local authorities. The privatisation of state monopolies is a straight read across from policy theme to policy initiative, with the programme of flotation of utilities (water, electricity, telecoms, gas) recently completed, and in which regulation has been framed to be a substitute for competition where there is none.

'Enterprise' and 'service quality' are more difficult to trace through to particular policies, since they are in a sense approaches or casts of mind rather than actions: they came fairly late to the piece. The focus upon enterprise was most overtly acknowledged with the designation of the Department for Trade and Industry as the 'Department for Enterprise' in 1988. 'Service quality', in the form of the Next Steps initiative in central government and the Citizen's Charter, are probably attributable to the fact that service quality became an increasingly important feature of competitiveness in the private sector in the 1980s, leading to increasing expectations in the population as a whole.

The importance of enterprise and of service quality as approaches or casts of mind is a direct result of the economic impact of Britain's transition from a manufacturing to a service economy; a shift that was not itself part of Government policy but which was dictated by exposure to the market. In a sense they became increasingly important as it became clear that Britain's competitive position among world economies was in decline at the start of the 1980s, that Britain was becoming a high value-added, service economy and — finally — that this change would require a cultural shift as well as altered systems and processes.

As a consequence, enterprise and service have received considerable attention throughout the decade, as the government has sought to inculcate different attitudes and patterns of behaviour in the economically active among the population. The emphasis upon enterprise has been pursued over the period through initiatives in schools, colleges and universities as well as through work with small- and medium-sized enterprises (notably through the Enterprise Initiative launched by the DTI in 1988); and the enhanced focus upon quality and customer service in the public sector has been given emphasis most recently by the introduction in July 1991 of the Citizen's Charter.

The range and scope of the changes that have taken place (and are still taking place) make synthesis difficult. Many of the initiatives outlined in the previous paragraphs were not evolved as part of a master plan, a planned programme of change, but were ad hoc responses to changing political and economic circumstances. Although with hindsight there are clear links between ideology and conviction and particular activities or pieces of legislation, the links were undoubtedly not as apparent at the time to those (both politicians and civil servants) engaged in framing them: each individual had a partial view and — to quote a senior civil servant — 'in the middle of a battle one's just dodging the bullets'.

As a consequence of the general untidiness of life therefore, policy trends and their concomitant legislation or initiatives cannot be neatly ascribed to the systematic working out of an ordered plan. But there is no doubt that the initiatives described in this section were fuelled by a determination to bring about a real cultural change in British life. In an interview with the *Sunday Times* in 1981, Margaret Thatcher said:

> What's irritated me about the whole direction of politics in the last thirty years is that it's always been towards the collectivist society. People have forgotten about the personal society. And they say: do I count, do I matter? To which the short answer is, yes. *And, therefore, it isn't that I set out on economic policies, it's that I set out really to change the approach, and changing the economics is the means of changing that approach. If you change the approach you really are after the heart and soul of the nation. Economics are the method; the object is to change the heart and soul.*[2]

It is too early to say whether the attempt of the last decade to shift the culture, modes of working and orientation of what has been described as a post-industrial nation[1] has been successful; or whether, if it *has* been successful, that shift will be sufficient to stabilise and eventually reverse the economic decline of the early 1980s. Definitions of the problem, as well as the design of a solution, are not value-free and remain political judgements. What *is* indisputable, however, is that a period of radical reforms has resulted in significant change in the public sector and therefore in all aspects of the management of its human resources: in the way organisations are structured; in staffing levels; in lines of accountability and authority; in freedoms and constraints; in managerial style and organisational behaviour. It is the impact of government policy upon these and other areas that is addressed next.

IMPLICATIONS OF RECENT GOVERNMENT POLICY

The policy developments described in the previous section have undoubtedly had an effect upon the various constituencies they were designed to address. Britain is becoming a service economy (in 1960 services accounted for approximately 45 per cent of GDP and 48 per cent of people in employment; in 1987 services accounted for approximately 60 per cent of GDP and 68 per cent of people in employment,[2] although the fact that this transition has been spread over 27 years makes it clear that government policy over the last decade has accentuated this trend rather than created it).

The initiatives associated with the main policy themes have been enacted. Parts of the transport framework have been deregulated; the education service and the NHS are being reformed; internal markets have been created; the executive functions of government departments are being regrouped as Agencies; competition has been introduced into the provision of services in local authorities. The central issue of this section relates, not to the effectiveness or otherwise in political, economic or social terms of the initiatives themselves, but to the impact that the initiatives have had upon the way people in the public sector manage people and are themselves managed. What has happened? What is happening?

Figure 11.3 shows the eight ways in which the impact of these changes has been most clearly felt in human resource management. They are:

1. a more 'managerial' approach generally;
2. adjustment of systems and processes;
3. new relationships;
4. new frameworks of remuneration;
5. contraction of workforces ('downsizing') and consequent organisational restructuring;
6. emphasis on quality of service provision and an increasing customer focus;
7. explicit management of change;
8. organisational culture shift.

The first five of these are tangible; the remaining three more nebulous — but no less significant. The remainder of this section reviews some of the ways in which each of these high-level changes is manifested in human resource terms and identifies the agenda that they suggest for those responsible for HR management in the public sector over the next five years. The final section of the chapter examines this agenda in detail.

A more 'managerial' approach

Although it should not be implied that no-one in the public sector 'managed' before 1979, it is indisputable that formal management skills have received considerable emphasis in the sector in the past thirteen years. This emphasis has been driven primarily (but not solely) by delegated financial responsibility and the thrust was the Financial Management Initiative (although Fulton was stressing management in 1968).

The creation of the Training and Enterprise Councils — TECs — (which have budgetary and managerial responsibility for training provision at local level); the Local Management of Schools initiative, the shift of Polytechnics from local authority control, the creation of NHS trusts and allocation of budgets to GPs and the creation of freestanding Executive Agencies have all been engines for change in this area. The transition has not been without pain, regardless of the area in which it has occurred.

Fig 11.3

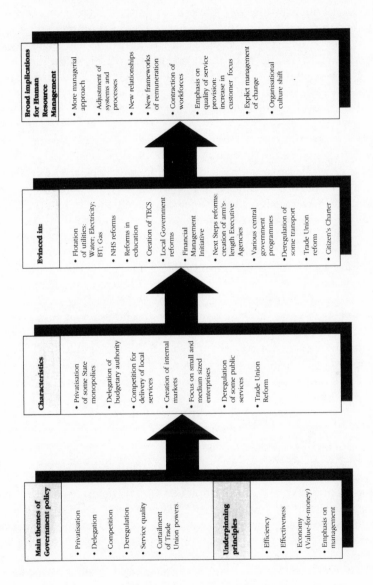

Figure 11.3 Main themes of government policy 1979-1991; broader implications for human resource management in the public sector

In the *education sector* for example, one or two large educational institutions — Universities, with total annual budgets of more than £60 million — have experienced an unhappy cycle of learning in the management of their resources, as that management task requires skills not previously specified in the job description of a Principal or a Vice-Chancellor. In the 1980s, some Deans of Faculty, finding themselves in charge of delegated budgets running to millions, observed that they had not joined academia in order to become managers (some GPs are making similar comments). As a consequence, therefore, the nature and make-up of the top team in academic institutions, as well as the tasks they must perform, has changed. Finance directors have joined senior management teams, and the past few years have seen an up-grading of the salary and status accorded to them.

In *central government*, the new Executive Agencies (57 to date with candidates for Agency status still going forward) have produced business plans to structure their work. A number have built their business plans around new, or newly-articulated mission statements and statements of core values; all have clear aims and targets set out in their framework documents. Here too, finance directors and personnel directors are being recruited, as the chief executives of the Agencies give thought to the achievement of the quantitative and qualitative targets they have agreed with their Minister.

In *local authorities*, senior officers are exploring the realities of their new roles in the light of an era of unprecedented change in local government. Chief Education Officers are restructuring departments and rethinking service provision and functions in the light of the new ability of schools and colleges to buy in (or not) services from the centre. In other parts of local councils, staff groups are exploring the realities of client and contractor roles as they seek to put forward and respond to efficient, effective and economic bids for service provision in waste disposal, transport, recreation and leisure facilities in the face of external competition; and are adjusting to being 'enabling authorities': no longer providing direct services but identifying strategic need.

In more than eighty *TECs* (Training and Enterprise Councils) throughout England and Wales, TEC chairmen, chief executives and directors — often from the private sector — are engaged in managing a total budget of more than £2 billion of public funds in a complex portfolio of tasks ranging from running government programmes for the unemployed (Employment Training; Youth Training) to stimulating the involvement of industry and commerce in Further Education. Their staff, the majority of whom are on secondment from the Department of Employment, are seeking to manage their work effectively in a private sector culture often radically different from that in which they have hitherto spent their working lives. Their chairman and boards of directors are learning the complexities of public sector management processes: notably in relation to public accountability and to how resources are allocated through the public expenditure round.

These are just some examples. The renewed emphasis upon management issues is apparent right through the public sector; in the increased focus upon:

- the role of the chief executive;
- empowering the chief executive;
- leadership in public sector organisations;
- the creation, and building, of effective senior teams;
- the creation or up-grading of the financial management function;
- the shift from administration to management; from the enforcement of defined processes and rules to the exercise of discretion;
- the overt linking of operational activity to the overall mission and objectives of organisations;
- the delegation of human resource management responsibility from the centre to the line;
- the evaluation of operational systems and processes for efficiency, effectiveness and value for money;
- the active pursuit of quality and high standards of customer care;
- active management of the cultural adjustment involved in changing organisations from one type of entity to another.

Making all this happen is part of the agenda for human resource managers in the public sector over the next three to five years; and the final section of this chapter reviews the task in more detail.

Adjustment of systems and processes

The major change in systems and processes resulting from recent government policy, and arguably the most important change, is the focus upon outputs — performance — rather than inputs. There has been, and continues to be, a shift from an exclusively product-determined service to one which takes account of customer need. The introduction of the Citizen's Charter has given further emphasis to a focus upon the outputs of the public sector and the quality of the services it provides to the public.

The impact of the focus upon outputs of systems and processes in the public sector has been to cause them to be re-examined; assessed for the fulfilment of criteria other than those against which, frequently, they were originally established. The focus of many organisations may, for example, have been upon quality of the *product* rather than quality of service: the private sector equivalent is the meticulous production of goods that few customers any longer want to buy. One of the effects upon work processes of the 'managerial revolution' of the past thirteen years has been to prompt consideration of how work systems can be adjusted to ensure that the public services provided by the public sector are framed in ways that are appropriate to their users or 'customers' and that the performance indicators used to evaluate them continue to be appropriate. For example, the Passport Office discovered from a survey of its customers that the turn-round time (in number of days) on the issue of a new passport (their primary performance indicator) was less important to their customers than *certainty* of receipt by whichever date was specified.

Organisations are looking at what they do, therefore, not just in terms of whether it is being done efficiently and effectively but in terms of whether the doing of it is making a direct contribution to the primary purpose of the organisation; its objectives (or 'mission', as some organisations in the public sector are describing it).

As a consequence of this shift the role of the human resource function, both centrally and as carried out by line managers is to inculcate or enhance, in staff accustomed to serving the needs of large bureaucracies, a sense of personal responsibility for efficiency and a commitment to a climate of continuous improvement. And at higher managerial levels, it is also to encourage senior staff to carry out critical appraisals not only of the way 'things are done around here' but of why some things are done at all, and of how what *is* done affects the recipients.

New relationships

In addition to the evaluation of work processes that is happening as a result of the focus upon outputs, new relationships are being established.

Some of the characteristics of a market have been simulated (in local authorities for example) by the establishment of client/contractor roles. The introduction of competitive tendering has had the effect not only of opening up to external competition the provision of local services like refuse collection or recreation and leisure provision, but of altering the relationship between groupings of employees in what was formerly a unitary authority.

A similar effect is being created in other parts of the public sector: for example, in central government and education where central services like IT are 'sold' to internal clients on a recharge basis, (as happens in the private sector too) and where the market testing of central services stimulates the perception of competition among service providers.

The political objective is to increase competition and thereby avoid the potential complacency of a monopoly position. The effects in management terms are to necessitate the accurate costing of activities (including labour costs) to arrive at unit costs that form the basis of service pricing, and to enhance the general efficiency and effectiveness of the function in order that it can compete effectively. The new management processes include the specifying of a service, management of the contract and monitoring of performance. (There is also the idea of comparative statistics as a surrogate for competition: if an operation costs £ x in Region X, what does it cost in Region Y?)

As a result of these changes the issues of concern for the human resource dimension in the adjustment of systems and work processes are not, on the whole, related to the specification of the criteria by which those processes should be evaluated, either for their overall 'fit' with the aims and objectives of the organisation or for the efficiency with which they are carried out. These are primarily line management tasks.

The effect in human resource management terms lies not only in the change to work processes but in the management of the changed relationship of one group of employees to another; in the exploration of the idea and meaning of the internal customer, and in the management of a change of culture. The human resource management function can add value to the process by helping with the 'how'; by facilitating the changed relationships. It can do this by contributing to the management team an understanding of human motivation and of the innovatory change management processes that will help ensure that an organisation's stated commitment to, for example, servicing the needs of internal or external clients, or creating a climate of continuous improvement, does not remain a paper at the back of a desk drawer or pinned up as an object of ridicule in the tea-room, but actually gets translated into changed behaviour patterns among large bodies of staff. The last section of this chapter suggests how this role — helping with the 'how' — should be fulfilled.

New frameworks of remuneration

The criteria for remuneration of employees in the public sector are also changing:

- New ways of working
- A focusing of the 'business' around clearly articulated aims and objectives
- The firm establishment of quality of output as the primary performance indicator
- The consequent changes in systems and processes.

These are driving public sector organisations toward systems of performance management and — more narrowly — performance related pay. The concept of a 'rate for the job' is being replaced by remuneration in the light of markets and performance and performance related pay is gradually being introduced in most parts of the public sector, with the concomitant development of different staff appraisal and development frameworks to guide, motivate and develop staff towards their optimum potential.

The pertinent human resource questions here include the following:

- How can a 'performance culture' be embedded in public sector organisations that may previously have had a culture in which length of service or seniority, as well as appropriateness, may have affected progression?[3]
- How do organisations accustomed to systems of progression based upon 'rules' adjust to the concept of managerial discretion?
- Job evaluation — given the emphasis upon quality of service delivery, how ought the jobs for the changed circumstances be evaluated?
- Criteria for appraisal — linked to the articulated needs of the 'business': what are they?
- Standards of performance — what skills, qualities, attributes, behaviours and attitudes does the changing organisation wish to reward? Does it know what

sort of human resources will be essential to the development and prosperity of the 'business' in the future?

* How best can the industrial and human relations aspects of the introduction of performance related pay be managed?

Contraction of workforces ('downsizing') and organisational restructuring

The fourth tangible effect of the policy initiatives — of the last few years in this case rather than throughout the decade as a whole, although there was a civil service recruitment freeze in the summer of 1979 — is a decrease in the number of people working in the public sector.

In 1987 one-third of all workers in Britain were employed by the State.[3] A by-product of government policy has been the transfer of some of those people from the public to the private sector, and the consequent contraction of the labour force in the former. Table 11.1 shows the decline in numbers employed by the State, notably in nationalised industries and in public corporations, where the overall number of staff employed has fallen by 60 per cent since 1978/79.[4] This contraction has occurred in several ways:

* through privatisation of public sector organisations (where the majority of staff are assimilated into the new enterprise);
* through natural wastage, early retirements and the non-filling of vacant posts;
* through temporary transfers of staff (many staff of the old Training Agency area offices, for example, currently constitute the greater proportion of TEC staff).

However, there are circumstances in which staff are not transferred. A number have taken early retirement; others have been made redundant. In the education sector, for example, some staff in educational institutions who are unwilling or unable to make the transition to what many regard as a 'new world' have elected to leave the sector. The same principle applies to staff in central government departments and Agencies, a (small) number of whom have taken voluntary redundancy.

The implications in human resource management terms of managing the contraction of labour forces and restructuring the smaller organisations are:

* the counselling and outplacement of staff;
* the design and negotiation with HM Treasury and other bodies of appropriate financial packages for staff taking early retirement or being made redundant;
* the provision of pre-retirement courses for staff;
* the reshaping of the smaller organisation (particularly relevant in the case of 'parent' departments of central government after the separation from them of Executive Agencies);
* the maintenance of motivation and morale among staff remaining in post.[5]

Table 11.1 Public sector manpower, 1978-89 to1989-90

thousands (whole time equivalents)

	1978-79	1979-80	1980-81	1981-82	1982-83	1983-84	1984-85	1985-86	1986-87	1987-88	1988-89	1989-90
Civil service	734	719	697	678	658	636	621	597	598	587	574	567
Armed forces	326	330	335	341	334	333	336	334	331	328	324	319
National Health Service	923	943	979	998	1,009	1,009	998	993	981	976	977	968
Other central government	211	210	207	205	210	210	207	207	207	204	206	205
Total central government	**2,194**	**2,202**	**2,218**	**2,222**	**2,211**	**2,189**	**2,162**	**2,131**	**2,117**	**2,095**	**2,081**	**2,059**
Local authorities community programme[1][2]						22	45	52	76	72	67	
Local authorities (other non-trading)[1][3]	2,073	2,115	2,092	2,064	2,040	2,043	2,041	2,040	2,054	2,089	2,097	2,062
Local authorities (trading)[1][3]	252	253	251	242	234	235	234	234	232	216	215	207
Total local authorities	**2,325**	**2,368**	**2,343**	**2,306**	**2,274**	**2,300**	**2,320**	**2,326**	**2,352**	**2,377**	**2,379**	**2,269**
Nationalised industries [1]	**1,843**	**1,818**	**1,785**	**1,656**	**1,538**	**1,444**	**1,396**	**1,124**	**1,049**	**856**	**781**	**709**
Public corporations [1]	**203**	**204**	**205**	**190**	**185**	**185**	**181**	**117**	**126**	**118**	**118**	**109**
Total public sector	**6,565**	**6,592**	**6,551**	**6,374**	**6,208**	**6,112**	**6,059**	**5,698**	**5,644**	**5,456**	**5,369**	**5,146**

1 At 1 July.
2 Community programmes ran between 1983-84 and 1988-89.
3 Including Northern Ireland.
4 Includes United Kingdom Atomic Energy Authority.

Source: Public Expenditure Analyses to 1993-94, Hm Treasury, Command 1520

Emphasis on quality of service provision, and increasing customer focus

The Citizen's Charter has given some impetus to the changes set in train by trends in government policy. Some of the characteristics of the public sector that have been implicit in the past have been given greater emphasis by the overall thrust and explicit statements of intent of the Citizen's Charter:

- overt and articulated commitment to quality in standards of service delivery;
- clear and agreed criteria by which such quality can be measured;
- the increased visibility of people engaged in the public service at all levels;
- the overt and articulated commitment of the public sector to a climate of continuous improvement;
- the clear intention that those engaged in work in the public sector will do their best in managing activities and delivering services to their fellow citizens.

Service quality and customer care is likely to be of continuing significance for human resource management in the public sector since the focus (though articulated in different ways) is shared by all three political parties.

The implications for human resource management of the above five points are threefold. First, there is likely to be a shift in emphasis between the human resource management department's internal 'customers' — the staff. The explicit commitment of entire organisations to the active pursuit of quality means that recruitment, training and development of *all* staff will be critically important. It will be nugatory for senior managers to set targets for performance and for quality if the body of the workforce is unable or unwilling to achieve them. This shift of focus may have important implications for human resource functions like training, pay, promotion, career development in the public sector, some of which have, in the past, paid much more attention to the alphas than to the epsilons.

All organisations give of their best to those individuals they have identified as being best qualified to drive the business forward. They must recruit and retain (and lead, motivate and train) those who are best able to equip them both to achieve the organisation's external aims and objectives and to manage it successfully. But no organisation consists solely of such an élite, and for public sector organisations to function to optimum efficiency in their changed climate they will need to exploit to the full the skills, intelligence and expertise of *all* their people. Achieving quality targets of any type will not be possible in organisations where, for example, 75 per cent of the work of the HR department is focused upon the top 12 per cent of staff.[6]

The second implication will be the impact upon training, which will acquire a high profile in organisations committed to enhancing the quality of their service provision and giving more emphasis to customers. Public sector employees are unlikely to adjust their behaviour, attitudes, and style of working overnight as a result of the production of a Charter or a Total Quality Programme. Although not sufficient in itself, training will be an important part of the process of inculcating the values associated with customer care and the focus upon outputs (especially for those in large bodies of staff). Methods of working will also be affected: a shift towards the effective *team* rather than the gifted individual; the decreasing importance of the rituals associated with highly differentiated hierarchies.

A more overtly managerial approach, the adjustment of systems and processes, new systems of remuneration and the contraction of the total workforce are all ways in which the impact of recent government policies upon the public sector is manifest. They are overt; tangible; they can be measured. For example, if an Agency gets into financial difficulties, or fails to meet the targets agreed with its Minister, it will be apparent. However two other implications of government policy are less tangible and less amenable to quantification: they have to do with the explicit management of change and with organisational culture shift.

Explicit management of change

There is a body of opinion that argues that the current focus on the management of change is essentially a case of the Emperor and his clothes; that the activity is little more than something that good managers always do, dressed up in a fashionable name.

There are persuasive arguments to support this hypothesis, and there is certainly no virtue in elevating into an art form the fundamental activities necessary to translate the policy initiatives of the last twelve years into effective organisational practice for the public sector. But it is true nevertheless that the cumulative impact of those policy initiatives implies a step change of a type infrequently experienced in the public sector. That step change means something significant, both for human resource management in relation to specific entities like remuneration, performance, organisational structures etc. and also for the management of change more broadly. This is what people in the sector are saying: one senior civil servant in a newly-established Executive Agency remarked recently that the last months had been the most challenging of his twenty-two years in the civil service. The point is that changes occurring in the public sector now are *not part of a continuum of change*; they represent a step change and as such require focused and — critically — perceptive management.

There are five essential characteristics of explicit change management:

1. recognition and understanding among the top management team of the nature of the changes that are going on;
2. determination of *how* the organisation in all its aspects is going to address those changes, including changing organisational culture; determination of *what* needs to be done;
3. communication of that vision and strategic direction to staff;
4. implementation of action plans;
5. recognition that the change required is not a matter of shifting the

organisation from A to B, but of shifting it from A to flexible: to the learning organisation.

These are not simple tasks, especially in some environments (Local Education Authorities for example, where the frequency of policy initiatives in Spring 1991 made interpreting their implications for staff almost a daily occupation). But it is this scanning of the external environment, and the concomitant development and communication of a strategic vision for the organisation — whether an LEA, an Executive Agency, a School or an NHS Trust — which constitutes one of the primary tasks of the person or people at the top of an organisation who are concerned to manage change effectively. Few things contribute more to organisational anxiety and uncertainty (and hence underperformance) at a time of potentially destabilising and disorientating change than ignorance; among managers and among staff generally.

The essential human resource management tasks raised by explicit management of change are, therefore, high level ones:

- developing a vision; having the ability to scan the external and internal environments and induce the implications of significant changes in them for the organisation and its people;
- communicating that vision within the organisation;
- carrying out an accurate analysis of existing organisational culture, including identifying gaps/differences (actual or perceived) between existing and desired cultures;
- engaging in strategic thinking for human resource management; translating the vision into a human resources strategy that addresses:

  — the organisational mission;
  — the leadership task;
  — appropriate organisational structures;
  — tasks: the jobs to be done;
  — staffing complements;
  — systems and processes;
  — definition of an organisational culture appropriate for the future.

Organisational culture shift

A further way in which government policy has driven change in human resource management practice in the public sector lies in recognising the need for change, sometimes minor, sometimes radical, in organisational culture. Although culture change is a corporate process, frequently driven by the Chief Executive or his/her equivalent, it is a process that in some senses has a natural 'home' in human resource management, being closely meshed with the behaviour of the organisation and of staff. (Some organisational change programmes are driven solely by directors of finance, but this is unusual.) Certainly, culture change cannot be achieved *without* the direct involvement of the HR function, since if it is not involved there will almost certainly be discordance between the culture of the organisation and the systems (of recruitment, career planning, development, appraisal and reward) which sustain and reflect that culture.

The subject of organisational culture in the public sector is problematic. On the one hand, it may be perceived as tentative, intangible, uneasily fashionable, the construct of behaviourists; having little to do with the realities of meeting Treasury targets, formulating a Business Plan for the first time, mastering the implications of an internal market or being held accountable for significant sums of public money. On the other hand, people in leadership positions in the public sector are increasingly aware that for their organisations to achieve their objectives and their targets, and to deliver quality services to customers, some aspects of their organisational culture will have to change. Altered systems and processes, new remuneration packages and a greater degree of freedom are not of themselves adequate to deliver the required change in practice: necessary but not sufficient, they will need to be complemented by changes in attitude, behaviour and management style if the new enterprises in the public sector are to realise their full potential.

As with the management of change, there is more than one view about how amenable organisational cultures are to being changed. Some argue that real culture change takes a decade or more to embed (the implication being that the process is essentially organic and cannot be managed);[7] others maintain that certain cultural levers exist that can be pulled to start the process of change.

However long it takes to change an organisation's culture, however, it is a task that senior executives in the public sector have to address. The nature and extent of change in their organisations (whether in central or local government, the health or the education sector), driven by external factors over which they have little jurisdiction means that organisational cultures *will* be affected. One measure of executive performance over the next five years will be the extent to which public sector managers are able to use the external thrust of change to shape their culture into something different; fit for their organisation's new purpose; supportive of its values and furthering its mission and objectives. This is a task of some magnitude, but one which cannot be avoided. Hierarchical public sector bureaucracies operating in a traditional manner are unlikely to achieve the qualitative and quantitative targets and objectives they have either defined or had imposed. The 'climate of continuous improvement' that government wishes to see characterise public sector organisations will not come about without understanding *why* it is that the climate does not already exist; *what* has to change in order to achieve it, and *how* senior management teams go about empowering their organisations to make it happen.

Embarking on the process of culture change in public sector organisations is in a sense the cornerstone of all the human resource management tasks reviewed in this section. Without some achievement in this area initiatives taken elsewhere — in restructuring; in new pay frameworks; in the assessing of work processes — are likely to be shallow-rooted: they cannot be 'bolt-ons' to the old culture; to the way in which things 'used to be done around here'.

The final section of this chapter focuses upon the nature of the step change that has taken place (and continues to take place) in public sector organisations, and the process of transition that is occurring. It then suggests a definition of the agenda for human resource management in the public sector over the next three to five years.

AN AGENDA FOR TRANSITION AND CHANGE

The previous section reviewed the broad implications for human resource management of recent government policy. This final section identifies the transition which is taking place, suggests a means of managing it, and identifies an agenda for HR management in the public sector. Not every organisation in the sector will need to address all the activities; while the relative weightings attached to individual areas will vary according to the particular phase of transition that organisations are in at the time. And finally, the agenda is not the sole precinct of those responsible for the management of human resources.

Before turning to the agenda however I want to examine briefly the reasons why any of it is necessary: to consider the characteristics of what I have argued is a step change for the public sector.

Organisational purpose and the old stereotypes in public and private sector

The driving force behind the management of organisations in the public sector is materially different from that in the private sector. In the latter the overall intent is frequently to provide a good return on capital investment or return on equity for owner(s) or shareholders. Without that, nothing much else prospers; not quality of service or products; not excellence in management, not innovation in design or originality in research. Without profitability the whole enterprise is threatened. For public sector organisations, the 'givens' are different. Although it is true that public sector organisations can find themselves the subject of a hostile takeover or an unwelcome merger, the recipients of public funds do not often go bankrupt;[8] face meetings of angry shareholders demanding an explanation of this or that course of action;[9] lose market share and go into slow decline. And critically, they are not 'in business' for the same purpose, since to the extent that public sector organisations can be said to share an ethos, it is that they are involved in managing for social result.

This fundamental difference — the absence of a focus on profitability as the key to continued survival — has in the past shaped the cultures of organisations in the public sector. The principle of financial accountability has always operated (the Public Accounts Committee and the National Audit Office for central government; the Audit Commission for local government; the funding councils for the education sector) but public sector organisations have in the past also largely been 'managed' by their controlling bodies. Traditional management models in the public sector provided for resource allocation and the 'hows' of day-to-day management to be decided elsewhere, leaving HR managers and line managers as administrators of rules rather than genuine managers of people. In pursuing delegation and local management, therefore, the cumulative impact of government policy has been to increase the power and authority, freedom of action — and the concomitant exposure to risk — of organisations in the public sector.

As a result, such organisations are effectively in transition; shedding some of their past cultural characteristics and adopting new ones. And while it is true that the process of change is continuous — the river flows on — the cumulative effect of government policy upon the public sector in the last decade does mean that the changes facing organisations now and in the next few years are particularly demanding.

Past stereotypes of *private* sector organisations have characterised them as essentially apolitical in their objectives, powered by the search for profitability, forced toward change by shifts in the market place. Their stability has been seen as being critically affected by competition, with customers that can choose to go elsewhere; and the real possibility of takeover, merger or ultimately bankruptcy if the appropriate balance is not struck between product, customers and price. The past stereotype of organisations in the *public* sector has been to some extent a mirror image. They have been regarded as having essentially political objectives,[10] and being powered by the desire to achieve not profit but social result. They have often been monopoly providers of services with captive customers; and consequently have been perceived as being free from the pressure of competition, unlikely to be allowed to go 'out of business' and less subject to risk. As a consequence they have been perceived as stable and slow to change. There are caveats to be entered when comparing the characteristics of public and private sector organisations in this way. Such a comparison risks being a parody of itself — and there is, of course, no one organisation, in either public or private sector, that embodies all the above characteristics.

Any mechanistic application of stereotype to organisations in either sector is therefore destined to be insensitive and inaccurate. But the significant point is not the accuracy or otherwise of the stereotype but the fact that it exists at all: and there is no doubt that stereotypes of organisations (in both their own and the 'other' sector), do exist in the minds of those that work in them. One of the things that has happened in the last twelve years is that the lines separating the public and the private sectors have become fuzzy; have been deliberately blurred by government by the application of market disciplines to the public sector, in particular the emphasis placed on results, which has caused the management style and priorities of the public sector to shift. In the process, it has adopted practices which are closer to those of the private sector.

This blurring of the lines has been accentuated by the exchange of personnel between the two sectors. Organisations in the private sector have been pressured by Government in the past twelve years to become more involved in the community; to contribute to the management of public sector organisations; to enhance their social conscience.[11] Companies release staff to serve as School, College or Polytechnic Governors; sit on TEC boards, participate in District Health Authorities. They second staff to Government departments and welcome civil servants on secondment; they participate in work shadowing schemes and make corporate donations to bodies committed to establishing links between industry or commerce and education.

Public sector organisations have also been active participants in the new partnerships. Their greatest contribution is perhaps represented by their focus upon the longer term and in their commitment to social objectives, since the canvas of the public sector is a broad one and its purpose comprehensive — the shaping, securing and servicing of British society.

A blurring of the lines: the case for radical thinking

The cumulative effect of Government policy has therefore been to blur the line to some extent between the private and the public sector. The old stereotypes of organisations in the two sectors are now simply inappropriate. Public sector organisations in particular find themselves functioning in a different operational climate. There has always been accountability: now there is an element of risk. There is increased visibility; there is a climate that says it encourages entrepreneurship (and intrepreneurship); venture; innovation. The traditional difficulty of constrained resources is being addressed by the right of organisations to vire between budget heads and to generate income.[12] People at the top of public sector organisations are transmogrifying from 'Permanent Secretary' or 'Grade 2' or even 'Chief Clerk' to chief executives; their role becoming more transparent to their client groups as a result. The key question in the public sector is no longer 'why?', but 'why not?': a fundamental shift.[13]

In summary then, the main themes of government policy in the last decade are having an effect upon the *climate* in which organisations in the public sector operate, and upon the *values* that inform their operation. The role of the human resources function has also changed, and the tasks of those in charge of managing people (both at the centre and in line management) need therefore to focus upon helping their organisations to function, through their people, effectively and vigorously in the changed environment; facilitating the change; ordering and structuring it so that the characteristics of excellence in the sector — its public accountability, its commitment to social equity and justice, and its purpose in shaping, furthering and servicing British society — are built upon and enhanced.[14]

The reasons why radical thinking in human resource management is necessary in the public sector are therefore fourfold:

1. The change that has taken place; the *rapprochement* between the private sector and the public sector is a step change and will have impact upon a large number of management processes.
2. It is happening already; is here *now.*

3. Many aspects of the change cross party political boundaries and are therefore unlikely to be removed (completely) from the political agenda under any different government.
4. Beneficial change in the public sector is a good of itself.[15]

Many of the old stereotypes of the public sector were inappropriate. In the changed context which has been created they are now impossible to sustain. The change can therefore be managed well or fumbled at; it cannot be ignored, and since organisations are staffed by people the role of the human resource function in helping organisations to manage the transition is critical.

The agenda for change

There are a number of components of the agenda for change; as shown in Figure 11.4. Some have to do with particular management processes — devising new performance management systems, for example, which is the subject of the Case Study at the end of this chapter. These are the tasks that are tangible; they have a beginning and a middle (although probably not an end) and will be easier to get right because they are in many ways part of the normal process of updating and renewal that go on in any well-managed organisation. They have been reviewed in the previous section.

Other components of the agenda are both less quantifiable and less familiar; not within the management experience of many individuals. They are also the areas that have to be got right if organisations in the public sector are to realise their full potential in the changed environment, and they will require both radical thinking and a willingness to adjust to a more open management style than is common in British public sector institutions.

There are four high-level tasks on the management agenda in this area, and taken together they constitute an iterative process, shown in Figure 11.5. These tasks are:

1. **perceiving** the changed circumstances and formulating the organisation's response to them; developing a vision;
2. **communicating** that vision: to the organisation; to stakeholders; to customers;
3. **listening** to the organisation; finding out what people are saying; finding out what the 'blockers' are that prevent them achieving the vision;
4. **acting** to remove the 'blockers'; to empower the people; to ensure congruence between the vision and what actually happens in the organisation.

Perceiving the changed circumstances and formulating the organisation's response to them; developing a vision

This is the role of the chief executive and his or her senior management team,

223

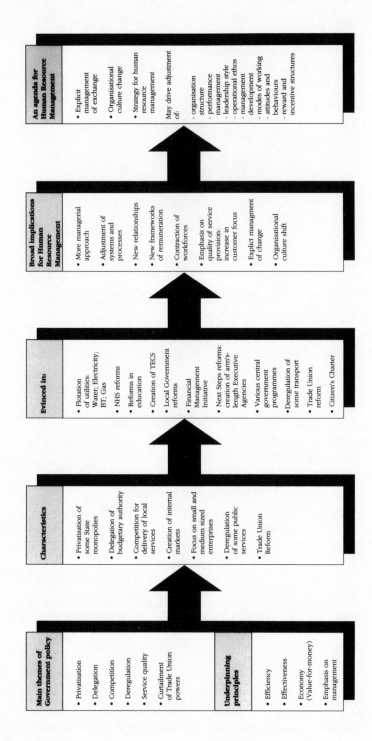

Figure 11.4 Main themes of government policy 1979-1991, and their implications for the management of human resources in the public sector

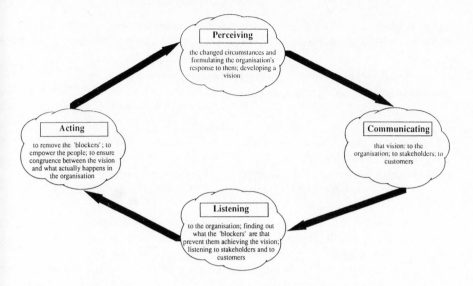

Figure 11.5   Four high-level tasks on the management agenda

including the head of the human resources function. It is their task to scan the external environment continually; to translate what they see as the impact of that environment upon the operating context of the organisation and to help the organisation adjust accordingly. For senior people in public sector organisations it means interpreting for their organisation the impact of government policy over the last thirteen years, and refocusing aims, objectives or 'mission' as appropriate. The process also involves identifying and articulating organisational values appropriate to the changed circumstances. These may embody commitments: to customers, to employees, to the community; to excellence in performance; to effective and efficient work processes; to innovation and a process of continual improvement — each organisation has its own particular focus.

Each of the four high-level tasks in the diagram is critical for the success of organisations in the public sector. This first one, however, is the cornerstone upon which the whole construct depends: if there is muddled thinking, undue haste or inadequate 'ownership' of the organisational mission and values at senior team level then the messages sent out will be inconsistent and unclear, and people at other levels in the organisation will regard the whole enterprise of high-level thinking about organisational purpose, management style and executive leadership as a 'quick fix' devised by management; something tacked on in a half-hearted way.

Getting this first step right is therefore very important, and it is something of which few senior managers in the public sector — including HR managers — have considerable experience. Their task is nothing less than to reorient their organisation; to adjust its mindset and to help it regroup itself around particular values and a particular ethos; to turn it into an organisation that cares passionately about quality, service, excellence, customer care — and to do all that with no increase in resources.[16]

Communicating the vision: to the organisation; to stakeholders; to customers

Employees, and the recipients of public services, as well as their funding bodies, are entitled to a clear articulation of what public sector organisations are there to achieve. The concept of the internal, as well as the external customer, is one which is valid, and the communication of organisational purpose and intent to both groups is an integral part of the role of the senior management team in public sector organisations.

The extent to which employees are involved in the framing of their organisation's mission varies. Some organisations have engaged in wide employee consultation before devising a mission statement; some have undertaken 'dipstick testing' of employee views; others have devised a mission statement and statement of core values at executive team level and then presented them to the wider organisation. (Knowing which method is appropriate is part of understanding the existing organisational culture; selecting an atypical method — for example instituting a consultation process in a secretive organisation — can be the first stage in a process of culture change.)

Regardless of how it is arrived at however, communication of the statement of mission and of organisational values constitutes the new credo. It is the organisation's signal of how it intends to be in the future; of what it regards as important. It is the ultimate statement of what the organisation intends itself to be evaluated by. The following Case Studies show two examples of such

---

Case Study — Royal Mail business mission

'As Royal Mail our mission is to be recognised as the best organisation in the world distributing text and packages.
   We achieve this by:

- excelling in our collection, processing,distribution and delivery arrangements;
- establishing a partnership with our customers to understand, agree and meet their changing requirements;
- operating profitably by efficient services which our customers consider to be value for money;
- creating a work environment which recognises and rewards the commitment of all employees to customers' satisfaction;
- recognising our responsibilities as part of the social, industrial and commercial life of the country;
- being forward-looking and innovative'

Case Study — Royal Mail business values

We each care about:

- our customers and their requirements
  - Reliability
  - Value for money
  - Accessibility
  - Courtesy
  - Integrity
  - Security
  - Prompt and timely response;
- all our fellow employees and their needs for:
  - Respect
  - Training and development
  - Involvement
  - Recognition and reward;
- The way we do our job and the way it affects our customers both inside and outside the business.

---

statements: the Business Mission and the statement of business values articulated by Royal Mail.

Making statements like those made by Royal Mail is dangerous. It means that failure can be identified; shortfalls pinpointed. Statements of organisational mission and values put organisations on the line and turn a searchlight upon dark corners. They take courage: especially in the public sector, where the primary relationship of accountability used to be between the organisation (or the *top* of the organisation), the Minister and the Treasury, and performance was usually thought of in terms of economy, efficiency and effectiveness — ie value for money. The new focus upon the (internal or external) customer or 'citizen' brings into play other entities and requires senior managers to formulate, and then express, views about the nature of relationships (the Royal Mail's *partnership* with customers); operating style (Royal Mail: *'forward looking and innovative'*) and management style (open or closed, secretive or participative, encouraging or punitive); command and control or negotiation and empowerment.

The general trend towards quality management will have particular impact upon communication in public sector organisations. The shift toward quality implies a move away from a bureaucratic approach, with rules and regulations and bounded areas of responsibility, towards one of increased team working, with an emphasis upon the explicit (and continuous) questioning both of purpose and of method. In the new environment managers at all levels become enablers, rather than instructors or regulators. All this will have a profound effect upon communications, and the openness of the senior team in disseminating information about the organisational mission and purpose, culture and values, is the start of the process.

Listening to the organisation, to stakeholders and to customers

Statements of intent or direction remain a dead letter if they are not subscribed to by those who work in the organisation and if the systems and work processes in place run counter to them. The third high-level task is, therefore, to open up channels for feedback from the body of the organisation to the senior management team; the top of the office. Finding out what people think is the only means open to management of identifying potential or actual 'blockers' to the organisation actually achieving the tasks it has set itself, *before* the impact of those 'blockers' is felt in the results. Traditional management evaluates performance against specified indicators at regular intervals; new management in the learning organisation listens to the organisation, to stakeholders and to customers, constantly gathering internal and external intelligence and then acting upon it.

The means used to listen vary according to the nature of the intelligence being sought. Staff attitude surveys can test organisational culture and issues of motivation and morale as well as the effectiveness of particular work processes. 'Best of . . . .' groups, cross-disciplinary and non-hierarchical, can address specific entities (eg Best of Recruitment; Best of Teamwork; Best of Support Staff Practice groups). Ad hoc Focus Groups, again drawn from the various echelons of the organisation, can gather information on a specific topic over a defined period and devise action plans. Customers and stakeholders can participate in all of these; alternatively specific groups can be established. The important thing is that 'live' information of an undoctored type is fed regularly and frequently to the senior management team of public sector organisations, so that they can take informed action quickly.

Action: to remove the 'blockers'; to empower the people; to ensure congruence between the vision and what actually happens in the organisation

This is the enabling step. It makes the difference between knowing what ought to be done and ensuring that whatever it is actually happens. It means identifying those old work processes and customs that undermine the new organisation values — and changing them. In an organisation like the Benefits Agency for example, now overtly committed to customer service, it made little sense for some offices to be closed between 12.00 noon and 2.00pm. The old resource allocation system, however, recognised and rewarded the completion of paperwork rather than customer satisfaction, so the offices closed in order that staff could catch up with the paperwork: a good example of disjunction between work processes and articulated organisational values.

Given the framework of change I have outlined, there are three ways in which the human resource management function may itself need to change if it is to play its proper part in the future in the strategic management of organisations in the public sector:

1. *The human resource management function must recognise that it has a significant part to play in facilitating transition and change.* The sea change described in the previous section will necessitate not only changes in work processes but radical changes in organisational culture. Changed attitudes and behaviours; changed organisational culture: these will not happen overnight as a result of senior management teams having negotiated their way through to agreement on organisational mission and values. The HR function must take a lead in ensuring that the organisation's people make the mission statement a reality. That process divides into work with the senior team as well as work with line managers within the body of the organisation. Beneficent organisational change cannot occur without the support and involvement of the top team, and the member with responsibility for the HR function can assist with top team building. He or she can ensure that individuals have a corporate sense of the whole organisation rather than their own function or department; that short-term action does not take precedence over long-term planning, and that the team does not focus upon simple issues because its relationships are not robust enough to cope with real ones.

2. *The human resource management function must help organisations achieve the human resources — the people — they need to achieve their aims.* For example it may need to devise different recruitment criteria to ensure that the organisation gets the right people to start with (and the 'right' people for the future will be different from those who were right in the past). It will need also to establish new types of training, to inculcate or to enhance different types of organisational and managerial behaviour. It will need to ensure that continuous professional development first embeds and then hones appropriate competencies and skills, congruent with the changed values of the organisation.

3. *The achievement of the four high-level management tasks described at the beginning of this section — perceiving, communicating, listening and acting — is an essential prerequisite for the explicit management of change; for cultural change; and for the successful implementation of any or all new systems and processes.* Each of those four tasks requires the involvement and contribution of those who already advise the chief executive on the recruitment, retention, pay, grading, promotion, motivation and performance of the organisation's human resources: the people through whom the organisation achieves or does not achieve its mission, objectives and targets.

The human resource function cannot therefore confine itself to a narrow portfolio of conventional 'personnel' operations: it is an essential part of the organisation's strategic management and must move to centre stage.

The Financial Management Initiative set a sound financial management *framework* for change in much of the private sector, and certainly in central government. If, however, the underpinning assumptions of the change as it continues to develop relate solely to volume and cost there is a risk that value may get lost, and that the public sector may therefore go in entirely the opposite direction from the private sector, which is increasingly emphasising the value and quality of customer-based service. The Citizen's Charter is an initiative designed to redress the balance, and to give focus to customer care and to quality in the public sector. If it is the FMI that set the framework for the last decade, it is the Citizen's Charter that has outlined the management tasks — including the human resource management tasks — for the next one.

The past thirteen years have been a catharsis: a substantial attempt to shift the culture, modes of working and economic orientation of British society. It is too early yet to evaluate how successful the radical changes have been in tackling the issues that they were devised to address. The sheer pace of change in many areas of public service has been unremitting and that, coupled with the effect upon the whole economy of a ferocious recession, has resulted in something of a hiatus. No-one therefore yet knows whether the experiment has been a success in its primary intent of arresting the decline in Britain's economic performance. The jury is out. But in 1959, in his famous lecture on 'The Two Cultures', C P Snow used a simile that risks being as appropriate in 1992 as it was then:

> *I can't help thinking of the Venetian Republic in their last half-century. Like us, they had once been fabulously lucky. They had become rich, as we did, by accident. They had acquired immense political skill, just as we have. A good many of them were tough-minded, realistic, patriotic men. They knew, just as clearly as we know, that the current of history had begun to flow against them. Many of them gave their minds to working out ways to keep going. It would have meant breaking the pattern into which they had crystallised. They were fond of the pattern, just as we are fond of ours. They never found the will to break it.*[4]

Whether or not the policy initiatives of 1979-1992 eventually prove to have arrested or reversed Britain's economic decline however, it is unlikely — especially given the 1992 election result — that the trends themselves will be reversed. The Thatcher and now Major administrations, with their focus upon privatisation, delegation, competition, enterprise, deregulation, service quality and the curtailment of trade union power, have had as profound an effect upon the public as upon the private sector. For those concerned with effective management in the public sector it is only possible to go forward from the present position, there *can* be no going back; and for anyone concerned to see a revitalised public sector playing its part in contributing to the regeneration of both the economy and British society therefore the next five years will be critical — and the task starts here.

> What we call the beginning is often the end
> And to make an end is to make a beginning.
> The end is where we start from.[5]

Case Study: —Human resource management at the Foreign and Commonwealth Office

1. The primary task of personnel management in the FCO has traditionally been to ensure that the manpower requirements — number, skills, grade, language ability — of the Diplomatic Service and home-based jobs are fulfilled and that the right people are put into the right job, in the right place and at the right time. In practical terms this means that over 700 officers in about 20 grades and with a variety of skills and abilities are being promoted, prepared with specialist training and posted, to about 200 Embassies, High Commissions, multilateral missions and consulates in any one year. (Several hundred other staff are also moved between jobs in the UK or brought home every year.) The secondary task (in the past) of the FCO's personnel managers has been to provide a thoughtful, efficient and effective personnel management service to around 5,000 staff: both those who might be described as 'clients' of the service (staff *qua* staff) and those with line management responsibilities including Heads of Mission overseas or Heads of London departments. These tasks were carried out in the FCO for some 20 years by the Personnel Operations Department (POD).

2. By 1989 the structure and work of the POD were under pressure from:
   — changes in the nature and tasks of the FCO;
   — societal issues (notably the trend for individuals to wish to participate in driving their careers);
   — existing management practice in the POD;
   — the need to operate a personnel management service of increasing complexity in a climate of sustained financial constraint, and conflicting demands.

3. In late 1989 POD therefore instigated a fundamental review of the personnel function in the FCO. The review analysed the personnel management needs of the FCO, of line managers and of individuals, and identified a new system that would fulfil them. It was the first study to be undertaken on such a scale by the FCO, and was carried out by a joint team of FCO staff and consultants. A significant feature of the review was the first comprehensive review of staff attitudes, through a survey that covered all staff at home and overseas. Over 2,000 staff responded to the survey, and the analysis of their views informed the design of a performance management system. The actual process of conducting such a comprehensive survey, and the participation in it of staff at all levels and grades and both streams, was itself an instrument in the introduction of significant organisational change.

4. As a result of the review, in early summer 1991 the FCO inaugurated a system of human resource management designed to mediate between the objectives of three constituencies:

* the needs of the *individual* (for coherent and systematic career development and for account to be taken of personal circumstances);
* the needs of line *managers* (for the centre to ensure the posting of an individual competent in terms of skills and personal qualities to act in

particular roles and posts);
- the needs of the *Service* (for a workforce equipped with the appropriate skills to fulfil the mission of the FCO).

The emphasis at the centre is now on the development of the individual and his/her career. This is reflected in revised priorities for Personnel Management Department (PMD), which has replaced the previous objectives and structure of POD.

5. The new system has four broad characteristics:

- clarification of role and function, identifying and making a distinction between the needs of the individual, the posting and the Service.
- delivery of conscious career management to all individuals equally;
- devolution of managerial authority from PMD at the centre to selection boards, consisting largely of line managers in London, who make recommendations on postings and promotions;
- separation of demand and supply, creating a healthy tension between the two.

Clarity of role and function

6. Roles have been clarified within PMD by the division of the overall personnel management function between three groupings with the following functions:

Career development unit	Postings group	Performance assessment unit
All career development and counselling divided by grade — deals primarily with individual staff	All postings overseas and appointments at home — deals primarily with line managers	Assessment of performance, promotability and potential for all streams and all grades

Conscious career management

7. The effort required to juggle the timetable of vacancies driven by fixed-term tours of duty in overseas and home postings, the development needs of individuals as their careers unfolded and the specific staffing demands of line managers overseas resulted in the management of individual careers being 'squeezed'. The needs of the FCO had to be accommodated (vacant posts had to be filled from the human resources currently coming free from other assignments; the question of whether those particular 'pegs' best fitted the particular 'holes' in career development terms became increasingly a secondary consideration). The new human resource management system is intended to ensure that the development needs of individual careers are given weighting at least equal to the needs of line managers and posts. There is also a closer match between the skills of the individual and the skills needs of the job, with more concentration on training if officers are to be given jobs which

make career development sense, but for which they have no experience. Even if the principle needs occasionally to be overridden by operational demands, conscious career management as an underpinning principle is overtly acknowledged and remains a conscious aim. An important sub-theme is equal to treatment for staff in all grades, cadres and streams. This addresses the problem of the different 'cultures' which have grown up in the FCO, as revealed by the staff attitude survey.

8. The effect has been to stimulate a desirable tension between the type and location of jobs falling vacant, and the availability, appropriateness, skills base, past performance and future potential of the individual.

Devolution of managerial authority from central personnel management function to line managers

9. The effect of enabling line managers both to specify the skills requirement for jobs within their command and to sit on selection boards which choose among candidates has resulted in power being shared between the central personnel function and line managers. This has also introduced much greater openness into the posting and promotion system — another tangible, and targeted benefit.

Separation of demand and supply

10. The selection of candidates for posts is now based on an agreed job description, compiled by line managers in a standard format which analyses the skills and qualifications needed for the coming vacancy. The needs of the post (and therefore the Service) — the demand side — are therefore unsullied by the characteristics of the supply side. The resulting system is demand-led not supply-driven; responding to the 'needs of the business' but also to the valid aspirations of individuals.

Why the introduction of human resource management into the FCO worked

11. There are three reasons why the introduction of human resource management into the FCO has been successful:

- **top team support** — support for this major organisational change;
- **extensive consultation** — of the whole of the FCO, led by the head of the personnel management function;
- **effective communication** — of the philosophy of change — a decision was taken at the most senior level to be open, throughout the organisation, about both the need for change and the various stages of the process.

12. In the longer term, senior managers have accepted that the new emphasis on individual career development will best help the FCO meet future demands. People are the FCO's main resource, and are now explicitly to be treated as such.

NOTES

1. *Again a political evaluation. The phrase was originally coined by the American sociologist David Bell.*

2. *This increase in the size of the service sector of the economy has not been able to offset fully the decline in manufacturing industry. Two million jobs were lost in industrial production between 1979 and 1981. (Randlesome, C, Brierly, Brunton, Gordon and King, Business Cultures in Europe, Heineman, 1990, p 167).*

3. *And in which there is more of a custom of criticising for failures rather than feting successes.*

4. *Given the Government's stated intention of rolling back the frontiers of the State the numbers employed in the public sector have remained remarkably static. Some of the apparent decrease is actually more a reclassification.*

5. *This last is particularly important, since most organisations assume both growth and staff turnover, and therefore a flow of promotion opportunities. The tasks in the public sector will be to find new ways of maintaining motivation and morale, and of managing human resources in a static organisation.*

6. *Unless the top 12% includes all line managers responsible for (and able in) the development of staff. Of the total civil service for example 80% are outside London and 50% are under 35. These are the people with whom the public come into contact as recipients of government services.*

7. *Or longer. Some civil servants claim that the spirit of the old Board of Education still haunts the Department for Education.*

8. *Or have not in the past; one East Midlands college has recently turned a deficit of £800,000 into an overspend of £5.5 million in the first year of its delegated budget. Education Vol 178, No 5, p 81.*

9. *Perhaps the Public Accounts Committee is the nearest public sector equivalent.*

10. *Some, like one or two local authorities, more than others.*

11. *One intention being to encourage the private sector to take over the role of statutory bodies (eg the Industry Training Boards) that have been abolished.*

12. *The right to retain it may still be a struggle, although attitudes and organisational culture in HM Treasury are shifting too.*

13. *A senior civil servant observed recently that something about civil servants'*

training in the past appears to have resulted in their being good at analysing the ten things wrong with any proposal, but less good at generationg innovative ideas for improving it.

14. *There is widespread recognition throughout the sector of the importance of effective human resource management in achieving the transition: see for example the Report to the Prime Minister on Making the most of Next Steps: 'the drive for better performance will mean . . . changes in attitude and approach and size, structure and method of working'; '. . . high performance comes more readily from people who care and who feel personally responsible and are ready to tackle challenges . . .'*

15. *Something that is in the best interests of both citizens and government in the UK. Hamish McRae argued recently that there is, particularly in Britain, a great desire to respect the public sector, to want to see it do well; that for most people in the industrial world the public sector symbolises the shabby and the second-rate; that as a result of the discovery that people want good public services both main political parties have focused upon quality in service provision, and that therefore 'the public sector is in with a chance'. But the emphasis on service quality, the Citizens Charter, etc will, in his view only really affect public sector management if there is a big cultural change. See 'Rebirth of the public sector' Hamish McRae, Independent, 31 July 1991.*

16. *This is a Herculean task. But if it can be acieved then the rebirth of the public sector that Hamish McRae described could come about.*

REFERENCES

1. Margaret Thatcher (Bruges Speech, 20.09.88).
2. Holmes, M, (1985) *The First Thatcher Government, 1979-1983*, Wheatsheaf, London.
3. Randlesome, C *et al* (1990) *Business Cultures in Europe*, Heineman, London.
4. Snow, C P, *Two Cultures* and *A Second Look* (lecture of 1959).
5. Eliot, T S, 'Little Gidding', V
6. Randlesome, *ibid*, p 169

12

ORGANISATION AND HUMAN RESOURCE MANAGEMENT : THE EUROPEAN PERSPECTIVE

By Mike Stanton

This chapter deals with organisation and human resource management issues in a European context, both within the European Community and beyond. It does not cover in detail the EC's proposed social legislation, because this is still in the process of formation and discussion. It focuses mainly on:

- Culture management and organisation dynamics
- Reward
- Organisation
- Manpower resourcing, development and training
- Industrial relations and the management of change

Terms and conditions of employment are not covered, because they vary widely, require detailed attention beyond the capacity of this chapter, and are dealt with fully in many publications, of which the most recent at the time of writing include the European Management Guide on Terms and Conditions of Employment (IDS/IPM 1991).

A complete guide to the European employment law situation can be found in *Employment Law in Europe*, published by Coopers & Lybrand and Gower, September 1991. The issues addressed are not only those of the European Community (EC). The roles of countries like Switzerland, Austria and the non-member Nordic countries cannot be ignored. The old Eastern bloc countries have, however, been omitted. Although the 'second revolution' of 1990–91 may allow many of them to join the European fold, it is too early to comment usefully on their likely effect. Initially their overriding concern is to introduce basic labour market and personnel management practices.

The process of converting the European collection of nation states into an integrated continental economy is well on its way. It has an inexorable momentum. It carries major implications for the management of the critical base resource of all organisations — people.

For we Europeans, particularly for those of us inhabiting an offshore island, this Europeanisation process is not an easy one. The issues and answers are not all obvious to us. But for our American counterparts it represents the normalisation of Europe — for them, the notion of a continental economy is familiar. Many American companies are applying American continental personnel and organisational principles to their European operations.

Europe (the EC) has 323 million people producing $5 trillion in GNP; the US's 250 million people produce $5.2 trillion; Japan's 125 million population produces $3.2 trillion. Europe's lower productivity stems mainly from the fragmentation of our continent into nations. The intention of the EC to bring about, by majority vote, free movement of goods, free movement of labour and professionals, and a common market for services, has enormous implications for the organisation and management of its human resources.

Surprisingly, standards of living do not vary much more widely across the European continent than they do across the American one. Given an average standard of living of 100:

Portugal	=	55	Mississipi =	66
Luxembourg	=	133	Connecticut =	134

Some companies have always functioned across European borders. Some of these are EC-based (Shell, Unilever, Philips); others are European non-EC (Nestlé, Ericsson); many are American (IBM, Ford). The personnel chiefs and staff of these companies are used to dealing with cross-border HR problems, with or without 1992. Many more companies have been joining their ranks recently.

The task of the strategically-minded HR or personnel director is to propose and implement personnel and organisation policies which will continuously improve the performance of their organisation. In the European context, this demands an understanding of the matters dealt within this chapter. Many of these are peculiar to Europe: differences of language, tax regime, etc, are not so significant within the US.

The information related in this chapter is based on practical experience across Europe, not theory. The experiences quoted are recent examples of approaches and changes made, many of them innovative, which have worked. Some of the thinking is inductive, because we have not yet arrived at some of the challenges which face us in the Europe of the late 1990s. We are still forecasting what these may turn out to be. Many of the examples quoted are from direct experience of consulting for the organisations involved; others are from indirect sources.

- flatter, more flexible, more organic Europe-wide organisation structures, market facing and focused on key competences;
- a more strategic, policy-making and international role for HR;
- greater sensitivity to national cultural differences among multinational members of boards of directors; consequent agreement to reach organisational objectives by a range of different routes;
- convergence of the HR policies of European and Multinational corporations (MNCs);
- the Euromanager becoming the glue between subsidiaries of European MNCs.

A Conference Board Europe survey indicates the challenges, trends and propensities for organisational change, as perceived by 59 HR executives working in 14 countries and 21 industries throughout Europe, to be as set out in Table 12.1. A low score indicates high urgency or likelihood.

So our attention must be directed towards management skills, flexibility, and flatter Europe-wide structures for organisation and for pay, for the benefit of our customers.

The Single European Act and the Social Charter will bring about a minimum level of social and employment standards, through qualified majority voting in EC countries. However, unanimity is still required for legislation on employee rights and taxation, which will therefore change more slowly and it remains to be seen what the implications will be of our opting out of the Social Charter at Maastricht. The very use of the term 'social' to denote the employee relations aspects of business, and the relationship of employers to the community at large, is one which the British are still getting used to.

The impact of the EC on the UK is perhaps most visible in its effect on the English language, which is now increasingly becoming the lingua franca of business world-wide (although it has not yet supplanted French in many parts of the EC bureaucracy).

CULTURE MANAGEMENT AND ORGANISATION DYNAMICS

A *culture* is a set of attitudes, values and beliefs which, in the absence of specific instructions, guide the behaviour of individuals. This kind of definition is now becoming familiar in relation to corporate cultures. But it is equally significant in relation to national cultures, and the styles and perceptions of management and organisation which go with them. In both cases, while we talk about changing and managing cultures and styles, it is in practice only the resultant behaviour which we really need to see change.

We all know about the obvious differences in national cultures which we observe when we travel — despite the best efforts of certain consumer brands to introduce a uniform greyness, the differences in language, food, architecture, dress, rules for proximity and physical contact between countries remain apparent, and seem, according to the latest evidence, to be becoming wider.

238

Table 12.1 Challenges, trends and propensities for organisational change

(i) What are the top ten most urgent challenges facing human resources managers in Europe in the next five years? (Rank 1 for 'extremely urgent' to 10 for 'relatively unimportant')

		Score
1.	Enhancing management skills	2.8
2.	Skill shortages	3.6
3.	Promoting flexibility	4.3
4.	Training	4.6
5.	Encouraging participation	5.6
6.	Containing wage rises	6.1
7.	Work/family issues	6.7
8.	EC Social Charter	6.8
9.	Hiring more women	7.1
10.	Industrial unrest	7.6

(ii)Which trends in the European labour market are likely in the next five years? (Score 1 for 'likely on a major scale' to 10 for 'impossible')

European convergence of:

	Score
Executive salaries	3.7
Benefit packages	5.1
Vacations/holidays	5.2
Wage levels	5.4
Collective barganing	6.6

Emergence of:

More trans-border migration	3.3
The 'Euro-executive'	3.4
Unified EC labour laws	5.1
Pan-European Trades Unions	5.9
Europe-wide pensions	6.0

(iii) How is your organisation likely to change? (Score 1 for 'will increase on a major scale' to 10 for 'will not be a priority')

	Score
Customer focus	2.4
Global strategy	2.7
Flat hierachies	3.6
Project management	3.9
Flexible pay schemes	4.3
Strategic alliances	4.4
Diverse personnnel mix	4.5
Acquisitions	4.9
Decentralisation	4.9
Non-pay benefits	5.5
Downsizing	5.7
Profit sharing	5.7
Subcontracting	6.1
Vertical intergration	6.4

Culture is, in fact, only one of the many softer aspects of organisation. All the business processes in use, the meetings held, reports generated, communications programmes, one to one interactions are collectively the life of the organisation. Each European country has its own set of assumptions about organisation dynamics, as has each business. For example, each country has a different perception of what organisational hierarchies are for, and how they should work. Table1 12.2 shows the width of the gap between Swedish perceptions at one extreme and Italian perceptions at the other. American data is included as a reference point.

Table 12.2   National differences in the perception of organisational hierarchical relationships systems

817 Managers from ten countries	Sweden	US	Netherlands	Great Britain	Denmark	Switzerland	Germany	Belgium	France	Italy
Sample size	50	50	42	190	54	63	72	45	219	32
% Agreement with: Most organisations would be better off if conflict could be eliminated forever.	4	6	17	13	19	18	16	27	24	41
% Agreement with: It is important for a manager to have at hand precise answers to most of the questions that his subordinates may raise about their work.	10	18	17	27	23	38	46	44	53	66
% Disagreement with: In order to have efficient work relationships, it is often necessary to bypass the hierarchical line.	22	32	39	31	37	41	46	42	42	75
% Agreement with: An organisational structure in which certain subordanates have two direct bosses should be avoided at all costs.	64	54	60	74	69	76	79	84	83	81
% Average agreement/disagreement	25	28	33	36	37	43	47	50	50	66

Source: Andre Laurent:The Cultural Diversity of Western Conceptions of Management; *International Studies of Management and Organisation,* Vol. XIII, No1-2, pp75-96

The most striking diversity is that against the third issue: how far would you disagree with the view that, in order to have efficient working relationships, it is often necessary to bypass the hierarchical line? Most Swedes, American and Dutch managers saw such bypassing as normal and necessary, but most Italian managers saw bypassing as unacceptable. The scope for misunderstanding and friction between managers of different nationalities working together is significant.

Hofstede ran his research inside big multinational corporations, each of which had a strong corporate culture, apparently international in its effect. Yet, contrary to expectations, he found that national differences were no smaller in these corporations, and in some cases became marginally wider. The only explanation offered seems to be that, to defend themselves against the effect of the corporate culture, managers will retreat further into their national cultures. These differences have been explored further by Fons Trompenaars, who believes that 'as national boundaries become blurred, cultural boundaries tend to be reinforced', and that its cultural diversity is potentially Europe's greatest strength, if only we can learn to capitalise on it. Human resources managers have a major role to offer here.

Yet even the idea of human resource management is culturally laden. Both Laurent and Trompenaars identified a natural divide between the Latin and North West European cultures. For the Anglo-Saxon culture the basic principle of job evaluation, namely separation of person and job, is understandable and usable, although with increasing difficulty. But for the Latin cultures, which base organisation much more on personal relationships and power which emanate from educational standing and the concept of the 'patron', job evaluation is an often unworkable imposition from outside. Pay for performance suffers from similar difficulties.

There is no one best way of organising. We have sought to imitate or even transplant American and Japanese practices with only partial success: our apparent commonality of language with the United States has perhaps encouraged this. The Latin cultures in Europe are still struggling to come to terms with the systems and methods orientation of the North West European countries, and the latter have not yet learned to respect the mutual relationships base of the Latin cultures. We also make different assumptions about the size and range of our personal privacy area, and the extent to which the public area of behaviour may intrude into it. We have to find a way to benefit from these and many other aspects of our multidimensional continent if we are to ensure that our people compete successfully with the rest of the world.

Well developed tools now exist for coming to terms with these difficult and complex issues within organisations. Their use needs careful, and culturally sensitive, application.

One specific area within which these differences must be managed, if they are not to cause damage, is international mergers. These will naturally become more common in the new Europe. Up to 50 per cent of mergers fail, and the most frequent cause of failure is cultural and human resource management difficulty. Substantial experience in managing international mergers effectively now exists, and needs to be learned from.

REWARD

In any context, reward structures should be configured so as to:

- retain employees at optimal cost within the appropriate labour market;
- contain and control business costs;
- reward desired performance (at enterprise, team and individual level);
- motivate — or, rather, provide a base platform on which to build motivation;
- minimise tax liabilities.

In a European context, this means designing reward structures appropriate to the employee with pan-European responsibilities, employees who are likely to be required to be mobile across the continent, and the retention of employees with special skills who are at risk of cross-border poaching. In practice, these employees will be mainly executives, professionals or technologists, although increasingly they may also include skilled craftsmen and technicians.

Variable cost/performance related structures

Many European companies are now introducing structures which combine a variable element of between 15 and 40 per cent with a fixed base to which no 'cost of living' or inflation-related increase applies. This variable element may contain up to three (or occasionally more) factors, for example:

- business performance
- division or team performance
- individual performance, often divided into measurable and non-measurable factors.

Figure 12.1 shows such a structure put in place by a European based global furnishings company headquartered in Austria. In this case, the pay curve/job family principle has also been used. The pay package is made up of three elements:

1. A divisional performance based element making up 10 per cent of salary.
2. A profit centre based element (20 per cent)
3. A personal objectives based element of 5 per cent.

This structure has been implemented worldwide.

Share option schemes

Such schemes, very popular and increasingly tax-effective in the UK, have not been adopted to any significant level by continentally-based European companies. This may change as the official British attitude to continental methods of employee participation begins to shift from outright resistance to

Bonus as % of salary

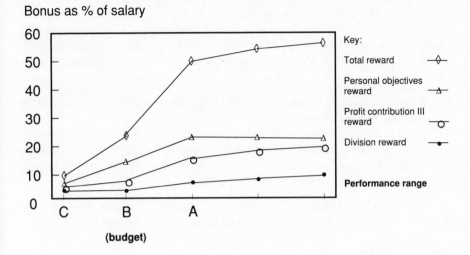

Figure 12.1 Performance curves

proposals for Europe to adopt, or at least accept, the 'Equity Option' as a legitimate and effective form of employee participation.

Pay comparisons

Pay comparisons are essential but full of pitfalls. Press reports on the comparative levels of directors' salaries are often misleading. One of the most difficult aspects is the reduction of pay data to a like-for-like basis.

Table 12.3 shows a comparison of the upper quartile cash pay levels and buying power of chief executives in six European countries, after allowing for tax/social security deductions and for the cost of living index; all figures are in £000 Sterling.

Table 12.3 Cash pay levels and buying power of chief executives

	Total cash pay	Buying power
Switzerland	109	68
France	88	55
W. Germany	108	51
UK	69	39
Netherlands	73	32
Denmark	76	27

Source: Wyatt Group reported in *Financial Times*, May 1989.

Although job evaluations are now often disavowed as a method of assessment of job value, because it is now recognised that jobs themselves do not possess value, they are a useful reference point for assessing relative market worth. Assessing the value of a job in a European context presents special difficulties, because of the national differences described above. The best solution is to go back to basics:

- What do the market data indicate to be the price of this kind of job for an organisation of a given size?
- What is the propensity of the individual (or job/skill group) to leave? In addition to the usual factors, this will now need to take into consideration the likelihood of a continental-based competitor recruiting an individual or categories of people with particular skills.

The thorough solution is to commission a bespoke survey of the price and demand for the type of job under consideration.

Tax considerations

Obtaining the most tax advantageous arrangements is a minefield best left to the specialists. Rules and hence transnational best practice vary widely and frequently from country to country.

Benefits

Other benefits are legion, and vary considerably from country to country, according to social history, culture and tax regimes. We deal here with only the two most common: pensions and company cars.

In a European context, the idea of flexible benefits (cafeteria benefits) may be appropriate, at least for the potentially mobile executive, although there are many pitfalls and risks in introducing these systems. Accurate assessments of costs and values are particularly difficult for both employer and employee. Such schemes are also highly dependent on employees making accurate forecasts about likely future circumstances, and on employers making good forecasts of likely take-up rates for various benefits. The employer needs to institute sufficiently good career planning to forecast future work locations — usually difficult, at least in the private sector — or else ensure that the flexible benefits system is able to absorb unpredicted changes in either individual or employer circumstances. Timing and nature of children's education needs, health problems, and arrangements for care of elderly relations, are among the most difficult of these.

Pensions

Probably the most significant barrier (closely followed by the growth of dual career families) to the international mobility of staff is the non-mobility of pensions. This is a complex area in which advice from international specialists must be sought.

As national borders become increasingly irrelevant to businesses, inevitably there will be an increase in the number of expatriates, adding to the five million Community nationals who already work in another member state. Multinational companies have always encountered problems in developing a coherent and robust expatriate benefit policy, but these problems could well increase in the future if the following trends continue:

- a tendency to move management around more frequently for temporary periods as part of their career development and to meet business needs;
- a move towards a senior, and occasionally middle, management team consisting of many nationalities.

A well-defined expatriate benefit policy is essential if expatriates are to be attracted, retained and motivated by multinationals at what, for many of them, will be an unsettling time. There can be a danger of developing ad hoc solutions which fail to ensure that a realistic cost is borne by each group company.

The provision of retirement benefits to expatriates will remain difficult until the community agrees on a flexible system which allows cross-border membership of certain pension schemes without tax disadvantages. This is unlikely to happen for many years.

Company cars

Provision of company cars varies widely between countries, as shown in Table 12.4.

Table 12.4 Provision of company cars throughout Europe

	Car holders (%)		
	Level 3 posts*	Level 4 posts*	
		Finance	*Marketing*
UK	97	96	99
Netherlands	92	56	90
Ireland	88	77	89
Germany	86	52	94
Italy	85	68	67
France	81	29	52
Sweden	81	53	84
Spain	78	36	52
Belgium	77	78	83
Denmark	70	not available	
Austria	68	31	78
Switzerland	32	5	36

*Level 3 = director or head of major function
 Level 4 = senior manager
Source: Monks Partnership European Company Car Survey, January 1991

Thus Spain and Germany have significantly lower incidences of car provision for senior managers in finance functions than for senior managers in marketing and for directors/heads of major functions. This may reflect different policies for levels at which 'perk' (as opposed to business use related) cars are provided.

Perhaps surprisingly, tax considerations appear not to be the major differentiating factor between countries. Switzerland has the lowest take-up rate, despite the tax efficiency of car provision in that country. Taxation of cars varies widely: several countries tax on the new list price of the car (Austria 18 per cent; Netherlands 20-24 per cent; Sweden 26-30 per cent) and some on mileage (Denmark and Germany for home to work travel). In the UK, cars are taxed by reference to a mixture of engine size (or value) and business mileage. Current trends in fiscal policy make it increasingly cheaper to pay cash instead.

ORGANISATION

The principal organisational decision to be made by any company which operates in several European countries is simply: will it best secure its own future by seeking to operate some or all of its functions on a pan-European basis, or by continuing to operate nationally? This decision is not necessarily one to which only rational judgement will be applied. Among the more emotional factors which may come into play are:

- What does past experience and organisation tradition indicate? For American companies, working continentally is the norm: reasons may need to be found for not doing so.
- Where would the most senior existing executives (and their spouses) who may be redeployed into European roles like to live?
- What is the preference of the most powerful existing operation?

Such decisions are based on a mixture of rationality, emotion, and power. These decisions must also be made in the light of expectations about what may happen to the organisation and its markets and customers in the future.

The latest thinking about organisational trends needs to be taken into account. For example, if the current thinking about the 'New Organisation' is right, any European organisation should, indeed must, deal in parallel with systems configuration and organisation structure.

Principal issues for consideration

The main issues to be addressed in arriving at a rational judgement about how Europeanised to become fall into five groups:

1. Conditioning Parameters — these include:

    - tax considerations; these must condition the corporate legal structure, and may influence organisation structure: forecasting the moment at which Europe-wide tax regimes will emerge may become critical;

- the characteristics of the market in which the business finds itself, including:
  — optimal distribution channels
  — the practice of key customers in relation to Europe.

2. Strategic considerations — the main purpose of any organisation is to promote coherence in the interaction of its people in order to fulfil its purpose. In most cases the purpose is defined in terms of strategies for serving customers, maximising shareholder value, and satisfying other stakeholders, including employees.

   Any rethink of organisational arrangements must therefore be made in the light of the corporate strategy — whether it is well articulated or not. If it is not, then one of the first tasks of the organisation designer must be to get it articulated to the satisfaction of the key decision makers and stakeholders. Matching the strategy to the corporate style and to national cultures within which it operates may be essential.

3. Organisational principles — the more we learn about organisation, the fewer principles seem to apply. Spans of control, centralisation/decentralisation, function/profit centre: these are all now questionable as principles. Different situations, different products or services, different histories, changing times, new electronic technology, current fashions; all demand organisational arrangements tailored to their need. For Europe, however, two specific principles do apply:

- The framework of company law: currently, apart from the still untested idea of the Societas Europea (SE), there is no choice but to work within the many disparate legal systems of the nation states of Europe.
- National differences must be taken into account: principles which have worked in one national culture must not be applied willy-nilly to another.

4. Practicalities and constraints — these are legion, but the one unique to the European situation, and unfamiliar to those from English speaking countries, is the enshrinement in law of the right of works councils to be consulted, as in the Netherlands and Germany, and the rights of trade unions to delay change pending their own independent investigation of the implications of a management side proposal, as in France and, to a lesser extent, Italy.

5. Culture and leadership — these 'softer' issues may have as important an influence on the eventual outcome of any organisation restructuring as any of the issues mentioned above. In a European context, they present special challenges.

The most difficult decision to make may be the decision not to 'go European' when all about you *are* doing so. One major chemical industry company with an existing strong presence in many European countries has, after skirmishing with the idea of a pan-European organisation, decided to go national. It has closed its embryonic European headquarters and is focusing on creating sets of nationally consistent human resource policies and practices. This is not an insular company: unlike many of its apparently more European counterparts, it has four nationalities on its executive board, it has a strong globalisation policy, and many of its most strategic resources are already globalised.

Figure 12.2 shows the decision process which should be gone through when

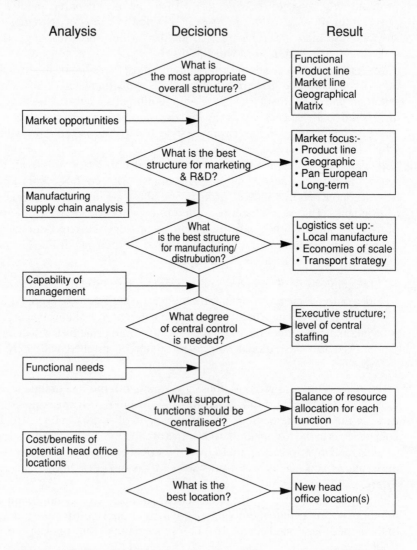

Figure 12.2 Developing pan-European operations — organisation structure

developing a pan-European structure. It is not exhaustive, but indicates the inputs, decisions and outputs not to be missed. The order indicated is not mandatory, although location of HQ, for instance, can only be decided after identifying which functions to centralise.

The management of change

The best judgement will be of little use unless the change process is properly managed. In practice, this demands early consultation with all those who may be affected, at all levels, including Government and trade unions. In some countries, notably the Netherlands and Germany, this is required by law, and if not properly done, can generate resistance which can become difficult to manage. Many change management issues are more to do with organisation dynamics than with structure.

MANPOWER RESOURCING, DEVELOPMENT AND TRAINING

This section covers management development as a subset of employee development, because the combined effect of flattening organisational hierarchies and the Europeanisation of development and training is increasingly blurring the boundaries.

Every country in Europe, with the exception of Ireland, will experience a reduction of around 20 per cent in the under 25 population by 1995, with only a slow rise thereafter. Together with the increasing proportion of technological and other knowledge workers, this will create serious scarcity at all levels. Some countries are better placed to respond to this than others.

The mid-1980s reports Competence and Competition[2] (Chris Hayes Associates), Challenge to Complacency[3] (Coopers and Lybrand), followed by Charles Handy's and John Constable's reports on The Making of British Managers[4] demonstrated that the French and German systems of vocational and management training produce higher quality people, in greater numbers, than the UK. Italian employees have the right to 150 hours of training time per annum. In the EC, programmes like COMETT and EUROTECNET are extending vocational training more widely on a European basis. Although the free movement of labour throughout the EC was enshrined in the Treaty of Rome, it is only becoming a reality as the effect of the 1985 EC legislation on the transferability of qualifications becomes effective. In France, despite this, the legal definition of a manager as a university or grande-ecole graduate may yet frustrate the ambitions of managers from countries with less formal and well-developed systems of management education.

Is there a need for the 'Euromanager'? Companies like ICL, CMB, and others with pan-European training initiatives think so, as does BP, which has put all its European HQ managers through a training programme in national culture differences. Saxton Bampfylde have gone so far as to hazard a definition and categorisation of the Euromanager, ranging from the senior statesman (aged over 45, in multinationals), through the ex-patriate (several years as deputy General Manager, XYZ, Spain) to the Euro-yuppie (multilingual, multicultural, peripatetic, and untried). More seriously, they find the deep background factors which create cultural flexibility are:

- small country origins, where English has often become a business lingua franca;
- hybrid origins: the products of a multinational marriage;
- hybrid education: children born into one culture but schooled in another;
- business school, particularly an internationally orientated one like INSEAD and IMD;
- a multicultural marriage.

Each country does not mean the same thing by the same word: the ideas of 'cadre' in France, 'Kader' in Germany and 'quadro' in Italy have different nuances — and no word for the idea exists in English at all, although the French usage, having entered the language through a military route, is catching on.

Research by M. Saias (Competitivite et strategies des entreprises face a l'horizon 93, in *Revue Francaise de Gestion*, May 1989, quoted by Bournois and Chauchat: Making Managers in Europe, *European Management Journal*, March 1990) indicates that there is a relationship between level of management skill and employee motivation (Figure 12.3).

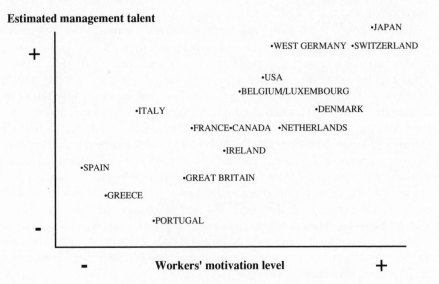

Figure 12.3 Management talent as a motivator

The practicalities of training presents some Euro-hazards too. Recently when training together managers from the German, French, Spanish, Belgian and British subsidiaries of a large manufacturer, we found the different expectations of teaching styles and levels to be a greater barrier than expected. The German preference for formal teaching, with much documentation and high specificity and accuracy, together with the French similar preference for a formal approach, but oral rather than written, and the British penchant for group work and open-ended sessions, meant that reduction to the lowest common denominator was not enough. We had first to teach learning.

For European success, management development — and the development of highly qualified non-managerial staff — is going to have to be well planned. It will need sophisticated market-based job profile/person profile matching systems, capable of handling both individual and employer needs, on a continental, multilingual basis.

On the broader level, perhaps countries which are investing in management and vocational training will prosper. Ireland is well placed in this regard; with its high birthrate and high quality English language education system, qualified Europeans may become a principal export.

INDUSTRIAL RELATIONS AND THE MANAGEMENT OF CHANGE

The industrial relations considerations worthy of consideration with regard to Europe relate mainly to the effect of EC legislation. The situation is fluid, and heavily influenced by the stances of national governments, notably that of the UK, and by the advice of employers' representative bodies and trade unions, namely the CBI in the UK; the effect of trade union comment has been marginal in the UK in recent years.

The essence of EC legislation, influenced by the confederation of employers in Europe (UNICE) and by the European TUC (ETUC) has been to attempt to create a minimum level of employee rights across the continent, embodied in a Social Charter. These rights include:

- freedom of association;
- recognition of trade unions;
- protection of individual employee rights;
- collective agreements.

Much progress has been made, agreement reached and legislation enacted, in the fields of individual employment protection, particularly with respect to collective dismissals/redundancies, transfers of undertakings and insolvency. However, legislation concerning the rights of employees still requires unanimity, so further progress may be slow.

Equal treatment legislation covering equal pay for work of equal value, social security and equality of treatment has already had its effect. The further extension of the 'social dimension' expressed in the Social Charter and enacted in directives, may not achieve the objectives envisaged by some in time for the end of 1992, but its advance will doubtless be inexorable, as time and changes of government and government policy in the various countries have their effect.

The co-determination provisions in individual countries, particularly Germany and the Netherlands, which have similar systems; in France and to lesser extent Italy, which have somewhat different systems, can have a major slowing effect on organisational change programmes proposed by employers, and may, if the process is not well handled by people familiar with the system, prevent certain changes altogether. Even apparently minor changes, such as new training programmes, may attract the interest of co-determination bodies in major employers, especially if they have international or European ramifications.

Terms and conditions of employment, and employee rights, are dealt with on a country by country basis in the IDS/IPM European Management Guides.

A more detailed exposition of potential provision for employee participation is given in the chapter of this book on Employee Communication.

REFERENCES

1. Coopers & Lybrand, 1991
2. National Economic Development Office and Manpower Services Commission (1984) *Competence and Competition: Training and Education in the Federal Republic of Germany, the US and Japan,* National Economic Development Office, London.
3. Coopers & Lybrand (1985) *A Challenge to Complacency: Changing Attitudes to Training,* Report to the Manpower Services Commission and the National Economic Development office, Imprint, London.
4. Constable, J and McCormick, R (1987) *The Making of British Managers,* the British Institute of Management (BIM), and Confederation of British Industry (CBI), London. Hardy, C (1987) *The Making of Managers* MSC, NEDC, BIM.

13

HUMAN RESOURCE MANAGEMENT IN ACTION: A JOINT APPROACH

Michael Armstrong and Roger Cooke

The message delivered throughout this book is that all managers are concerned equally with the management of human resources: it is not the preserve of the personnel function. And it is perhaps this feature which most clearly distinguishes human resource management (HRM) from personnel management. HRM is business- as well as people-orientated. Personnel management has tended to put people first, taking less interest in the strategic needs of the business.

CHARACTERISTICS OF THE HRM APPROACH

The HRM approach has three main characteristics: it is strategic, integrative and enabling.

The strategic approach

HRM takes a long-term view of where the business is going. Top management assumes full responsibility for seeing that there is strategic fit between business and human resource strategies. It ensures that human resource strategies emerge from and support business strategies. It takes into account any human resource opportunities or constraints that might affect the strategic direction in which the organisation is going.

The integrative approach

HRM is integrative in two senses. First, it integrates human resource and business activities. It provides for a sense of purpose in the management of people which starts at the top and permeates the organisation.

Secondly, it integrates HRM processes to achieve synergy and added value. For example, a performance management system can be the vehicle for cascading corporate objectives downwards throughout the organisation thus concentrating people's minds on what matters to the business. It can underpin such core values as innovation, teamwork, quality and the pursuit of excellence. Additionally it can be used to clarify roles and objectives, to improve the ways in which managers lead, guide, motivate and develop their staff, and to provide a basis for career planning, management development programmes and performance related pay. It can thus become a unified and powerful force for improving organisational effectiveness.

The enabling approach

The enabling approach involves:

- creating an environment in which managers can obtain, develop and motivate the people they need;
- empowering individuals and teams with the skills and confidence they need to perform well;
- developing an organisation climate which is conducive to innovation, growth, quality, commitment and high level performance.

SHARING THE RESPONSIBILITY

If these are the main characteristics of the HRM approach, how can they be put into effect? Top management sets the direction, line management deploys its human resources to get things done, so where does the human resource function come in?

The answer to this question is that human resource management should be seen as a business partnership. The roles of each member of that partnership may differ but all members share the responsibility of taking the business forward. It is a matter of emphasis. Each party is concerned with strategy, integration and enabling the organisation to perform effectively. In the case of top management, the emphasis is on the formulation of strategy, on ensuring that everyone in the organisation is aware of the part they have to play in achieving strategic goals and on monitoring performance. Line management is largely responsible for the implementation of the business strategy but is very much concerned with integration and enabling the business to make the best use of its resources. The human resource function is heavily involved in integration and enabling, but always operates within the context of the business strategy.

The rest of this chapter explores in more detail the respective roles of top, line and human resource management.

THE ROLE OF TOP MANAGEMENT

The roles of top management in strategic human resource development are to:

- define or redefine HRM philosophies;
- take into account human resource factors in formulating business plans;
- prepare 'agendas for change';
- act as custodian of the human resources of the organisation.

HRM philosophies

HRM philosophies refer to the ways in which people are treated in an organisation. Two basic philosophies can be identified, but each organisation will need to develop its own in the light of its special requirements. First, the 'hard HRM' philosophy, which has been adopted by a number of US organisations and which means dealing with employees as just another factor in the input-output equation, to be managed as efficiently and tightly as any other resource. HRM strategies are concerned with improving employee utilisation (the cost efficient approach) and, in effect, getting employees to accept that their interests coincide with those of the organisation — the principles of mutuality and commitment. An HRM industrial relations strategy will develop direct links with individuals and groups of workers, and may bypass the trade unions and their representatives. Employees may be involved in the improvement of quality and productivity but will not contribute to business decision making.

Alternatively, the 'soft HRM' approach pays more attention to the fact that employees cannot be treated just like any other resource. The way in which they are managed is based on an understanding of the values and needs that guide and motivate them. There is more emphasis on strategies for gaining commitment by informing employees about the company's mission, values, plans and trading conditions, involving them in deciding on how tasks should be carried out, and grouping them in teams which work without strict supervision. But it stops short of advocating worker participation in corporate decision making.

HRM philosophies may be expressed clearly and positively as an integral part of the business philosophy as in IBM where the emphasis is on 'respect for the individual'. They can also be represented as a statement of core values, as in Book Club Associates where they were defined as follows:

- **People** — members of the organisation are treated fairly and as responsible human beings. They are given the opportunity to develop their skills and careers, and the firm is constantly aware of the need to improve the quality of their working life.
- **Partnership** — all employees are treated as partners in the enterprise, to be involved in matters that affect them and to be kept informed about future plans and results.

255

- **Professionalism** — the effective and dedicated use and development of skills is a prime requirement.
- **Productivity through people** — higher productivity and profitability are achieved by effective leadership and the development of a committed, highly trained, well-motivated and well-rewarded work force.

HRM philosophies reflect the culture of the organisation but they can help to underpin and, indeed, change it. In organisations with strong cultures there is likely to be a clear philosophy, although this may not have been articulated, especially if a particularly hard HRM approach is adopted.

Business planning

The business plans formulated by top management will impact on the organisational structure and will determine resourcing plans for recruitment, retention, training, development and, if necessary, downsizing. They will also affect reward and employee relations strategies. But this should be a reciprocal process — business plans create HR plans but are in turn affected by human resource considerations.

Agendas for change

Top management articulates agendas for change for implementation by line managers. But on what may be the most important items on the agenda — human resource matters — the head of the HR function has a key role to play by prompting and advising top managers and by providing 'levers for change'.

Custodian of human resources

Top management is the custodian of the human resources of the organisation in the same way as, collectively, directors are the stewards of the functional and physical assets of the business. Chief executive officers will be particularly concerned with resourcing and reward matters for senior managers — who is appointed, who stays or goes, how are they rewarded? They will also be concerned with the overall organisation structure and with critical questions relating to the role of the centre and the extent to which authority is devolved to business units. Decisions in these areas will have major effects on human resourcing and employee relations plans.

THE ROLE OF LINE MANAGEMENT

Within the framework of company personnel policies and procedures and in line with their budgets, line managers are accountable for achieving their results by making the best use of their human resources. The desirable trend to increase the accountability of line managers has been accompanied by a recognition that they have to be given the maximum amount of authority over their own resources. This means, for example, not only recruiting and developing staff but also making pay decisions (subject to policy guidelines and budgets) and handling employee relations issues themselves without any help from industrial relations specialists.

In particular, line managers:

- define their human resource requirements;
- set up and maintain organisation structures;
- set objectives and define performance measures for their staff;
- monitor performance against objectives and take any corrective action required;
- appraise staff;
- provide 'on the job' training and counselling;
- motivate and reward their staff;
- develop teamwork;
- develop a 'total quality' approach amongst their staff;
- create a cooperative climate of employee relations;
- handle departmental or shop floor industrial relations issues;
- communicate with staff and involve them in decision making;
- deal with discipline and grievances;
- maintain a healthy and safe working environment;
- implement equal opportunity and other personnel policies.

THE ROLE OF THE HUMAN RESOURCE FUNCTION

The above list of managers' human resource responsibilities is a formidable one. Some will be good at meeting them, some will not. Many will benefit from the guidance and help that personnel professionals can provide. And the organisation as a whole will benefit if the human resource function takes on the responsibility of monitoring the implementation of personnel policies and procedures, identifying any cases where standards are not being met and advising on any actions required.

At top management level, the head of the human resource function should be part of the team which, acting on a collegiate basis, is deciding where the organisation is going and how it is going to get there, and thus monitoring its performance. The HR director can and should make a powerful contribution to the deliberations of this team and to initiating new approaches to the management of human resources.

Factors affecting the role of the HR function

There is no one 'right way' to structure the role of the HR function. It depends on a number of factors which will determine the boundaries between what the HR function and line managers do, the amount of power exercised by the function, extent to which it is centralised or decentralised, and indeed, whether there is an HR function at all.

These factors include:

1. **The strategic characteristics of the organisation** — this covers strategic behaviour such as the ways in which strategic guidance and control is exercised.

   Goold and Campbell[1] as described in Chapter 1 identified three main styles adopted by corporate offices to the strategic management of diversified businesses: strategic planning, strategic control and financial control. The role of the HR function will vary according to the strategic approach adopted. In strategic planning and control companies there may be a small but influential headquarters personnel function, while in a financial control company there may be no HR function in the centre at all.

   Miles and Snow[2] suggested that there were three types of strategic behaviour and supporting organisational characteristics, each of which might result in different roles for the HR function:

   - A 'defender' strategy is characterised by a narrow and relatively stable product-market domain, a functional structure, and skills in production efficiency, process engineering and cost control. The basic HRM strategy of defenders will be to 'build' human resources — they typically engage in little recruiting above entry level while training and development involves extensive, formal skills-building programmes (the 'make' approach).
   - A 'prospector' strategy is typified by the continued search for new product and market opportunities and experimentation with potential responses to emerging environmental trends. Prospector companies 'buy-in' talent, the emphasis being on identifying skill requirements and acquiring them in the labour market. This involves the use of sophisticated recruitment techniques and 'on the job' development.
   - An 'analyser' strategy is adopted by organisations which may be operating in two differing types of product-market domains; one stable; one changing. They therefore exhibit a range of behaviours which are typified by a limited basic product line, the search for a small number of related product or market opportunities and cost-efficient technology for stable and new products. Analysers 'allocate' human resources. They match their HR strategies to the nature of the product and the stage of the product life-cycle.

2. **The organisation** — the extent to which the organisation is centralised or decentralised; the degree to which it is formally structured or operates on a relatively informal, fluid and 'organic' basis.

3. **The corporate culture** — including values (especially those concerned with people), norms, organisation climate and management styles.
4. **The type of business** — manufacturing, retail, distribution, research and development etc.
5. **The size of the organisation.**
6. **The sector** — public, private, voluntary.
7. **Operational characteristics** — diversity, locations, national, European or global.
8. **The technology** — high-tech or low-tech, mass production, batch production or process.
9. **Type of employees** — professional, 'knowledge workers', skilled, unskilled.
10. **Employee relations climate and arrangements** — co-operative and trusting or conflict ridden and suspicious, degree of union power, consultation and communication systems.
11. **The traditional role of personnel** — its power, influence, acceptability and credibility.
12. **The need for personnel expertise** — because of the nature of the organisation and its human resource requirements and problems, or because of the relative weakness of line management in human resource matters.

Human resource function models

Because of the diverse factors mentioned above there is no such thing as a typical HR function. David Guest[3] has, however, distinguished four basic types:

1. **A paternalistic welfare model** where the emphasis is on looking after employees as a path to ensuring that they in turn look after customers. Marks & Spencer provides the stereotype of this model.
2. **A production model** where the central role of the personnel department is to support continuity of production by ensuring that staff are in place and that a clear and consistent set of industrial relations guidelines exists. Ford provides the typical example of this model.
3. **A professional model** reflecting demonstrated and acknowledged competence displayed by high-quality personnel department staff in the core area of selection, training and development, pay and industrial relations. Companies such as Shell and ICI fall into this category.
4. **A human resource model** reflecting a people orientated focus throughout the organisation, including respect for the individual, full utilisation of individual abilities, and sophisticated policies for employee involvement. IBM is the stereotype of this model.

Role of the human resource function

The diversity of circumstances in which HR functions operate and the various models describing how they fit in with particular types of organisation, mean that it is dangerous to generalise about the role of the function. It is possible to suggest that there are two fundamental contributions it can make. First it can, in Karen Legge's[4] words, provide 'unique, non-substitutable expertise'. Secondly, it can use this expertise to provide professional support services in such fields as recruitment, training, salary administration and maintaining personnel information systems more efficiently and economically than anyone else.

More specifically, members of HR departments can:

- provide guidance on HR strategic directions;
- act as internal consultants;
- encourage and support innovation in the form of new approaches to HRM;
- facilitate change — they can help to articulate agendas for change and operate the various powerful levers for change available to them such as performance related training, performance management systems and reward systems;
- provide the support services in the fields of resourcing, development, pay and employee relations required by management to fulfil their human resource responsibilities;
- act as the guardian of company human resource principles and policies, controlling and coordinating their application as necessary to achieve consistency.

Achieving the role

To achieve their role the members of the human resource function must be business orientated. They must intervene when appropriate and demonstrate that they understand the critical success factors affecting the use of human resources. As Michael Armstrong[5] has written:

> Personnel directors who remain in their corner nursing their knowledge of the behavioral sciences, industrial relations tactics and personnel techniques, while other directors get on with running the business cannot make a fully effective contribution to achieving the company's goals for growth, competitive gain and the improvement of the bottom-line performance. It is not enough for personnel directors just to understand the business and its strategy; their role must be built into the fabric of the business.

And human resource directors are well placed to make a significant impact on performance because they can:

- reach the ear of the chief executive on key resourcing and remuneration issues;

- take a balanced view of human resource needs because they are not so preoccupied with short-term results;
- provide levers for change in the shape of such processes as performance management and reward systems.

To be fully effective they must be capable of seizing opportunities to intervene. They must understand the economics of the business — which means knowing its cost and profit drivers and, on this basis, decide what contribution they can make to achieving competitive advantage.

For example, a major brewer did not appreciate that its practice of supplying beer to its tied outlets at well below the usual price made it essential to extract more profit from those outlets. The personnel director fastened upon this point and switched personnel resources to an ambitious recruitment and training programme designed to improve the sales performance of publicans and their staff.

At Book Club Associates, Michael Armstrong seized the opportunity of new owners and a new chief executive to take control of the corporate planning function and, on the basis of an analysis of critical issues, developed a performance plan, the aim of which was to promote 'a climate of enterprise and endeavour.' The proposals were prefaced by the following remarks:

> BCA is a successful business. It must be kept that way. There is no secret to our success. It has been achieved solely by the people we employ and the way in which they have been organised and managed. But it could be said that this success is partly fortuitous. And in the face of the changes and turbulence ahead of us we cannot afford to rely on chance. Our future is utterly dependent on having an explicit and coherent strategy for developing and maintaining the highest standards of performance.

A performance management programme was then developed and progressively implemented with help from Coopers & Lybrand. This involved relating pay more specifically to performance and increasing commitment and involvement by better communications and ensuring that employees participate more in the affairs of the firm.

CONCLUSION — STRATEGIC GOALS FOR HUMAN RESOURCE MANAGEMENT

Making human resource management happen is first a matter of seeing that top management, line managers and the members of the human resource function get their acts together. How they do this will depend largely on the circumstances of the organisation but a strong and common orientation to the economic as well as the human resource needs of the business will be an important unifying factor.

But a preoccupation with the roles of management could lead to the neglect of the whole point of human resource management — the integration of the needs of the business with the needs of those who work there. Employees should be brought into the partnership to be involved in the formulation of human resource policies and to be involved in the development and implementation of personnel systems and processes. HRM is about gaining commitment and achieving mutuality. This means that the strategic HRM goals of the organisation must be shared with all concerned.

These strategic goals may include some or all of the following:

- creating human resource strategies which are consistent with the strategic direction in which the business is going;
- developing a flatter and leaner organisation where clearer accountabilities and the resources required to meet them are devolved as close to the scene of action as possible;
- encouraging the development of organisational processes which promote flexibility, teamwork and rapid response to new situations;
- fostering a performance-orientated and value-driven organisation which encourages high levels of commitment, competence, innovation, quality and customer service;
- promoting unified vision in organisations which will be staffed increasingly by specialists;
- identifying present and future skill requirements and taking steps to satisfy them through recruitment, training and development programmes;
- seeking alternative and more cost-effective methods of meeting human resource needs;
- investing in performance and competence related training;
- developing remuneration systems which relate rewards to contributions, provide incentives for improved performance and deliver messages about the expectations of the organisation;
- balancing the needs of the organisation and its individual members.

REFERENCES

1. Goold, M and Campbell, A (1986) *Strategies and Styles: The Role of the Centre in Managing Diversified Corporations*, Blackwell, Oxford.
2. Miles, R and Snow, C (1984) 'Designing strategic human resources systems'. *Organizational Dynamics*, Summer.
3. Guest, D (1989) 'Personnel and HRM : can you tell the difference', *Personnel Management*, January.
4. Legge, K (1978) *Power, Innovation and Problem Solving in Personnel Management*, McGraw-Hill, Maidenhead.
5. Armstrong, M (1989) 'Personnel director's view from the bridge', *Personnel Management*, October.

BIBLIOGRAPHY

Armstrong, M (1988) *A Handbook of Personnel Management Practice*, Kogan Page, London

Belasco, J A (1990) *Teaching the Elephant to Dance*, Hutchinson, London

Blackstone, T and Plowden, W (1988) *Inside the Think Tank: Advising the Cabinet, 1971-1983*, Heinemann, London

Butler, R (1990) *'New Challenges or familiar prescriptions', The Redcliffe-Maud Memorial Lecture*, RIPA, London

Butler, R (1991) *FDA Lecture on the Future of the Civil Service*, 15 October

Cabinet Office (1988) *Service to the Public Office of the Minister for the Civil Service*, Occasional Paper, HMSO, London

Carr, D K, and Littleman, I D (1991) *Excellence in Government: Total Quality Management in the 1990s*, Coopers & Lybrand, London

Cassels, J S (1983) *Review of Personnel Work in the Civil Service*, report to the Prime Minister, HMSO, London

Cooke, R and Armstrong, M (1990) 'The search for strategic HRM', *Personnel Management*, December

Coopers & Lybrand (1990) *Performance management in local government*, Executive Briefing

Davies, A and Willman, J (1991) *What Next?: Agencies, Departments, and the Civil Service*, Institute for Public Policy Research, London

Dawson, S (1986) *Analysing Organisations*, Macmillan, London

Eliot, T S (1963) *Collected Poems, 1909-1962*, Faber, London

Flynn, N (1990) *Public Sector Management*, Harvester Wheatsheaf, London

Fraser, A (1991) *Making the most of Next Steps: The Management of Ministers' Departments and their Executive Agencies*, HMSO, London

Heider, J(1988) *The Tao of Leadership*, Bantam, London

Hennessy, P (1989) *Whitehall*, Secker & Warburg, London

Jenkins, K, Caines K and Jackson, A (1988) *Improving management in Government: The Next Steps*, HMSO, London

Jenkins, P (1987) *Mrs Thatcher's Revolution*, Pan, London

Kakabadse A (1991) *The Wealth Creators: Top people, top teams and executive best practice*, Kogan Page, London

Loden, M (1985) Feminine Leadership, *The Times*

Lord Fulton (1968) *The Civil Service*, Report of the Committee chaired by Lord Fulton, Command 3638, HMSO, London

Machiavelli, N (1977) *The Prince*, Ed George Bull, Penguin, London

Major, J (1991) *The Citizen's Charter: Raising the Standard*, HMSO, London

Mayes, D (1986) 'Britain's position in the World', *Catalyst*, Vol. 2, No. 1 (Spring)

—— (1991) *Improving Management in Government: The Next Steps Agencies*, Review 1991, HMSO, London

Moss Kanter, R (1983) *The Change Masters: Innovation and Entrepreneurship in the American Corporation*, Simon & Schuster, Hemel Hempstead

—— (1989) *When Giants Learn to Dance*, Simon & Schuster, Hemel Hempstead

Pedler, M, Burgoyne J and Boydell T (1991) *The Learning Company*, McGraw-Hill, London

Peters, T (1988) *Thriving on Chaos*, Macmillan, London

Peters, T and Waterman, R H (1982) *In Search of Excellence*, Harper & Row, New York

Peters, T and Austin, N (1988) *A Passion for Excellence*, Fontana, London

Plant, R (1987) *Managing Change and Making it Stick*, Fontana, London

Plowden, E (1989) *An Industrialist in the Treasury: the Post-War Years*, Deutsch, London

Porter, M E (1990) *The Competitive Advantage of Nations*, Macmillan, London

Randlesome, C, Brierley, W, Brunton, K, Gordon, C and King, P (1990) *Business Cultures in Europe*, Heinemann, London

Senge, P M (1990) *The Fifth Discipline: The art and practice of the learning organisation*, Doubleday, London

BIBLIOGRAPHY

Tomkys, R (1991) 'The Financial Management Initiative in the FCO', *Public Administration*, Vol. 69, Summer (pp. 257-263)

Warner Burke, W and Litwin, G H 'A causal model of organisational performance', *The 1989 Annual: Developing Human Resources*, pp. 277-288

Young, H (1990) *One of Us*, Pan, London

Index

INDEX